THE RISE OF URBAN AMERICA

FIFTY YEARS
OF RAPID TRANSIT
1864–1917

James Blaine Walker

ARNO PRESS
&
The New York Times

NEW YORK • 1970

338.4
W181f

Reprint Edition 1970 by Arno Press Inc.

Reprinted from a copy in The University of Illinois Library

LC# 70-112581
ISBN 0-405-02480-0

THE RISE OF URBAN AMERICA
ISBN for complete set 0-405-02430-4

Manufactured in the United States of America

CHARLES T. HARVEY OPERATING CAR BY CABLE POWER ON FIRST ELEVATED RAILROAD IN GREENWICH STREET, IN 1867

FIFTY YEARS OF RAPID TRANSIT

———o———

1864 to 1917

———o———

By JAMES BLAINE WALKER

Illustrated

———o———

From the Press of
THE LAW PRINTING COMPANY
6 Church Street, New York City

1918

CONTENTS

CONTENTS

PREFACE

"RAPID TRANSIT" in New York City means the transportation of passengers from one part of the city to another by trains of cars, as distinguished from transportation by single cars or "street cars." It is distinctly a modern development covering roughly a half century, although practical, rapid transit operation dates back only to 1871.

Located on a narrow island between the Hudson and East rivers, New York City presents probably the most difficult situation in regard to internal traffic of any city in the country. Bounded on West, South and East by water, the only outlet for growth was toward the North, with the result that early in the Nineteenth Century it became a long, narrow city, with its business section at the southern end and its homes at the northern extremity —an extremity that has always receded as the business section grew and pushed it further away.

When Wall street was the northern limit the traffic problem was simple, but when that limit had been transferred to Twenty-third street the population had grown to such an extent that it was a difficult matter to provide facilities to take its business men down town in the morning and up town at night. Omnibuses were the first public conveyances following the stage coach days. Then came horse cars, then elevated railroads, then electric trolley cars and finally subways. Each class in its day was overcrowded. This was due principally to the phenomenal growth of the city, which added to the traveling population faster than transportation facilities could be provided. A secondary cause was the policy of traction corporations, which have always found "dividends in the straps" and have postponed extensions of their lines to the last minute in order to enjoy as long as possible the swollen revenue which came from overcrowded trains and cars.

In the year 1870, when the first dummy engine trains ran on the first elevated railroad, the entire street railway travel of the city was about 115,000,000 passengers. In 1880 this had grown to 288,000,000—more than doubling in ten years. Each succeeding decade has seen a corresponding increase until at the present time (1917) the passenger traffic in the greater city is upwards of 1,900,000,000 a year. This growth is out of all proportion to the increase in population, for while in 1870 the average citizen took 100 street car rides in a year he now takes upwards of 350. In other words the more traveling facilities provided the more people make use of them.

This enormous traffic is now handled by electric surface or trolley cars, trains on elevated railroads and trains in the subways or underground railroads. It demands the use every day of about 13,000 passenger cars operated over 2,300 miles of track. If laid in a straight line these tracks would stretch from New York to Salt Lake City. The capital invested in these enterprises is enormous. The outstanding stocks and bonds of the several companies now aggregate $1,121,296,001. The universal fare is five cents and one may ride twenty miles for one fare. The total amount of fares collected during the last fiscal year was $94,547,916.

About one half of this traffic is rapid transit traffic— that is traffic handled by trains of cars on elevated or underground roads. The other half is carried by single cars operated on surface tracks. Electricity is the universal motive power—the third rail on elevated roads and subways and the underground or overhead trolley on the surface lines. A few of the latter use storage battery cars.

The pursuit of a suitable and adequate system of rapid transit has been constant. The sought for ideal has been at times almost in sight; again it has disappeared, only to be revived as the struggle for it grew in strength. Romance and tragedy, few successes and many failures marked the quest. In its service men whose ideas made possible the successes, like the traditional poor inventor, have lived to see those ideas turned to profit by others; have sunk their all in vain attempts to materialize their dreams only to retire bankrupt and see other men reap golden harvests from their crops.

The history of rapid transit is replete with flashes of genius and the sordid spirit of greed. It tells of battles, of schemes, of great ambitions. The struggle for public franchises alone, staged in the Legislature and the City government, provides material for a thrilling drama. Most of the actors in the earlier scenes have gone from this world, but a few remain, and with their recollections and documentary relics it is still possible to recast the forgotten parts. The writer has endeavored to do this in the following pages, which embrace the most interesting phases of an interesting research.

JAMES BLAINE WALKER.

PELHAM MANOR, N. Y.
November 1, 1917.

CHAPTER I

First Suggestions of Rapid Transit.

LIKE other great conceptions the rapid transit idea was born during the Civil War, but it is impossible to account for it on any theory that it served a war purpose. The trans-continental railroad and telegraph grew directly out of the demand for better communication created by that great struggle. The demand for rapid transit came from the development of New York City and its growth northward, just as the demand for elevators came from the development of buildings and their growth skyward. The elevator also was a production of the Civil War period. Both were incidental, however, and in no way related except by time to the conflict of arms. By the year 1860 buildings had grown to so many stories that stairways became inadequate, and the city had pushed so far to the North that the busy New Yorker demanded some quicker mode of conveyance from his home to his office than was supplied by the horse-drawn vehicles of the period.

It is really remarkable how many great things were either accomplished or initiated during the Civil War, when one might suppose that the energies of the whole people would have been so absorbed in the mighty struggle that there would have been little opportunity for the conception of new projects. Yet one finds the period singularly prolific of notable advances in art, science and material progress. This development was so marked that it attracted attention even at the time. For instance, in an editorial on the revival of the Atlantic cable project, the New York Herald of June 11, 1864, remarked:

"Whoever shall undertake hereafter to present a philosophic history of these times will be compelled to linger over and to emphasize the fact that, during the bloodiest epoch in their national career, the progress of the American people in social and political enterprise outstripped that of any previous period from the founding of the Commonwealth.''

The writer then cites the electric telegraph completed across the continent, the new railroad to the West, the generous contributions to the starving in Ireland and to the suffering operatives in England, the revival of ocean subsidies and the establishment of the postal money order system.

Rapid Transit in New York had its birth in the year 1864, when the armies of Grant and Lee were contending for the final mastery. The city then lay mostly below Twenty-third street. Harlem had been ''discovered'' and a few, venturesome pioneers had built homes there. The great majority of the citizens, however, dwelt south of Forty-second street. Some of the north and south avenues were not even opened north of that street. Many of the streets were unpaved, and citizens ploughed through mud and dust to reach the crude horse car or the crowded omnibus. A six-story building was a ''skyscraper'', a trip to Albany on the steam trains took a whole day; national banks were a novelty; the Brooklyn Bridge was unborn; electric lighting was only a dream and the Government was just establishing the money order system.

To the present generation the New York of those days seems much more remote than the time would suggest, so rapid has been its growth and so many have been its achievements. The city has been practically rebuilt in the meantime, and the ''sights'' of that era have been well nigh forgotten. Then the Fifth Avenue hotel, at Twenty-third street and Fifth Avenue, was the new uptown rival of the Astor House, down at Broadway and Vesey street. Both now have been destroyed, the former to make room for a modern office building, the latter to permit the building of the Broadway subway.

It was a time when women wore hoop-skirts; when Barnum's American Museum and Niblo's Garden flourished; when Maggie Mitchell was making herself famous in "Fanchon" and negro minstrelsy was in its glory; when the Academy of Music was the home of grand opera, and Brignoli, Zucchi and Massimiliani sang in "Il Trovatore" and other early Verdi operas; when Theodore Thomas was building up his famous orchestra and giving "symphony soirees" at Irving Hall. It was the year which saw the re-election of Abraham Lincoln as President and the admission of Nevada as a State of the Union.

The city had become a metropolis, but its metropolitan life was just beginning. In spite of war prices its people had plenty of money and lavished it on all kinds of pleasures. The newspapers commented on the gaiety of the winter season, the extravagance of the women and the expensive restaurants, of which Delmonico's set the pace. In one editorial it was stated that women of fashion thought nothing of paying $100 for a bonnet; yet the paper criticized the omnibus companies for raising their fares from six to ten cents and the theaters for preparing to increase the price of admission beyond fifty cents. It was the day of fractional currency, or "shin-plasters", when a man had to look twice to tell the difference between a bill for three cents and one for a half dollar.

A picture of the city at that time is drawn by James Grant Wilson in his History of New York, a picture worth reproducing here to glimpse the condition of the community when rapid transit was first projected:

"The City stretched her limbs anew and began that progress which in a quarter of a century more transformed her from a struggling, provincial town into a metropolis. Three potent factors in that

transformation were the introduction of the electric
light, the use of elevators and the achievement of
rapid transit, or rather the continued struggles
toward rapid transit, the desired end receding
as the means for attaining it proved successively
inadequate.

"In order fully to appreciate the power of these
factors, * * * we have first to remember what
the New York of 1865 was. Above Forty-second
street it could scarcely be said to exist, being only a
dreary waste of unpaved and ungraded streets di-
versified by rocky eminences crowned with squat-
ters' shanties. Railway passengers from the North
still left their trains at Twenty-seventh and Thirtieth streets. Street railways were comparatively
few, and there was no speedy and comfortable way
of getting from one end of the city to the other.
Below Eighty-sixth street there were in 1865 25,261
vacant lots. The grading of Madison avenue was
still in progress, and the state of the city as regards
transit facilities is set forth in a striking way by the
hopeful language in which a pamphlet of that day
speaks of the new street as likely to 'prepare the way
for an extension of the Fourth Avenue Railroad' and
thus give new access to the Park. Unable to get
anywhere on Manhattan Island, people sought the
suburbs and rapidly built up Southern Connecticut
and Eastern New Jersey, with Long Island and Staten Island."

And here it may be well to state that 'rapid transit',
as used in these pages, applies to transportation by
trains inside of the city, as distinguished from the steam
railroads which supplied rapid transit from and to distant points. In 1864 the steam roads offered the only
quick mode of traveling, and to them, as the historian
notes, was due the building up of the suburbs in West-

chester county, N. Y., in Connecticut, in New Jersey, Staten Island and Long Island. In 1864 there were three of these roads running into New York City—the Hudson River Railroad, the New York and Harlem Railroad and the New Haven Railroad. The former two are now parts of the New York Central system, while the latter still retains its individuality and name. In New Jersey there were the beginnings of the Erie, the Pennsylvania and the Northern Railway. On Long Island the Long Island Railroad ran to Islip, Oyster Bay, etc., and the New York and Flushing, the Brooklyn, Bath Beach and Coney Island and the Brooklyn Central and Jamaica railroads to the places named in their titles.

Street cars of the kind drawn by horses had been in use for many years. They were introduced in 1832, when the first car in the world to run on tracks was operated in Fourth Avenue between Prince street and Fourteenth street on the route of the New York and Harlem road. Originally a horse railroad, this line was changed to steam operation a few years later. About 1852 the horse car movement, which had languished owing to the bulky and unwieldy style of cars used, took on new life by reason of the improvement in the type, and by 1855 lines were in operation in Fourth, Sixth, Third and Eighth avenues. By 1864 the number of such lines had increased to twelve, and in that year they carried about 61,000,000 passengers. The population of the city then was about 700,000. Today (1917) in Manhattan and the Bronx (approximately covered by the old city) with four times the population, the street railroads carry in a year about 1,000,000;000 passengers, sixteen times as many as in 1864. In other words, while in 1864 every citizen on the average took about eighty-seven street car rides in a year, he now takes about 357. The age of rapid transit has not only multiplied the traveling facilities but enormously increased the usefulness of street car travel to the citizen.

Tradition has it that an ox cart was the first form of

street transportation used in New York. In 1746, it is said, a line of such carts ran from the Battery up Broadway to Houston street. This form of transit, if it ever existed, proved too slow for the New Yorker, and early in the Nineteenth Century omnibuses were introduced. By 1850 Broadway was so crowded with these vehicles, operated by several rival companies, that the later notorious Jacob Sharp began his fight for a surface railroad in that thoroughfare. It took him thirty-five years to get it, the franchise having been granted in August 1884 by the "boodle" aldermen. According to figures compiled by Sharp in one of his campaigns for a franchise, about 230 omnibuses passed Chambers street going up Broadway and 240 down each hour. For thirteen hours his count, taken in August 1852, showed that 3,035 omnibuses and 4,719 other vehicles passed up, and 3,162 omnibuses and 4,723 other vehicles passed down Broadway at this point. This meant an omnibus service at thirteen seconds' headway.

By the year 1864 conditions had become intolerable. Broadway became unsafe for pedestrians, and we are told that the rivalry between omnibus drivers was so great that they recklessly drove over men, women and children in their haste to beat their nearest competitors to waiting passengers. In the rush hours the omnibuses were so crowded that passengers had to hang on to straps, as they were forced to do in the more crowded street cars. As omnibus fares were ten and the street car fares six cents, the latter carried by far the greater number of passengers. The newspapers of the period denounced the conditions and scored omnibus and car companies. Reckless driving, and crowded omnibuses were not the only grievances. The drivers were accused of swearing at passengers and giving them bad money or tickets in change. In its issue of October 2, 1864 the New York Herald savagely attacked the omnibus nuisance, and called upon the capitalists of the city to establish cab lines to relieve the suffering citizens. Here is a quotation from that editorial:

"Modern martyrdom may be succinctly defined as riding in a New York omnibus. The discomforts, inconveniences and annoyances of a trip in one of these vehicles are almost intolerable. From the beginning to the end of the journey a constant quarrel is progressing. The driver quarrels with the passengers, and the passengers quarrel with the driver. There are quarrels about getting out and quarrels about getting in. There are quarrels about change and quarrels about the ticket swindle. The driver swears at the passengers and the passengers harangue the driver through the strap-hole—a position in which even Demosthenes could not be eloquent. Respectable clergymen in white chokers are obliged to listen to loud oaths. Ladies are disgusted, frightened and insulted. Children are alarmed and lift up their voices and weep. Indignant gentlemen rise to remonstrate with the irate Jehu and are suddenly bumped back into their seats, twice as indignant as before, besides being involved in supplementary quarrels with those other passengers upon whose corns they have accidentally trodden. Thus the omnibus rolls along, a perfect Bedlam on wheels.

"It is in vain those who are obliged to ride seek for relief in a city railway car. The cars are quieter than the omnibuses, but much more crowded. People are packed into them like sardines in a box, with perspiration for oil. The seats being more than filled, the passengers are placed in rows down the middle, where they hang on by the straps, like smoked hams in a corner grocery. To enter or exit is exceedingly difficult. Silks and broadcloth are ruined in the attempt. As in the omnibuses pickpockets take advantage of the confusion to ply their vocation. Handkerchiefs, pocketbooks, watches and breastpins disappear most mysteriously. The foul, close, heated air is poisonous. A healthy person cannot ride a dozen blocks without a headache. For these reasons most ladies and gentlemen prefer to ride in the stages, which cannot be crowded so outrageously, and which are pretty decently ventilated by the cracks in the window frames. The omnibus fare is nearly double the car fare, however, and so the majority of the people are compelled to ride in the cars, although they lose in health what they save in money. But it must be evident to everybody that neither the cars nor the stages supply accomodations enough for the public, and that such accommodations as they do supply are not of the right sort. Both the cars and the omnibuses might be very comfortable and convenient if they were better managed, but something more is needed to supply the popular and increasing demand for city conveyances.''

A very convincing argument for rapid transit, but the writer concludes his editorial by urging the establishment of a cheap cab system. This is proof that the rapid transit issue was not a burning one in October, 1864. Forty years later the papers were writing the same kind of editorials, but in place of calling for a cab system they were hammering the Rapid Transit Commission for not providing more subways.

The disgraceful conditions on the omnibus lines above described, it seems evident, were promoted rather than alleviated by competition, for in those days Broadway was filled with rival omnibus lines. Is there not a lesson in this now for city authorities in considering the grant of motor 'bus franchises to several competing companies?

CHAPTER II

THE FIRST RAPID TRANSIT BILL.

WHILE the transit conditions existing at the opening of the year 1864 demanded relief, the public authorities did little or nothing to provide it. As indicating the complete absence of anything like a rapid transit programme at that time, I quote the following, which is the only mention of the transportation question in the inaugural message of Mayor Charles G. Gunther, delivered January 4, 1864:

> "The proper regulation of the city railroads is a matter of public interest in a city like New York, where a large portion of the population is compelled to use this means of conveyance to and from their places of daily avocation. These companies, enjoying a valuable franchise and paying little for the use of the streets in comparison with the revenue derived therefrom, while they increase so materially the expense of cleaning and repairing, should be compelled at least to extend their tracks as far as the avenues they occupy are graded, and also to run cars as often as the local population reasonably demand; nor should they be permitted to use a rail endangering either life or property."

It may be inferred from this that rapid transit was not a question of vital import in January, 1864. The only relief which the Mayor points out in his message is the extension of the tracks of the existing surface railroads and the prohibition of the T rail. He ignores the congestion of traffic and the crowding of cars and omnibuses.

The railroad companies, however, were quick to act on the Mayor's suggestion. In February the New York and Harlem Railroad Company had a bill introduced in the Legislature to give it the right to extend its line down

Fourth Avenue and Broadway to Whitehall street, in accordance with a resolution passed by the previous city administration in 1863. This bill also provided that the railroad company should buy out the Broadway 'bus lines, the idea apparently being to substitute a street railroad for the latter in Broadway south of Union Square. Similar rights for a railroad in Broadway had been sought for years by Jacob Sharp, and the property owners were generally opposed to it. They and the newspapers opposed the New York and Harlem bill, and it was killed by an adverse report in the Senate on March 25, 1864. That not all the property owners were opposed to a Broadway railroad, however, is shown by the fact that D. Appleton and Co. and Lord and Taylor were among the signers of a petition sent to the Senate asking for the passage of the New York and Harlem bill.

It was at this session of the Legislature that the first rapid transit bill appeared. On March 21, 1864, articles of incorporation of the Metropolitan Railway Company were filed with the Secretary of State, and a few days later a bill was introduced in the Senate to give this company the rights to build—AN UNDERGROUND RAILROAD in Broadway from the Battery to Thirty-fourth street and then under Sixth Avenue to Central Park! This will be a surprise to the present generation, many of whom think that the existing subway, opened in 1904, was the first underground transportation project of the city. It is a historical fact, however, that the first project for a rapid transit railroad, conceived in 1864, was a subway project. The elevated railroad was a later conception and grew out of the subway proposal, as will be told in a subsequent chapter.

The father of the subway idea and the promoter of the Metropolitan Railway Company of 1864 was Hugh B. Willson, a Michigan railroad man, who had been in London during the construction of the London Underground railroad and was present at its opening in January, 1863, when the first three and three-quarters miles was placed in operation. Willson examined the new railroad carefully and traveled on it frequently. He was so impressed with its merits that he conceived the idea of building the same kind of a road in New York, and on his return to that city, in June, 1863, he, in his own words "set to work to secure the aid of prominent men to enable me to present to the public a plan similar to that of London. At first my efforts were not successful. All were deeply engrossed in the War, and it was not till the autumn that I made any substantial progress."

It was not until January, 1864, however, that Willson's work began to take form. He then obtained the cooperation of Henry V. Poor. Poor interested others, and the two succeeded in getting enough support to justify the incorporation of a company with a capital stock of $5,000,000—a large amount for those days. This was the Metropolitan Railway Company alluded to above. The list of incorporators includes many well known names. Here it is:

Jonathan Sturges
Simon B. Chittenden
Danford N. Barney
John J. Cisco
William H. Osborn
Luther C. Clark
John T. Agnew
Uriel A. Murdock
Samuel Marsh
Francis Skiddy
John Taylor Johnston
Wehrmit Keight
Edwards Pierrepont
David Dows
Abiel A. Low
Nathaniel Marsh
James B. Johnston
Samuel Sloan

Charles H. Russell
Sheppard Gandy
William R. Kirkland
Edmund T. H. Gibson
John J. Phelps
Sidney Webster
Henry V. Poor
James Bryce
Hugh B. Willson
John Lowery
George A. Townsend
William Butler Duncan
John H. Wainwright
Edward S. Jaffrey
James T. Sanford
William E. Dodge, Jr.
Charles Lanier
James F. D. Lanier

Edward Jones
William Kelly
John J. Astor, Jr.
Moses Taylor
Isaac Bell
Robert S. Hone
Henry F. Vail

Edward C. Brodhead
George Bliss
Wyllis Blackstone
Wilson G. Hunt
Courtlandt Palmer
Elisha Riggs
Thomas Slocomb

The company was incorporated under the general railroad law of 1850, and the life of the corporation was 100 years. The $5,000,000 capital stock was divided into $50 shares.

With such backing, the new project received the attention of press and public. Everybody began to talk about riding underground, and there was a great demand for information as to the operation of the London road. This was operated by steam locomotives, and the same power was to be used in the Metropolitan line in New York. Such operation was taken as a matter of course, as electricity as a power was then unknown. There were some timid souls who expressed fear of catching cold by suddenly going into a tunnel on a hot day, but there was no serious objection to steam as a motive power at first. Later its use was deprecated by a few engineers who favored propulsion by pneumatic power, but in the scramble for rapid transit rights which Willson's project started all promoters of subways contemplated the use of steam locomotives burning coke to reduce the smoke nuisance to a minimum.

In the Legislature, however, the Willson project was not received with enthusiasm. The corporations of those days had great influence with the Legislators, and as no corporation already operating favored the new scheme it got short shrift in the Railroad Committee of the Senate, to whom it had been referred. In two weeks after the bill had been introduced it was reported adversely by "Senators Beach, Williams and Woodruff, from the

Committee on Railroads." The majority of the Committee gave as their reason that there would be another bill for a Broadway underground railroad at the next session, "and this would prove an obstacle in the way unless disposed of now." The obliging Senate adopted the report on the day it was made, April 8, 1864.

News of this summary action on a project in which New York City was so vitally interested aroused general indignation. Petitions were circulated asking for a reconsideration of the bill, and the press denounced the action of the Legislature in unmeasured terms. On April 11 the New York Times said editorially:

"The defeat of the Underground Railroad in the Legislature, coupled as it was with the rejection of Mayor Gunther's proposition to compel the street railroads to pay 10 percent. of their receipts to the City treasury, is a fresh and alarming illustration of the enormous power over our property and comfort which is now wielded by the omnibus proprietors, railroad corporations and political jobbers. The Legislature on which we have been in the habit of relying seems to have surrendered itself completely to their hands.

"The Underground Railroad promised to be an immense boon to the city. It was perfectly feasible; a similar road has been in successful operation in London for one year; it encroaches on no vested interest; takes no one's land or house; interferes with no traffic or thoroughfare; offers cheap, comfortable and speedy transit from one end of the island to the other; requires no money from the public, will add nothing to municipal taxation and is undertaken by men of the highest character and standing both social and commercial. In short, there is not a single objection to be made to it on the part of the public or the Government, and yet the Committee of the

Senate has reported against it, under the lead of a Senator from this city, and it has been laid on the table, for what reason is not stated. We wonder how much longer the people of this city will permit themselves to be thus plundered by men who are ostensibly their servants and dependents.''

The outburst of popular indignation had its effect on the Legislature. On the day on which the above editorial was published, namely April 11, Senator Angell, chairman of the Railroad Committee of the Senate, asked that the Underground Railroad bill be taken from the table and referred to the Committee of the Whole Senate. He said he considered the matter one of grave importance in which New York city was vitally interested. He presented a petition signed by Brown Bros. and Co. and 1,600 citizens of New York, asking a reconsideration of the bill. The motion prevailed, and the bill was taken from the table and referred to the Committee of the Whole. The spasm of reform, however, was short lived, and nothing came of it. The Legislature adjourned on April 26 without any consideration having been given to the measure by the Committee of the Whole. This ended the matter for the time, but the fight for rapid transit was on and it was waged from that time forward with increasing interest and fierceness.

CHAPTER III

PIONEER PLANS FOR A SUBWAY.

WHILE the first subway operated in New York City is justly regarded as one of the engineering wonders of the world, the fact that its construction was not undertaken until 1901 is equally marvelous, considering that its prototype was conceived and planned in 1864. The plans made in that year for the Broadway Underground proposed by the Metropolitan Railway Company, organized by Hugh B. Wilson, covered almost the identical route of the present subway from the Battery to Central Park, called for the construction of twelve miles of railroad under the streets and a tunnel similar to that of the first subway, built nearly a half century later. The chief points of difference were that the 1864 subway was to be only a two-track line and the tunnel was to be of brick and stone masonry instead of steel and concrete and was to be operated by steam locomotives instead of by electric motors.

Mr. William Barclay Parsons, who made the plans for the existing subway, Mr. August Belmont, who financed its construction and others connected with its development, hold the opinion that only the application of electricity to traction power purposes permitted the building of the first subway, and that it was because of the objections to steam power for use under ground that the early day plans for subways were discarded in favor of elevated railroads, which, as everyone knows, were the first rapid transit roads to be placed in operation. Research indicates, however, that it was not power but politics and the war for franchise rights which postponed the building of the first underground road. Steam had been successfully used in London's underground railroad as early as 1863, and if Hugh B. Willson and his backers had been able to obtain the necessary rights from the Legislature, it is clear from the historical review of the period that the first rapid transit road in New York would have been a subway and that it would have been in operation by 1870, or about the time the first elevated road began actual business. The engineer who planned the Willson road has left behind a complete and exhaustive study of a steam subway. In fact, aside from the question of power, the builders of the first subway might have constructed their road from the plans made by that engineer. His name was A. P. Robinson, and he deserves everlasting honor as an American engineer who was far ahead of the times. It is not desired to belittle the work of the men who planned and built the existing subway, but if they did "pioneer" work, what shall be said of Robinson, who about fifty years ago saw, and projected on paper and justified by cogent argument an underground road having all the important features of the present line?

After his defeat in the Legislature of 1864, Willson perfected his scheme and made preparations to go back to the next Legislature for the franchise which had been denied the Metropolitan Railway Company by the previous session. With his associates he had ample financial backing and was enabled to retain first class engineering talent. Poor was the Secretary of the company, of which Danford N. Barney was president and Uriel A. Murdock treasurer. The directors included ten of the most influential of those named as stockholders. Willson was one of the directors. In the fall of 1864 they retained Mr. Robinson to "prepare for the company a statement of the character and cost of the proposed work." This modest statement of his task was made by Mr. Robinson himself in the introduction to his report. This report, which was dated January 1, 1865, was printed in New York by Clayton and Medole, book and job printers in the Trinity Building, No. 4 Thames Street. It is a pamphlet of forty-one pages, illustrated with maps

Plate 1.

SECTION OF TUNNEL WITH DETAILS

of Sewers, Water and Gas Pipes and Ventilation

Scale 8 feet to an inch

A. P. ROBINSON'S PLANS FOR SUBWAY, 1864
Section of Tunnel Showing Sub-Surface Structures and Ventilation.

of the route, drawings of cross-sections of the proposed subway and colored prints of the proposed stations. It is written in argumentative style, the author evidently feeling that he was proposing a daring innovation and needed to justify it.

Robinson first compared the physical conditions in New York with those of London, and pointed out the great differences existing. He then went into an analysis of traffic conditions in the American metropolis, showing that every north and south avenue except one was occupied by a horse car line at that time, and that even with the numerous omnibus lines the facilities were utterly inadequate. At the rate of increase he showed that a rapid transit line was a necessity. But read a few paragraphs from his report on this subject and marvel that the future was so clear to him in 1864:

"The average increase for the whole period of sixty years," he writes after tracing the growth of traffic for that length of time, "is nearly twenty-five per cent. for each period of five years, and if we apply this ratio we shall find that in the year 1870 we may reasonably calculate upon a population of not less than 1,272,000, and in 1880 of not less than 2,000,000 (the actual figures for those two years were 942,292 in 1870, and 1,206,590 in 1880), or about double the present number. This will cover the entire island. If at the same time the proportion of passengers to population increases in anything like the same ratio as has been shown for the past ten years, we shall not be beyond bounds in estimating that in 1870 we shall have at least 100,000,000 passengers requiring transportation through our streets on the railways, and in 1880 200,000,000. (The actual figures were 115,139,553 in 1870 and 288,000,000 in 1880.)

"When we take into consideration the fact that the increase of population must take place prin-

cipally in the upper part of the city, and that in consequence of the large area occupied by the Central
Park the extension northward must be more rapid
for the same increase than in past years, and that
the distance traveled by each passenger must be
correspondingly lengthened, we can then begin to
appreciate how totally impossible it is that the necessities of this population in the means of transit can
be satisfied by any system of horse railways that can
be devised. The streets would be absolutely blocked,
and the time occupied by the trip would be a loss
from the occupations of the day which would be un-
endurable. Speed must come in to fill up the deficiency, and this is inadmissible unless the vehicles,
of whatsoever description they may be, are entirely
separated from the ordinary traffic of the streets.
Steam must necessarily be used, for the want of some
other available power. Compressed air has been suggested, but experiments have not yet demonstrated
the practicability of its use for considerable distances."

No better grasp of the traffic problem of New York
City has been shown by our modern experts. Robinson,
after carefully surveying the field and calculating the
increase of traffic, accurately guaged the coming develop-
ments and foresaw the time when a horse railroad in
every street would be insufficient to move the throngs demanding transportation. He did not use the words,
"rapid transit," but he did say that "speed must come
in to fill up the deficiency." And he proposed to provide
it by building what we would now call a rapid transit
line beneath the surface—namely a subway. It was only
the necessity of the times that made him advocate steam
as a motive power. He realized its weak points, but it
was the best available. He noted the experiments made
with air as a motive power in the tunnel near Sydenham
Palace in England, but concluded: "All these plans are

yet experiments, and until they are more fully developed
we must confine our attention to steam, and the alternative must be its use either upon railways elevated above
the streets or placed in excavations or tunnels below
them.'' He then proceeded to show why subways are
better than elevated roads, concluding the argument as
follows:

"The statistics I have indulged in convince me
that it is only necessary to look to the local travel
(unless it be to the transportation of freight at such
hours of the night as would not interfere with the
passenger business) for such amount of traffic as will
work the capacity of your road to the utmost; and I
am satisfied that every consideration of economy,
safety and convenience justifies the adoption of the
plan you propose, viz. an underground railway. In
no other way can the public exigency be met.''

Robinson recommended that for economy and convenience of operation the road be built "as near the surface of the street as possible," and to accomplish this
he discussed the question of routes and their relation to
the sewer system, which he wished to disarrange as
little as possible. He pointed out that Broadway follows
the ridge of the island and that sewers in the cross streets
generally can flow both ways from it. For this reason
he recommended a route up Broadway from the Battery
to Fourteenth Street; thence under Union Square and
through Broadway to Twenty-third Street; thence under
Madison Square to Fifth Avenue and through Fifth
Avenue to Fifty-ninth Street at the southern end of
Central Park. This was a slight variation from the
route set forth in the articles of incorporation of the
Metropolitan Railway Company, adopted before Robinson had been retained. This route was described as follows:

"The road is to be constructed in a tunnel under-

ground from a place at or near the Battery in the
City of New York, following a line under or near
Broadway to Thirty-fourth Street, and then following a line under or near the Sixth Avenue to or near
the Central Park; with two branches from the last
mentioned place, one branch running to a place at
or near the Harlem Railroad, and the other branch
running to a place at or near the Hudson River Railroad all in the County of New York. The whole
length of such road, as near as may be, is to be
twelve miles.''

Here we have the main outlines of the present subway
—a trunk line running from the Battery to Fifty-ninth
street, with two branches, one going up the East Side and
the other the West Side. The main difference is that
in today's subway the dividing line is at Ninety-sixth
Street instead of at Fifty-ninth Street—a difference due
to the northward growth of the city in the meantime.

A novel treatment for the Battery end of the line
was proposed. In his plan Robinson advocated starting
the road on the surface at a connection with the South
Ferry, where the "immense travel from this point to
Hamilton and Atlantic Avenues in Brooklyn and also
to Staten Island" was to be considered. His line began
at the Battery "with a circle for the turning of trains"
(exactly what we have today in the subway) and skirt-
ing the inner edge of the Battery ran in an ever-deepening
cut to Bowling Green, where it entered the tunnel under
Broadway. He proposed to span this cut with on ornamental iron bridge to carry the travel through Battery
and Whitehall streets.

The existing subway has an inside height of about 13
feet two inches; some of the new subways under construction will have a height of 15 feet. In 1864 Mr. Robinson proposed to make his tunnel 16 feet high in the
center and 25½ feet wide (for two tracks) at the widest

part, which was at the level of the platforms of the cars. This width, he says, would be ample for two tracks carrying cars nine feet wide and would allow 2½ feet in the center and on each side. The tunnel was to be arched, with an oval-shaped roof and sides sloping slightly inward. At present a width of 15 feet for each track is allowed.

Employment of concrete for floor material and of asphalt for water-proofing in the existing subway is generally regarded as a modern and up-to-date method. Robinson specified both in the following description of his tunnel:

"The foundations should be of granite blocks cut to the required form, as skewbacks for the invert; underneath which should be a base of concrete. The spandrils should be well loaded with concrete, and the whole well covered with asphalt. A center drain is provided, emptying into cisterns at all the depressions, from which drain pipes should be provided to carry the water to the sewers. As these cisterns would necessarily be below the level of any sewers in their immediate vicinity, in some cases it will be necessary to construct these drains for some distance before finding outlets for them. But in one case, namely at Canal Street, it will be necessary to pump the drainage which may collect there for a short distance in each direction. This, however, would be but a slight matter, as there would seem to be no cause for any serious accumulation of water if the tunnel is properly constructed. Even the Thames tunnel is kept dry without difficulty."

In the matter of stations Robinson planned better than the designers of the present subway. Instead of kiosks occupying valuable space on the sidewalks, he proposed the purchase and use of appropriate buildings on each side of the street, except in parks etc., where he suggested the erection of suitable structures on city property. For convenience of train operation, he placed the stations at intervals of a half mile apart. Terminal stations were to be erected at Bowling Green and Fifty-ninth Street, with eight intermediate stations and a special station at South Ferry. At stations the tunnel was to be widened so as to give station platforms, which were to be on a level with the platforms of the cars, 12¼ feet wide and 150 feet long.

For the terminal and other stations to be built on public property Robinson proposed to erect structures of iron and glass, with glass floors, directly over the tunnel, and to dispense with the roof of the tunnel under them, so that the daylight would pass through the glass structure and illuminate the station platforms beneath. This was to save artificial lighting of stations during the day. His drawings of these unique structures (Plates 3 and 4) are reproduced on other pages. All stations were to be equipped with everything needful, including telegraph offices. Robinson figured that the cost of stations built on purchased property would be about $125,000 each, and he proposed to rent part of the buildings for enough to earn interest on the cost.

The problem of ventilation, which bothered the designers of the existing subway not a little and was confessedly only partially solved when operation began, was handled by Robinson in an ingenious manner. Whether his plan would have been effective is a question. He gave the credit for the invention of it to Hugh B. Willson, the promoter of the company in whose interest Robinson was working. The plan was to get ventilation through pipes "running laterally to convenient openings", and connected with hollow iron gas lamp posts about 15 inches in diameter, erected on the surface of the street at the edge of the sidewalks. These were to be placed 100 feet apart on each side of the street.

Robinson's plan for the operation of his subway is

interesting enough to give in its entirety. Here it is:

"The true theory in all public conveyances is that the oftener the vehicles run the greater is the public convenience, and the greater the number who will ride. If a car with a capacity of 80 passengers can be filled every four minutes, it will be fair to assume that one with capacity for at least fifty can be filled every two minutes. Hence a system should be adopted by which trains can be run at the shortest intervals consistent with safety, provided the capacity required for each train is not too small to enable it to be run with economy proportional to the larger train.

"In my estimate of the total amount of local travel to be expected in this city for the horse railroads in 1870, I have placed it at 100,000,000. Making due allowance for the number which would be carried in stages, the entire movement will probably be 150,000,000. It has not probably been less than 100,000,000 during the past year.

"This would amount to 410,000 per day. If we assume that but one eighth of this number would prefer the speedy and comfortable cars of the tunnel, we should have to provide for 51,250 passengers, or 25,625 each way. As a question of safety it is important that there should never be more than one train between two adjacent stations at a time. If we calculate upon a running speed of twenty miles per hour, the distance between stations being one half of a mile, the time would be one and a half minutes. Allowing one half minute for stopping and the average time from station to station would be two minutes, the trip from Bowling Green to Central Park (4 3-5 miles) occupying less than twenty minutes. (*)

* It now takes just about twenty minutes for an express train in the present subway to make this run.

Without violating the condition that there shall be but one train at a time between two adjacent stations, we should then be able to dispatch a train every two minutes, or thirty per hour. (@) This is probably as often as the trains could be dispatched or run with safety. If we assume that the 51,250 passengers are distributed through 18 hours, or from six o'clock in the morning until twelve at night, we have to transport each way every hour 1,423 passengers, or 47 in each train. This is the average for the day, but when it is considered that the great proportion of the travel is in one direction in one portion of the day, and in the opposite direction in another, it will be found necessary to provide accommodations for a considerable greater number in order to carry the average and seat every passenger.

"From an inspection of the table giving the statistics of the operation of the horse railways it will be seen that the average number carried per trip each way, in 1864, was 34. It is not probable that the trip in one direction will average 15. In order, therefore, to make an average of 34 each way, they must have carried at least 53 in the other direction. Making allowance for changes on the route and it is probable that the average load was not less than 40. To have averaged 34 passengers per trip each way and to have given each passenger a seat, they should, therefore, have had capacity for 40, while in fact they had but seats for 20. In estimating accordingly for a travel of 51,250 passengers daily through the tunnel, with a train every two minutes, I assume that we should require seats for at least 80.

"I submit herewith two drawings of steam cars suitable for such a traffic. I propose a car 40 feet

---

@ The quickest movement in the present subway is 33 trains per hour. but these are ten car trains carrying more than 100 per car.

long, exclusive of engine apartment, divided into eight
compartments running cross-wise, with a door to
each compartment on the right hand side of the car.
Each compartment would be five feet wide, with
seats vis-a-vis. The width of the cars being nine
feet, from out to out, or about eight feet inside, there
would be comfortable and abundant room for seating
ten passengers in each compartment, or eighty in the
car. The compartments need not be separated above
the backs of the seats. The doors should be arranged
to slide, all being connected and moved simultaneously by an apparatus operated by the brakeman
at the rear of the car. Each car should have its gas
holder and burners, or other suitable lighting apparatus.''

In Plates 6 and 7, reproduced on another page, Mr.
Robinson shows two types of cars, one having the engine in it and the other having it in a separate car. He
figured that either car would perform the service required and haul another car of equal capacity if necessary for an expenditure of 12 pounds of coal per mile.
With two cars to a train the capacity of the subway would
be more than 100,000 passengers per day allowing a seat
for every passenger. He advocated the use of coke in the
engines, which could be made to condense their own steam
and thus render the exhaust scarcely perceptible.

Nor was the proposed system of ticket selling behind
modern practice, for Mr. Robinson eliminated ticket col-
lectors altogether and would have had passengers pay
at the stations before entering. He was also up to date
in planning for electric signals, but in using electricity
to start his trains he was guilty of a serious lapse, for
he actually proposed to have every train at every station
at exactly the same moment. He wanted to have electric
clocks in each station, all on the same circuit and ticking
together, and an electric starter, which would give the

signal to move to all stations at the same instant. How this would work he tells as follows:

"There would be a car at every station at the same time. At a common signal all would leave. There being no train on the track between stations, every engine driver would move with confidence and know that he has only to run his half mile in one and a half minutes. The platform operator at each station would know the second when a train was due. If not arrived, or if so far behind as to render it impossible to start from the station at its proper time, or if stopped by accident, he would send the proper signal to the starter so that he would not give the next starting signal, or the circuit controlling this might be so arranged that any station operator could disconnect it in an emergency so that it could not be operated."

In presenting his estimate of the cost of the road, Robinson is careful to state that it corresponds with the currency then circulating, namely the money of war times, when gold was at a big premium. The figures are interesting in comparison with present prices. He estimated that the work would cost $8,487,006, divided as follows:

ESTIMATE OF COST.

Taking out and relaying 60,000 square yards of Russ pavement from Battery Place to Union Sq. at $3. $180,0

Taking up and relaying 37,000 square yards Belgian pavement from 14th to 59th Street at $2........ 74,0

692,000 cubic yards earth excavation at 50 cents...... 486,0

560,000 cubic yards earth carted away at 50 cents.... 280,0

372,000 cubic yards earth refilled at 20 cents........ 74,

101,000 cubic yards rock excavation at $10.......... 1,010,0

92,000 cubic yards rock carted away at 25 cents...... 23,0

9,000 cubic yards rock refilled at 25 cents............ 2,

6,114	Ms. brick masonry at $20....................	1,322,280
4,100	cubic yards rubble stone masonry at $6.......	324,000
1,022	cubic yards granite masonry at $25..........	525,550
5,000	cubic yards concrete at $7..................	245,000
2,200	cubic yards ballast at $1...................	52,200
85,000	square feet asphalt covering at 6 cents.......	53,100
00,000	square feet cobble paving at 12½ cents......	62,500
5,000	lineal feet center drain at 50 cents...........	12,500
,700	lineal feet side drain, 12 in..................	1,700
00	lineal feet pile foundation at Canal St. at $40....	20,000
25,000	lineal feet 18 in. sewer pipe at $1.50..........	37,500
,880	lineal feet 48 and 54 in. brick sewer in Canal Street at $10	28,880
50	man holes at $60	15,000
0	street basins at $200..........................	10,000
	House connections	10,000

,000	lineal feet 20 in. water mains					
,600	" " 24 " " "				6,500,000 lbs. at 5c. $325,000	
4,500	" " 30 " " "					
,100	" " 36 " " "				1-3 off for old pipes 97,500	
						$227,500

00	lamp post ventilators, 1,000 lbs. each at 5c........	25,000
2,500	lineal feet 15 in. pipe........................	12,500
00	lineal feet lamp and gas pipe, labor etc...........	25,000
	Bridge at Bowling Green	50,000
1	miles track complete at $25,000 per mile..........	275,000
0	engines and cars combined at $8,000.............	320,000
0	cars (80 passengers each) at $4,000..............	80,000
0	cars (50 passengers each) at $2,500..............	100,000
	Station grounds at northern terminus...............	350,000
	Terminal and way stations	1,400,000
		$7,715,460

Add 10 per cent. for contingencies, engineering, superintendence, etc.	771,546
	$8,487.006

In a foot note Mr. Robinson pointed out how certain savings might reduce this cost, but he figured the total average cost, including the equipment, at $1,550,000 per mile. This, he said, is less than the cost of the London Underground, which up to January 1, 1864 was $1,670,000 per mile. This he held is a good showing, considering "the extraordinarily high prices now prevailing". Upon a gold standard, he said, the cost of the New York road probably would not exceed one-half that of the London Underground.

Robinson estimated that the tunnel road in its first year would carry 20,000,000 passengers and that the average fare paid would be 7 cents, yielding a gross revenue of $1,400,000, and that rents from station buildings would yield $100,000 more—a total of $1,500,000. The expense of operation, excluding interest on cost, he estimated at $541,200, leaving a profit of $958,750, equal to about 12 per cent. on the cost. An interesting item in his expense allowance due to the war is $35,000 for the "Government tax on gross receipts."

Summing up the advantages of a subway at the end of his report, Robinson wrote:

"I can conceive nothing so completely fulfilling in every respect the requirements of our population as such a road with such an equipment and worked in the manner suggested. There would be no dust. There would be no mud. Passengers would not be obliged to go into the middle of the street to take a car. They have simply to enter a station from the sidewalk and pass down a spacious and well lighted staircase to a dry and roomy platform. The temperature would be cool in summer and warm in winter. There would be no delays from snow or ice. The cars would not be obliged to wait for a lazy or obstinate truckman. The passenger would be sure of a luxurious seat in a well lighted car, and would

Plate 2.

SECTION OF TUNNEL AT STREET STATION.

Scale 16 feet to an inch.

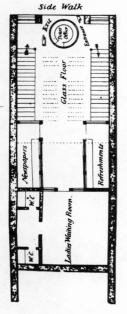

Side Walk

Plan of Arrangement of Station Rooms on Street Level.

Scale 16 feet to an inch.

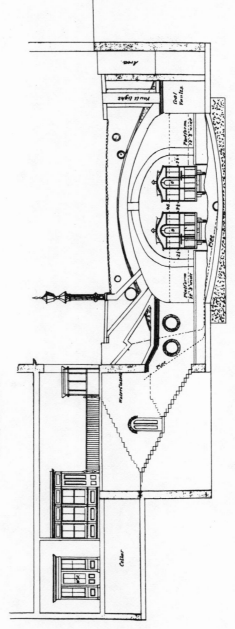

A. P. ROBINSON'S PLAN FOR SUBWAY, 1864

be carried to his destination in one-third the time he could be carried by any other conveyance. These would be the advantages to those who ride, and for the other great public in the streets there would be no collisions, no broken wheels or fractured axles, no frightened horses or run-over pedestrians. Everything would be out of sight and hearing, and nothing would indicate the great thoroughfare below.''

To us who enjoy the advantages of underground travel there is nothing new in the above statement, but how must it have sounded in the ears of our fathers in the last year of the Civil War? No doubt the scheme was looked upon by many as an idle dream, but that there were a few brave men who believed in it is shown by the fact that Henry V. Poor and his associates were ready to put $5,000,000 into the enterprise. But Robinson and his backers shared the fate of those advanced thinkers who are ahead of their times!

CHAPTER IV

FIRST RAPID TRANSIT BILL PASSED BY THE LEGISLATURE AND VETOED.

IN November, 1864, one of the most momentous general elections ever held in the United States took place. At it Abraham Lincoln, after a campaign in which he was villified and ridiculed shamelessly not only by the opposition press but by papers which called themselves loyal to the Union, was triumphantly re-elected to the Presidency. New York State had given him its electoral vote and with it had elected a Legislature strongly Union in both branches and a Governor, Reuben E. Fenton, also a strong Unionist. The majority in the Legislature was composed of Republicans and Union Democrats, all of whom were known and spoken of as Unionists. The opposition was composed of Democrats entirely.

Hugh B. Willson's first bill for a charter for the Metropolitan Railway Company to build an underground railroad in Broadway, as we have seen, was defeated in the Senate of 1864. It was not introduced until towards the close of the session, and Mr. Willson made no great effort to press it. "It was, however, too late in the session", he wrote later, "to hope to get it passed through both houses, and I did not attempt to press it at that session." It is probable, too, that he foresaw the election of a new set of Legislators and felt that nothing he could do at the session of 1864 would help him with the session of 1865. So he made up his mind to lay the project befor the new Legislature, and meanwhile devoted himself to laying the foundations for a successful appeal to that body.

"During the recess of the Legislature of 1864," he wrote, "I devoted myself with untiring energy to the popularizing the subject of an underground system of railways, and frequently discussed with Mr. Robinson

(A. P. Robinson, the engineer) the engineering and other features of the project.   He became convinced of its feasibility and regarded it as superior to any other system that had yet been presented to the world for city traffic.   In the autumn he was engaged to investigate the various routes and make a report on the undertaking.   I gave him all the aid in my power, and the result was the production of a report almost exhaustive of the subject.''

This report Willson had printed and circulated, and with it he went to Albany and had introduced a bill to give the Metropolitan Railway company the legal right to build and operate a subway as therein planned.   The bill was carefully drawn so that it infringed no private rights.   It was introduced in the Senate on February 7, 1865, by Senator Laimbeer, a Union Senator from New York City.   At the same time Senator Laimbeer introduced another bill for a pneumatic tube line for freight traffic, to run underground in Nassau, the Bowery and other streets.   Thereafter both bills were considered together.

On February 15 the Senate Committee on Railroads held a hearing on both bills.   This committee was composed of Senators Angell, Williams and Beach, Unionists, and Hobbs and Woodruff, Democrats.   There was no opposition, everyone appearing being in favor of the bills. On March 15 friends of the bill had a hearing before the Assembly Committee on Railroads.   At this time the Albany correspondent of the New York Times wrote as follows to his paper:

"This proposition to construct an underground railroad is ably advocated before the committees of the two houses and has thus far met with no opposition.   The Senate committee reported the bill for the consideration of the Senate last week, and the Assembly committee express themselves as favorably impressed with the arguments advanced in favor of the project, although they have not yet taken any action in regard to their report.''

Within a few days, however, opposition appeared. Stories were circulated to the effect that the scheme was impracticable and that the men who put any money into it would lose; also that the new line was not needed and could not get traffic enough to make it pay. On March 20 the New York Times in an editorial attacked the shallowness of such arguments. ''The only persons to whose interests it can prove in the slightest degree prejudicial,'' said the Times, ''are the street railway companies and the omnibus proprietors.'' The writer then pointed out that these interests were always complaining that they did not have conveyances enough for their traffic, yet when any effort like the underground project was made to relieve them of a portion of their burden, they rushed up to Albany and used every means, fair and foul, to defeat it. ''The one point for the Government to satisfy itself about'', said the Times, ''is whether the proposed excavation will affect the houses, sewerage or streets of the city injuriously; whether the line is needed and whether it will pay are not matters for the consideration of the Legislature. It is no part of its business to prevent speculators from sinking their money in unprofitable enterprises. It may be satisfied that people who propose to invest their money in digging a tunnel seven miles long have good reason for believing they will get it back again; and if they are disappointed, nobody else will suffer.''

The bill came up in the Senate for passage on March 24th. Seventeen votes were required for passage. The vote was 14 to 12, and although the affirmative scored the 14, the bill failed for lack of the required number. Senator Laimbeer, who voted for the bill, moved to reconsider and to lay that motion on the table, which was carried. Friends of the measure at once exerted themselves to save it. Some of the negative votes, it was said, came from

Senators who resented the previous turning down of a bill to give the New York & Harlem rights to build a railroad in Broadway. These differences were smoothed out, petitions for the bill were received from New York City, and on April 3 it was reconsidered and four days later came up again for passage. This time it was passed by a vote of 19 to 7. It came up in the Assembly on April 27 and was passed by that body by a vote of 89 in the affirmative. In the debate preceding its passage by the Assembly the opposition was led by Assemblyman Brandreth, of Westchester county, who expressed the fear that the construction of the underground would "disturb" the surface of Broadway. Even in those days the country member was solicitous for the streets of the metropolis! Assemblyman Creamer, of New York, also spoke against the bill, while it was championed by Assemblyman Van Buren, of New York, and Assemblyman Veeder, of Kings County.

Friends of the underground railroad were naturally jubilant, and the prospects for a subway seemed bright. But they reckoned without the Governor, Reuben E. Fenton, who astounded the community by vetoing the bill. On May 20 some weeks after the Legislature had adjourned, he sent it to the Secretary of State, Chauncey M. Depew, without his signature and with a note of disapproval. His reasons for withholding his approval were set forth in his veto message, which was included in a general letter transmitting other vetoes and was as follows:

"Neither can I approve the 'Act to authorize the Metropolitan Railway company of the City of New York to construct a tunnel under Broadway, and for other Purposes.' This bill appears to have been elaborately drawn and seems to have provided against any improper infringement of private rights. I am inclined to think that the structure contemplated, or something occupying the same prominent route from the foot of Broadway to the upper part of the city, may be made practicable and may be deemed necessary. Rapid access to and from the business center of New York is of vital importance, and it is not improbable that some more systematic, direct and well-guarded measure will finally be inaugurated. My objections to this bill are that, although a specified route is laid down, there is no requirement that the road thus authorized shall be speedily completed. There being no obligation that it shall be constructed with reasonable rapidity (the General Railroad Act allowing five years for the construction of the road from the date of commencement) it might be possible that, through financial disasters or other causes, the central thoroughfare of our commercial metropolis would be obstructed or unsettled for a vexatious period. Even should the work be vigorously prosecuted, Broadway must be rendered, at intervals and for short distances, for a short time, unpleasant and uncomfortable to travel and business, and it seems to me, therefore, that the Legislature should have provided against the contingency of prolonging the inconvenience through the financial vicissitudes to which such enterprises are too often subjected.

"But a controlling objection to the approval of this bill is found in Section 4, which authorizes the trainsfer of State and City property for the use of this company. It reads as follows:

" 'The Mayor, Aldermen and Commonalty of the City of New York are hereby authorized to permit the use by said Metropolitan Railway company of such portion of any lands heretofore granted by the people of the State of New York to the said Mayor, Aldermen and Commonalty, or of such other public lands or places in the said city, as they may deem proper, to allow the said company to occupy either temporarily or permanently for the public convenience, in the construction, operation and use of the said railroad and tunnel, and upon such terms and under such regulations as may be prescribed by the said Mayor, Aldermen and Commonalty.'

"By the provision of that part of the section cited it will be perceived that the whole of the Battery, if so much shall be deemed necessary, which is in one sense the property of the State, may be converted into a passenger and freight depot. The same use might be made of the other public parks and places of the city along or near the contemplated route. I can see grave objections to such a diversion of the parks or public grounds, which are designed for the benefit of the people, and which are essential to their health and conducive to their pleasure. I cannot consent, on my part, to such use of these grounds, without feeling that I had violated the trust reposed in me by the people."

For similar reasons the Governor also vetoed the bill for a pneumatic tube underground express line, which had passed the Legislature with the Metropolitan bill.

It is difficult to imagine a Governor in these days vetoing a subway bill on any such grounds. The Battery park, for which Fenton displayed such solicitude, was later turned over to the elevated railroad, which now maintains there a structure infinitely more unsightly than the station and bridge which the Metropolitan Railway Company of 1865 planned to build there. In those days, however, criticism of the Chief Executive was not as common as it is now, and the newspapers, with one exception, were silent as to this veto. That exception was the New York Times, which on May 22, the day the veto message was published, contained the following editorial:

"The Underground Railroad—We are sorry that

Governor Fenton has refused his signature to the bill authorizing an underground railroad in this city. We have always regarded such a road as the only measure which would afford substantial relief to our over-crowded streets and facilitate transit from one part of the city to another. It is perfectly certain that there is not room on the surface of the city to accommodate the traffic which its business requires. Being situated on a long and narrow island, its surface is restricted and its streets are narrow. A careful calculation shows that, even with its present population, enough railroads cannot be placed in its streets to accommodate all who wish to ride, without stopping its business traffic. This evil, of necessity, increases from year to year, and will absolutely compel, sooner or later, resort to such a road as that which the Governor has just refused to permit. *We think his action will be regretted by all classes of people in this city, except those who are interested in existing and prospective street railroads.*"

The writer has italicized the last sentence, which is the only one casting any reflection, and that by implication, upon the Governor. The sting, however, was there, and it immediately brought forth a defence of the Governor in the New York Tribune, then edited by Horace Greeley and as pro-Fenton in State politics as it was pro-Union in national affairs. In an editorial published the next day, May 23, Horace rebuked the Times and asked if such criticism was fair in view of the Governor's reasons for vetoing the bill. "Now, we favor an underground railroad," continued the Tribune, "and hope to see it constructed under Legislative charter and by the company which procured the passage of the bill just vetoed." It defended all the Governor's vetoes and suggested that they be published and generally circulated in pamphlet form. It also criticised the Legislators as corrupt and impugned the motives of those who voted for the measures vetoed by the Governor.

There was some truth in the Tribune's remarks. Its fault lay in failing to distinguish between good and bad bills. Many, perhaps most, of Fenton's vetoes were justified, notably that of the bill to allow the New York Central to increase its rates from two cents to two and one-half cents a mile, but a study of the Metropolitan underground railroad bill reveals nothing to warrant its disapproval.

The Times did not reply to the Tribune, further than to repeat its previous expression of regret at the defeat of the underground project. Both papers, like all their contemporaries, were absorbed with the closing scenes of the Civil War, reporting the Mrs. Surratt trial and discussing the appropriate punishment for Jefferson Davis, the recently captured President of the Confederate States. Possibly in more normal times the underground railroad promoters would have been given more consideration. Certainly the veto of Governor Fenton caused much less stir then than a similar step would now.

There was one man in New York City, however, who resented the Tribune's harsh criticism of the men who voted for the underground bill, and that was Thomas B. Van Buren, Assemblyman from the Fifteenth district, New York City, who not only voted but spoke for the bill. He wrote a letter to the Tribune, which gave it space without comment in its issue of May 27. After a general introduction Van Buren wrote:

"Now, sir, although under the ban of so severe a punishment as never being returned to the Assembly, and fearing that the present city railroads, having succeeded in their opposition to the underground road, may not see fit to invest in the pamphlet you propose, I wish to state through your columns that I am one of those who voted not only but labored zealously to pass the bills creating an underground railroad and a pneumatic express.

"The opposition to these measures came from these representing the interests of the existing city railways, and I venture the assertion that no bill creating a corporation has for years been presented or passed, which so thoroughly guarded public and private rights as the bill creating the Metropolitan or Underground Railway. * * *

"I believe that no projects have been before the Legislature for years which would have proved of such benefit and advantage to the public as these two railways. They were to interfere with no vested rights, obstruct no streets, violate no contracts. They would have provided cheap, clean, rapid and safe means for carrying passengers and freight, and would have made the upper portion of our city the most delightful residence in the world.

"For Governor Fenton personally and for his motives and independence I have the very highest regard, but I claim for myself the same purity of motive and the same right of independent action. The grounds upon which the veto of the underground road are based do not seem to me sound. The right given to the Mayor and Common Council to allow the said company to use 'either temporarily or permanently, for the PUBLIC CONVENIENCE, such portions of the public lands in the city as they may deem proper and under such regulations as they may prescribe', does not seem to me fraught with such dread consequences as to demand the exercise of the veto power; and I do not believe that the public of New York entertain such a holy reverence for the Battery as to regret its being used, or a part of it, for such purposes."

To the unprejudiced reader of this chapter of Legis-

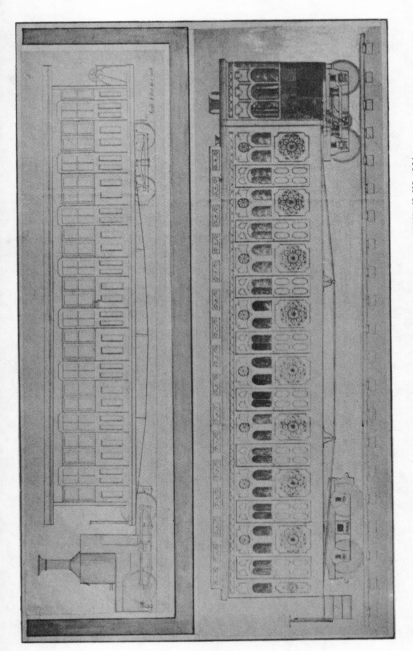

TYPE OF CAR PLANNED FOR METROPOLITAN SUBWAY IN 1864.

lative history it would appear that the first underground railroad bill was defeated by the corporations then owning the street railroads, who did not want the competition of a subway. Fenton's action gave the opponents of the scheme time to organize rival projects and ultimately to defeat it. He thereby deferred underground transit in New York City for almost half a century.

CHAPTER V

LEGISLATIVE COMMISSION ON RAPID TRANSIT.

WHILE Willson and his associates naturally felt aggrieved at the action of Governor Fenton, who had deprived them by a pen stroke of the fruits of two years of labor, they accepted the Executive's interference with the best grace possible, and set to work to remove the cause of his objection. With their counsel they went over the terms of the bill and addressed a communication to the Executive, in which they bound themselves and their company to waive all rights to which the Governor had taken exception. The Governor, however, refused to sign the bill, even with this waiver.

Willson's project and the publicity it obtained during the Legislative session of 1865 started a perfect avalanche of rapid transit schemes, and the newspapers of that year are filled with a variety of plans for providing better transportation facilities. Subways, depressed railroads, elevated railroads and railroads built through blocks, were proposed, some practical and others fanciful in the extreme. Many of them, no doubt, originated with the companies owning the existing street car and omnibus lines, who had fought the Willson project in the Legislature and before the Governor. Anticipating that the Metropolitan company would apply to the next Legislature for the rights they sought, these interests devised a number of rival schemes and companies to contest for the Broadway underground franchise. On the other hand many men of inventive turn took advantage of the public interest in the matter to bring forward their ideas of providing rapid transit.

It would be useless to describe or even name these different projects. Suffice it to say that among them were several proposals for elevated railroads which commanded respectful attention from the press. One of these was the Harvey and another the Montgomery plan. The former, brought forward by Charles T. Harvey, contemplated a railroad elevated on pillars erected at the sidewalk line and operated by cars propelled by cables driven by power from stationary steam engines. The other, advanced by Richard Montgomery, consisted of a similar elevated structure operated by cars drawn by steam locomotives, the structure to be built of corrugated steel bars, invented by Montgomery, and for which great strength and lightness were claimed. The latter never got beyond the stage of newspaper plans, but the Harvey scheme we shall hear more of later, as it was the progenitor of the present elevated railroad system.

In November 1865 another election was held for all State officers except the Governor and for members of the Legislature. The Republicans were again successful, electing General Barlow Secretary of State and a majority of both branches of the Legislature. The Unionists had 28 Senators to four for the Democrats, and the Assembly stood 94 Unionists to 34 Democrats. At the same time the Democrats elected John T. Hoffman as Mayor of New York City, a man who subsequently became Governor and played a prominent part in the rapid transit game.

Before the new Legislature met Willson made another attempt to get Governor Fenton to sign the bill passed by the previous session, subject to the waiver by the company of all privileges to which he objected. This effort was backed by more or less newspaper support. The New York Times in an editorial in its issue of December 14, 1865 said:

"Why does the Governor still refuse his signature to the Underground Railroad bill? The bill was passed by the last Legislature, if we remember rightly, by twenty-two votes in the Senate and upwards of ninety in the Assembly—a vote which

would have passed it over a veto if it had been previously passed and vetoed by the Governor. It has,
therefore, received the constitutional vote, though
not upon the constitutional condition, to become a
law *without the Governor's signature.* For some
unexplained reason Mr. Fenton withholds his signature.

"The measure is one of very grave importance
to the people of New York. Its feasibility and util-
ity are no longer matters of experiment."

After alluding to the success of the underground road
in London the writer continues:

"The names of the gentlemen who compose the
company which offers to undertake this enterprise
constitute a sufficient guaranty that the work will be
promptly undertaken and carried forward to completion; and as the law limits them to five years from
their organization, nearly two of which have already
elapsed, they have certainly not any too much time.
We trust the bill will without further delay be
signed; and as the company has with great liberality
come forward and under the advice of able counsel
tendered to the Governor a relinquishment of any
portion of the franchise which he may require, there
ought to be no reason to apprehend that we shall not
soon have the privilege of seeing this much-needed
enterprise actually begun. The question is one which
will not bear further trifling with. Every month's
delay is an immeasurable loss to the city in a business point of view and an incalculable sacrifice of the
comfort and convenience of residents."

The Governor again refused to yield, and Willson and
his associates prepared to resort to the new Legislature
to obtain the passage of another bill. The measure they
submitted was identical with the bill which the Governor

had vetoed, the promoters holding that it was the province of the Legislature, if it deemed it wise, to amend it to conform to the Governor's suggestions. They should have made the amendments themselves, for later in the session the fact that their bill contained the objectionable features was used to advantage by their opponents. Chief among these was a deserter from their own camp, one Origen Vandenburgh, who had been employed by Willson during the previous session as a lobbyist at Albany. This man now appeared with a bill of his own for the same rights to build a subway under Broadway for which the Metropolitan company was an applicant. He sought to justify himself in this course by making the statement that the president of the Metropolitan company had told him that that company would not make another effort to get the franchise. In this, however, he was flatly contradicted by Willson.

The fight in the Legislature opened early. Before the session was ten days old, namely on January 10, 1866, the following resolution was introduced in the Senate by Seator Lent:

"Resolved that the engineer of the Croton Aqueduct Board be requested to report his opinion as to the practicability of constructing a railroad under Broadway in the city of New York, and especially as to the effect of the attempt to construct the same upon the Croton and other pipes and the sewers, and the damage if any which may be caused to the city and to the individual property owners thereby, and what precaution ought to be taken to guard against the same, and to provide for the payment of damages, and what legislation is necessary in reference to that object."

After lying on the table for a day, this resolution was adopted. The engineer of the Croton Aqueduct, to whom it was addressed, at that time was Alfred W. Craven, one

of the leading engineers of the day and an uncle of Alfred
Craven, who from 1910 to 1916 was chief engineer of the
Public Service Commission in charge of the building of
the new Dual System subways. In response to a request
from A. P. Robinson, when the latter was preparing his
report for the Metropolitan company, Alfred W. Craven
had stated that with proper precautions the underground
road could be built without seriously damaging the water
system.

But what Alfred W. Craven found unobjectionable in
1865 he declared highly objectionable in 1866 in his response to the Senate resolution. On February 2, 1866,
the president of the Senate laid before that body Mr.
Craven's report, in which the Engineer of the Croton
Board said:

"I assume that the inquiry refers to a road constructed upon the same general plan as that vetoed
by the Governor last year. Also that the grade, loca-
tion, plan of the tunnel etc. are the same as proposed
in the report of A. P. Robinson Esq., civil engineer.
In reply I beg leave to state that to set forth in specific detail the extent and cost of the work of remov-
ing and relaying pipes, and the reconstruction of
sewers necessarily resulting from the building of
such a road would require more time than appears to
have been anticipated by your honorable body. I
have been compelled, therefore, to confine myself in
general terms to the principal points involved;
which, together with the aid of the accompanying
maps and profiles, will enable you to form at least an
approximate estimate of the complicated difficulties
to be encountered so far as the water pipes and
sewers are involved; the damages to the inhabitants
whose daily comforts and daily absolute necessities
are dependent upon the uninterrupted use of these
public works; the losses of manufactories suspended;

the risk of destruction of property by fires during
the total or partial interruption of the water supply,
and other interests affected.

"*First, the Water Supply*: It must be borne in
mind the chief supply of the whole city is drawn
from the large main pipes through Fifth Avenue
and Broadway, directly on the site of the proposed
railway. From these main pipes the water is distributed east and west to the river limits. At whatever point the work on the railroad should be in
operation, it would at once involve the necessity of
the removal of these main pipes from the section
where the work might be in progress. During the
time taken for this removal and the reconstruction
of the numerous lateral branches, the inhabitants
in the intersecting streets would be cut off from
water entirely, while the rest of the city, from river
to river, south of the point of work, would be dependent solely on the utterly inadequate supply
coming through the small cross-mains, reaching districts for which they were not intended by the way
of lateral connections with the remote parts of the
general system or net work of pipe distribution.

*   *   *   *   *   *   *   *   *

"When it is considered that even now, when all
the mains are in operation, complaints of an insufficient head of water throughout the lower part
of the city are constant and urgent, you will more
readily understand the condition to which the inhabitants might be reduced if that head were materially diminished, as it most certainly would be,
by the construction of the proposed railway, however well devised or skillfully conducted might be
the operations.

"The above statement implies the possibility of
prosecuting the work on the road in the most careful
and deliberate manner, commencing at the Battery

and working in regular sections. But it is undeniable that if the road were to be finished in any reasonable time it would be necessary to work it in many points simultaneously. This, while it would decrease the number of persons deprived of water, would also diminish the supply through the laterals to the rest of the city.

"The extent of damages to individuals and to companies growing out of the construction of the suggested railroad it is impossible to estimate with even approximate correctness. The area of population covered, the extent and variety of interests involved and the different degree of inconvenience and loss sustained by each class of sufferers, all make up a whole so complicated that the actual experience alone of proved results could warrant any summing up of the total loss or damage. That the municipal government, which has guaranteed to consumers the use of this water, would be obliged to make good the losses growing out of the interruption seems probable. I do not advert to the cost to the city of making all these changes in the mains, because the cost of removal and reconstruction would depend on so many contingencies that it is impossible to arrive at any degree of accuracy, and because also it is proposed the railway pay this."

When the above report had been presented to the Senate and published, there was consternation in the camp of the advocates of an underground railroad and corresponding rejoicing in the ranks of the surface railroad companies and in the Jacob Sharp lobby. This lobby had been at work for years trying at each session to get passed a bill giving Sharp and his associates the rights for a surface railroad in Broadway. These lobbyists were no amateurs like Willson and his friends, but seasoned Albany operators who worked intelligently if

not always legitimately.   There is little doubt that to
them was due the failure of the Willson subway scheme.
Opposition by such a prominent engineer as Craven,
occupying probably the greatest engineering position in
the public service at the time, was, of course, a powerful
argument against it.   The press so regarded it, and at
first it was heralded as the death knell of the underground.

But the friends of the latter were not vanquished yet.
They rallied presently and began to pour into the Legislature petitions and documents calculated to offset the
Craven report.   One of the strongest shafts hurled in
this way was a letter from A. P. Robinson, the engineer
of the Metropolitan Railway company, who had planned
the Willson subway.   Mr. Robinson not only defended
his plans and asserted that the road could be built without damaging the water system, but he produced a letter
written by Craven a year before in which Craven had
made practically the same assertion.

Mr. Robinson quoted in full the following letter:

CHIEF ENGINEER'S OFFICE

CROTON AQUEDUCT DEPARTMENT, February   , 1865.

H. B. Willson Esq.

Care Senator Angell, Albany, N. Y.

Dear Sir: I beg leave to acknowledge the receipt
of Mr. A. P. Robinson's report upon the contemplated Metropolitan Railway in this city, and also
his report on the contemplated Pneumatic Railway,
together with a note from you, asking whether in my
opinion the proposed works would injuriously affect
any of the sewers or other interests committed to
our charge.   In reply I beg leave to say that the
works proposed would, of course, involve the necessity of very considerable changes in the position of
water mains, sewers and appurtenant constructions

now occupying space below our street surfaces; and
that during the time required for such alteration
there will be unavoidably much inconvenience felt
in the immediate locality of the work. The inconvenience or damage will extend beyond the immediate locality just so far as the water supply and
sewerage may depend upon the water mains and
sewers, the operations of which by reason of the prosecution of your work are suspended. The extent
of this damage or inconvenience would of course be
lessened or increased according to the manner in
which the work would be carried on.

I have no doubt, however, that the works you
contemplate can be so constructed, and the necessary
removals and changes in the water mains, sewers,
etc. be made in such a manner that, after the whole
work is completed, the public works will not be
found to have been permanently injured, either in
regard to their condition or efficiency in operation.
As the professional member of the Board, responsible for the good condition of the public works referred to, and also for the maintenance of and uninterrupted enjoyment of their use by the inhabitants,
I feel obliged to add that the bill authorizing your
railway should make provisions:

1st, That the Department charged with the proper
maintenance of the water mains, sewers and pavements should have such supervision and control over
your operations as the public interests might require;

2d, That the city shall be secured against all
liabilities for damages sustained in the prosecution
of this work. What I mean by this is not only the
damage resulting from the carelessness or ineffi-
ciency of workmen, but all the damage, including
that which is inseparable from the nature of your
proposed work.

As the contemplated operations involve the necessity of the entire reconstruction of long lines of sewers, with alterations in the grade and direction of many of them, and also make necessary a very considerable change in the position of some of our large water mains, you will, I know, readily concede that temporary inconvenience and damage will be unavoidable under the most favorable fortune, while any negligence or failure might very greatly increase that which, under the best circumstances, will be a very great annoyance. You will, therefore, see that in calling your attention to these points, and begging you to make proper provision for them in any bill you may ask of the Legislature, I am only doing what is made imperative by my official responsibility.

I am etc.

A. W. CRAVEN, C. E.

Mr. Robinson then added:

"Mr. Craven here requires very reasonable, proper safeguards and guarantees for the public; and in accordance with his suggestions the clauses in the bill passed last winter referring to these points were prepared after full consultation with the other members of the Croton Board, as well as with the Corporation Counsel.

"I believe that the public works to be affected remain in about the same state now as then. No extensive sewers have been constructed, nor have any new water mains been laid down.

"A work which then presented no serious difficulties to the mind of Mr. Craven becomes now impracticable; and because we have a water pipe three feet in diameter, lying eight feet below the pavements, and a few petty brick sewers three feet wide by four feet high in the route proposed, there is not

in his opinion engineering skill enough in this country to construct this railway. This is the standard
as to the ability of the profession in the United States
gravely put forth by a representative member. I
have entertained a pardonable pride in my profession, and a still higher pride that I am an American
engineer; for although we cannot point to works of
the magnitude and extent of many in the old country, we can show as brilliant conceptions and as bold
achievements as any that the world can boast; and
I should indeed feel humiliated if I could for a moment believe that you would indorse the meagre
standard here given us by a refusal to report a bill
for the construction of this work for any of the
reasons set forth in the communication of Mr.
Craven.''

This spirited rejoinder to Mr. Craven's change of
front no doubt helped to soften the blow which the latter's unfavorable report dealt the Willson underground
project, but it did not prevent the defeat of that project
in the Assembly.

It would be useless to recount the several attempts
made at this session of the Legislature (1866) to get
charters for an underground railroad. Three or more
bills for this purpose were introduced, and as many more
for rights to build elevated railroads of one kind or another. Broadway was the route most desired, and the
fight for the underground rights was waged over this
thoroughfare. The reason for this was that Broadway
was then as now the main business artery of the city, and
the traffic on its surface was greater than that of any
other street, so that the great need for relief of congestion was a new road of some kind along Broadway.

As before stated, the horse railroad interests looked
with hungry eyes on this thoroughfare and for years had
sought the priceless franchise for the surface rights.

ROBINSON'S PLAN FOR SUBWAY STATION IN PARKS — 1864.

Property owners had resisted their efforts successfully, and when the Legislature of 1866 met were prepared to continue their resistance. Owners of the horse railroads, too, argued that if Broadway underground rights were granted to rivals the construction and operation of a subway would delay, perhaps for all time, the building of a surface road in that street. As they were still fighting for the surface rights, they naturally opposed the grant of the sub-surface rights sought by Willson.

The main fight in the Legislature of 1866, therefore, was between Willson and Vandenburgh. Both had bills introduced, and soon the Committees on Railroads of the two houses had a lively time with the clashing interests. Efforts were made to bring the rivals together, and a bill was introduced to embrace both interests, but Willson and his friends would not accept the compromise plan, and it came to naught. Vandenburgh, who undeniably had great influence with the Legislators, finally prevailed, and his bill was favorably reported in the Assembly.

Willson made one last appeal to the Senate for justice. He was desperate at the prospect of losing everything which the success of Vandenburgh in the Assembly made imminent, and prepared a memorial which he submitted to the Senate and had published. Here it is:

"To the Honorable, the Senate of the State of New York:—

"The petition of Hugh B. Willson, of the city of New York, a loyal citizen of the United States, respectfully showeth:

"That he was the originator of the undertaking known as the Underground Railway in this city. Having been in London several times during the construction of the Metropolitan Tunnel Railway of that city, and for some months after it was opened for traffic in January, 1863, he had great opportunities for obtaining practical information as to the

engineering difficulties to be overcome. Those few
months, during which he traveled almost daily
through the tunnel, sufficed to convince him that
the undertaking was a great success, and that
a similar line in New York would not only be equally
successful, but would in fact afford the most econ-
omical and effectual method of relieving our crowded thoroughfares. Hence on his return to this city
in the summer of that year your petitioner determined to present the project to such influential parties as he might be able to convince of its adaptation to the wants of the community.

"This task your petitioner at first found difficult
of accomplishment, owing mainly to the absorbing
interest of the war, but he finally succeeded after
several months of earnest labor in effecting through
the instrumentality of friends a powerful organization of capitalists, under the name of the Metropolitan Railway Company, whose articles of association
were filed March 22, 1864. Prior to that organization, and in order to demonstrate to the gentlemen
in question the practicability of the undertaking,
your petitioner and one of his friends employed Mr.
R. T. Bailey, an experienced civil engineer, to examine and report on the same, and the company so
formed, in the autumn of the same year, had a still
more careful survey and detailed report on the proposed work made by Mr. A. P. Robinson, another
distinguished civil engineer, and no other scientific
reports or practical information have ever been procured to be made and published by any other parties.
These reports were in fact demonstrative of the
whole question involved as to the possibility of constructing so vast a public work in the heart of a
great city without damage to property of any kind
whatever and without embarrassing the traffic.

"Your petitioner begs further to represent that

the said company, in which he was a director, and which he has labored ever since most assiduously to promote, had a bill introduced into the Legislature to authorize the construction of the proposed tunnel and railway, the day after the articles of association were filed (March 23, 1864) and your petitioner attended for several weeks at Albany to endeavor to obtain its passage, but found the session too far advanced to secure that object, although it received a favorable consideration in the Senate on a vote of 19 to 7.

"The following session (1865) the same bill was again introduced, and your petitioner spent nearly three months at Albany as the chief agent of the company, and with the assistance of others succeeded in getting it through the two branches of the Legislature when it failed to receive the approval of the Governor for reasons which your petitioner fully appreciated and regrets could not have been made known in time to have enabled the company to amend their bill in respect to the objections stated by His Excellency. This unfortunate circumstance rendered it necessary for the Metropolitan Railway Company to renew their application for a new bill at the present session, when they found themselves opposed by two other parties, who, without any just claims to the franchise, are using the most strenuous efforts to obtain it.

"Your petitioner begs further to represent that these two parties have combined and made enormous demands upon the Metropolitan Company, which the gentlemen in its direction refused to accede to, and he is apprehensive that the undertaking will be wrested out of their hands by a bold act of piracy. Your petitioner in such an event will be left without any legal means of obtaining justice or indemnity for nearly three years of arduous labor and anxiety and an expenditure so large as to prove ruinous to himself and family.

"Your petitioner under all these circumstances feels that he may with propriety appeal to the sense of justice of your honorable House, and prays that it will be pleased to cause an investigation to be made into the claims of your petitioner and his friends before the passage of any such bill.

"H. B. Willson
"New York, March 21, 1866."

This proved to be the swan song of Willson and the Metropolitan Company. Though first in the field their labors were to go for naught and the first subway project was to be throttled in deference to the wishes of the powerful corporations which controlled the horse car lines in New York City. Willson had the sympathy of the public, and the New York Times in an editorial expressed the belief that he had "suffered unfairly."

The day after the memorial was published a letter in reply from Thomas B. Van Buren appeared in the Times. Van Buren had been a member of the Assembly in 1865 and had supported the bill which Governor Fenton vetoed. He followed Vandenburgh on the latter's desertion of the Willson cause and became one of the incorporators of the company formed by the bill which Vandenburgh succeeded in putting through the Assembly. In his reply he denied Willson's charges of a combination and "hold-up". He excused his own course by making the statement that Mr. Barney, the president of the Metropolitan Company, had told him that he intended to "drop the enterprise entirely". As he "hated to see the project dropped", he and Vandenburgh got up the bill which was introduced in the Assembly. Finding two other bills pending, he explained, he sought to get the promoters of the three measures together on a new bill, which would give representation to all. To his letter to this effect,

he said, the Metropolitan Company made no reply, and
he finally compromised with the backers of the third bill
and the measure they agreed upon was favorably reported in the Assembly.

Willson answered this statement by a letter published
in the Times of March 31. He declared that Van Buren's
proposal of compromise was answered and refused by
the Metropolitan Company, for the reason that it proposed that Mr. Barney desert the Metropolitan and join
Vandenburgh's Company. He also claimed to have in his
possession a letter written by Vandenburgh in which the
latter offered to buy out the Metropolitan Company for
$112,500, of which $12,500 was to be paid in money some
months after the Vandenburgh bill should become a law,
and the balance in the latter company's stock. He explained the allusion to Mr. Barney's alleged desire to
"drop the enterprise" by saying that, in the autumn of
1865, Mr. Barney had a serious illness and asked his associates in the Metropolitan Company to allow him to retire
from active participation in the company's affairs, but
that later when he recovered his health he changed his
mind and consented to remain at the head of the company.

The Vandenburgh bill had been favorably reported in
the Assembly on March 15. On March 24 the same Committee on Railroads reported adversely on five bills for
elevated railroads on Broadway and other streets. On
March 29, in spite of Willson's appeal, the Assembly took
up and passed the Vandenburgh bill. On April 4 it
passed the bill providing for the construction of the Montgomery "corrugated" elevated railroad in Broadway.
There were prospects, too, that the Broadway surface
railroad bill would get the approval of the complacent
Assembly. The New York Tribune of April 5 editorially
condemned the granting of any more surface railroad
rights, saying:

"We most earnestly protest against any more

tracks being laid in our crowded streets until some one of the projects contemplating an elevated railroad and one of those intending an underground railroad shall have had a fair trial''.

After the passage of the Vandenburgh bill by the Assembly the fight was transferred to the Senate, which killed the bill in spite of a favorable report by the majority of the Committee on Railroads. Before this result was reached, however, there were exciting scenes in the Senate, culminating in the mention of alleged charges of bribery.

Meantime the Senate Railroad Committee gave a public hearing on all bills affecting Broadway, and a large delegation of wealthy men from New York City attended. Among them were William B. Astor and A. T. Stewart. The latter argued against the *giving away* of franchises, and offered $3,000,000 for the rights which the pending bills proposed to confer for nothing. When asked to make a *bona fide* offer for the Broadway underground franchise, however, Mr. Stewart declined. In general the millionaire delegation opposed all railroads in Broadway, but especially the underground and elevated projects.

It was on April 14, a few days after the millionaires had been heard, that the Senate had the most thrilling day of the session. On the previous day Senator Folger, on behalf of the majority of the Railroad Committee, had reported in favor of the Vandenburgh bill and Senator Humphrey, for the minority, against it. The report had been tabled temporarily, and the next day Senator Humphrey, for the majority of the Railroad Committee, reported favorably on the Broadway surface railroad bill. Senator Low dissented from this report and moved to take the underground and elevated railroad bills from the table. The motion prevailed and a debate ensued.

After a few commonplace speeches, Senator LaBau

electrified the Senate by stating that he had been informed two weeks previously that the majority of the Railroad Committee would report as it had done. He could tell the gentlemen composing that majority, he continued, that there were rumors about the porticos and halls of the capitol and on the streets of Albany, to the effect that each of them had received $10,000 for their action on these bills. This action gave color to the foul rumors, and the gentlemen owed it to their own vindication to favor the reference of the bills to the Committee of the Whole.

Immediately the debate turned from the bills to the sensational remarks of Senator La Bau. The three Senators composing the majority of the Railroad Committee disclaimed having received anything for their votes against the underground and in favor of the surface road. Other Senators were "astonished" that such language should be used on the floor, while a few pointed out that Mr. La Bau had not made any charges but had simply stated that the ugly rumors were in circulation. La Bau himself, who hailed from the First District of New York City, disclaimed any intention of indorsing the rumors, but had merely stated them and pointed out to the Senators how they could disprove them by their votes on the pending motion.

On the vote the lobby was defeated, and the bills went to the Committee of the Whole, the Senate thus refusing to indorse the report of the majority of the Railroad Committee. On April 17 the Vandenburgh bill was considered in Committee of the Whole, when the motion to report it favorably was defeated by a vote of 14 to 12. The Senate later refused to order it to third reading by a vote of 17 to 12, and the President declared it lost. A motion to reconsider was made, but this too was defeated, 17 to 9. The elevated and surface bills went the same way, so that the Senate killed everything granting railroad rights on Broadway.

But the rapid transit idea would not down. On the

last day of the session, April 20, 1866, the Senate received
"a memorial and remonstrance from S. P. Ruggles",
requesting the appointment of a commission by the Governor to report at the next session what accommodation
was required in the way of railroads in New York City.
Friends of rapid transit saw in this suggestion at least
a promise of something in the way of progress, and at
the afternoon session the following resolution was offered
by Senator Andrews, of Otsego, and adopted:

"Resolved:—That a select committee of three be
appointed, to sit during the recess with the Mayor
of New York, the State Engineer and the Engineer
of the Croton Board, to ascertain and report to the
Senate the most advantageous and proper route or
routes for a railway or railways, suited to rapid
transportation of passengers from the upper to the
lower portion of the city of New York, having in
view the greatest practicable benefit and safety to
the public and the least loss and injury to property
on or adjacent to said route or routes."

Before adjournment Senators Andrews, Low and C.
G. Cornell were appointed as such committee by the
President of the Senate. This action, together with the
passage of a bill which attracted little attention at the
time, gave New York its first rapid transit line—the elevated railroad. This bill was an amendment to the General Railroad law of 1850. It was passed by the Legislature of 1866 and authorized any number, not less than
ten, persons to form themselves into a company to build
a railroad to be operated "by means of a propelling rope
or cable attached to stationary power." It also authorized such a company to charge fares not exceeding five
cents per mile, with a minimum fare of ten cents. The
bill was passed in the interest of Charles T. Harvey, the
father of the elevated railroads, who had invented a plan
for the propulsion of trains on an elevated structure by

cables operated by steam power furnished by stationary engines along the route.   In the clash of rival underground and elevated schemes, this amendment to the railroad law slipped through without attracting much notice and without its importance being generally recognized.   How it gave New York the first elevated road will be told in a subsequent chapter.

CHAPTER VI

WORK AND CONCLUSIONS OF THE SENATE COMMITTEE ON RAPID TRANSIT IN 1866.

CREDIT for the first systematic study of the rapid transit question by a public authority belongs undoubtedly to the Special Committee of the Senate appointed at the session of 1866, as told in the preceding chapter. That committee's work was the first of many efforts by the public authorities to solve the rapid transit problem. It did its work intelligently and well, and had its recommendations been followed New York would have had rapid transit of the right kind long ago, and the present generation might not have known the universally execrated "strap-hanging." But greed conflicted with progress, and the battle for franchises prevented for many years the carrying out of this well-conceived plan.

In its report, which was presented to the Legislature of 1867, the Committee unanimously recommended subways or underground railroads as the best and quickest means of relief, although it suggested that permission be granted Charles T. Harvey to try out his elevated railroad on an experimental stretch of track. The tenor of the report, however, was favorable to the underground, and the arguments therefor were set forth in full. An east side line and a west side line of subways were recommended, and every member of the Committee, including the city officers named ex officio, signed the report. Even A. W. Craven, engineer of the Croton Board, who had held the Metropolitan underground project impracticable earlier in the year, now certified to his belief that an underground system was the best solution of the problem.

The Committee met in New York City on June 1, 1866, and organized by electing Senator George H. Andrews chairman and James F. Ruggles secretary. It at once advertised for plans and suggestions to meet the objects

CHARLES T. HARVEY
INVENTOR OF THE ELEVATED RAILROAD.

sought in the Senate resolution, and gave four months time for their preparation and submission. By October a great many plans had been submitted, and in November the Committee met and began their consideration. Days were set for the consideration of each plan, and the engineers and promoters were invited to come before the Committee to explain the advantages of their respective projects. The Committee devoted two months to this work, made up its report and on January 31, 1867, transmitted it to the Legislature.

That the Committee studied and understood the problem before it is shown by the nature of its report. After reciting the appointment and organization of the Committee and its method of proceeding, this report says:

"It is proper here briefly to recite some of the circumstances which demanded the appointment of this Commission. Since 1860 there had been no legislation which tended to afford additional facilities for the transportation of passengers in the direction indicated in the resolution—that is, on lines running lengthwise of the city. In the meantime the population had largely increased, and the inexorable demands of business had continued to appropriate for its necessities essential portions of the most densely inhabited lower districts, thus separating more and more widely the residence from the store and workshop.

"The Central Park, bounded on the South and North by 59th and 110th streets, on the East by the Fifth Avenue and on the West by the Eighth Avenue (and between 77th and 78th streets by the Ninth Avenue) an area more than half a mile broad by more than two and a half miles long, containing some 862 acres, not only excluded from its boundaries all tenements, but all property within the area on either side of it extending nearly to the rivers and for some distance above and below the Park has advanced so enormously in value within the past six years as practically to exclude the laboring classes from residence in a district more than three miles long and extending nearly the whole width of the city. For a large population, then, this area on either side of the Park, unavailable for its greater portion for domiciles for the working classes, requires in effect to be traversed by some method affording rapid means of transit from the extreme upper to the lower portions of the city.

"That magnificent park, the Central, is correctly designated, occupying as it does the central portion of the island. In the form of a parallelogram, or nearly so, it substantially divides the city lengthwise into two districts, and considered in connection with the width of the island north of Grand street left the Commission no option but to recommend two lines of transit in preference to a single, central line. Such a line (even if the park did not present an insuperable obstacle) would still fail to afford the accommodation demanded by the necessities of the population. The requirements of travel can only be properly met by two lines, which shall run as nearly as may be through central portions of two longitudinal sections of the city on its eastern and western sides."

When one considers the fact that the above was written a half century ago, before the first elevated road was built, one must credit the Committee of 1866 with extraordinary foresight. In later years the accuracy of its conclusions became apparent and its plan for two longitudinal lines, one on each side of the city, was carried out in the elevated construction, but it took nearly forty years (till 1904) before its recommendation for subways was put into practical effect, and then the authorities made the mistake of zigzagging one route lengthwise of the island, instead of building two complete lines, one on each side. It is only now, a half century after the Committee of 1866 pointed the way, that the present system of underground roads is being expanded into the double system then recommended. This will be accomplished by the Dual System routes adopted by the Public Service Commission for the First District, which will continue the first subway down Seventh Avenue and up Lexington Avenue from 42d street, thus making a complete East Side line and a complete West Side line. Lack of money when the first subway was built is some excuse for the erratic laying out of its original route, as will be further explained in the chapters devoted to that work. But the mistakes of modern times make all the more remarkable the clear vision and correct attitude of the men of 1866.

New Yorkers of the present generation, familiar with the long fight which has been waged to get the New York Central tracks off the surface of the streets on the West Side of the city, will hardly believe that the same problem engaged the attention of this Committee in 1866. Yet here is what its report said:

> "The traction of freight and passenger trains by ordinary locomotives upon the surface of the streets is an evil which has already been endured too long and must speedily be abated."

Had anyone told the man who penned that sentence that the city still would be struggling with that "evil" in the seventeenth year of the Twentieth Century he probably would have refused to believe it. Yet the tracks, or most of them, are still in the streets they occupied in 1866!

The conclusions of the Committee of 1866 were epitomized in a set of resolutions, which, the report says, were "unanimously adopted" after "protracted and careful consideration of all the plans submitted." These resolutions were as follows:

"Resolved, That in the opinion of this Commission the best method of speedily attaining the design contemplated by the Senate resolution passed at its last session is by the construction of underground railways.

"That in view of the prospective increase in travel there should be one line of such railway from the Battery to City Hall Park, under Broadway, connecting at the City Hall Park with two or more lines of underground railway, each with double tracks, east and west of the line of Broadway.

"That to accommodate the larger passenger transportation the following routes are recommended, each connecting with the said first mentioned track at the City Hall Park:

"One under Chatham street to the Bowery and Third Avenue to the Harlem River.

"The other under Park Place (or Murray or Warren street or by the most feasible route) to Hudson street, thence under Hudson street to Eighth Avenue, thence under Eighth Avenue to Broadway, thence under Broadway to Ninth Avenue, thence under Ninth Avenue to the Harlem River.

"The line under Broadway between the Battery and City Hall Park to be constructed only as part of one or more of the through lines."

Reasons which led to the above conclusions are given at length in the report. The Senate resolution called for a plan which should have the elements of speed, safety, cheapness and rapidity of construction. As surface roads could not be relied upon for speed, the Committee dismissed them from consideration at the outset. There remained only elevated roads or subways to be considered. Out of many plans for the former submitted the Committee found only one worthy of recommendation, namely that offered by Charles T. Harvey, which, the report said, "appeared to have been the most carefully prepared, the most free from engineering difficulties involving the question of safety and the least objectionable as to the application of the motive power." Harvey asked for the privilege of building one half mile of his structure in the southern portion of Greenwich street as an experiment, and the Committee recommended "that permission be granted by the Legislature to that extent."

After dismissing two plans for a depressed railroad on the ground of expense and the length of time it would take to get title to the property required, the Committee took up the underground method and discussed it at length. A comparison of the physical conditions in New York with those of London was made, and the report referred to a communication from Mr. James P. Kirkwood, an engineer, which stated that in London the underground road passes through several open cuts and that in no place has it an uninterrupted line of tunnel equal in length to the distance from the Battery to Fourteenth street. Without similar open cuts in the New York tunnel the Committee feared that "the generation of steam would be attended with difficulties hardly to be overcome." To eliminate this objection the report suggested the trial of a pneumatic method of propulsion, concerning which it presented as an appendix a statement by Mr. M. O. Davidson, an engineer, "who has recently returned from England, after devoting much time there to a critical investigation" of that method.

"The successful application of this principle upon a large scale" said the report, "would be a practical solution of the difficulties which embarass an underground plan relying upon locomotive engines for power, in the matter of ventilation and injurious concussion and the accommodation of the tunnel to the grade of the surface."

The following summary of the conclusions of the Committee ended the report:

"1. That commercial, moral and hygienic considerations all demand an immediate and large addition to the means of travel in the city of New York.

"2. That if every avenue lengthwise of the island were to be occupied at once by surface rails, the relief afforded thereby would not be adequate to present requirements, and in three years' time the pressure, with all its accompanying annoyances, inconveniences and dangers would be as great as it is today.

"3. That the steam roads upon the surface now in use should be removed from the island of New York as soon as other sufficient and rapid means of transportation can be substituted.

"4. That a central line would not suffice to meet the present requirements for increased facilities.

"5. That elevated railways erected on supports in the middle or on the sides of the present streets of the city cannot be fully adapted to the transportation of freight, and have never been tested in any practical way so as to warrant an unconditional recommendation of them for transportation of passengers.

"6. That a system of railways running wholly through blocks would involve an expense for right of way and resulting damages, which would render it impracticable to convey passengers for long distances at rates of fare as low as the necessities of the case require, and would moreover involve too great delay in the acquisition of the right of way required.

"7. That the continual increase of population and the consequently growing necessity for transportation throughout the city will very soon demand the construction of several lines of railways other than surface roads. That more than the two roads herein recommended may be eventually required and

successfully operated, and the opening of new avenues and the erection therein of viaducts upon the
scale hereinabove mentioned may be found to be of
the greatest advantage and improvement to the city,
and while gratifying the public taste will effect the
desired object.

"8. That underground railways passing under
streets present the only speedy remedy for the present and prospective wants of the city of New York
in the matter of the safe, rapid and cheap transportation of persons and property."

Here were appended the signatures of the entire
Committee as follows:
George H. Andrews, H. R. Low, Charles G. Cornell,
                                    Committee of the Senate.
John T. Hoffman, Mayor of New York.
Alfred W. Craven, Engineer of the Croton Board.

In appendices to the report descriptions of the several
plans submitted are given. Among them were the fol-
lowing:
From A. P. Robinson, an underground railway.
From O. Vandenburgh, an underground railway.
From M. O. Davidson, a pneumatic system of under-
ground railway.
From S. B. Nowlan, an arcade and basement plan.
From John Schuyler, a depressed railway.
From James B. Swain, for the Metropolitan Transit
company, an underground, surface and elevated railroad.
From Charles T. Harvey and others, an elevated rail-
road.
From Gouverneur Morris and Isaac D. Colman, an
elevated railway.

It will be observed that, while the Committee recommended an underground railroad, it expressed no favor
for any one of the several plans submitted for that kind
of a road. Evidently it was not able to agree upon any

specific plan and decided to let the rival claimants for a franchise fight it out before the Legislature. This is just what those claimants proceeded to do, but they fought so hard that it was some years before any underground franchise was conferred, and that was for a pneumatic railroad which never got beyond the experimental stage.

As it is not worth while to reproduce or even to describe all the plans considered by the Committee, a glance at a few of the principal suggestions may be interesting.

A. P. Robinson, who had drawn the plans submitted to the Legislature by the Willson company, offered the Committee a plan on behalf of the Manhattan Railway Company, an organization formed two years later than the Metropolitan Railway Company, organized by Willson. On behalf of the Manhattan Company Robinson now submitted practically the same plans he had drawn for the Metropolitan company, which have been described in a previous chapter.

Willson's former associate and later antagonist, Origen Vandenburgh, submitted an underground plan in his own name. It was clearly derived from Robinson's plan, the only difference being that he proposed to build two tunnels instead of one—one for each track—and alleged that it could be built so far above water level that the sewers could run under it. He also proposed to lay the rails in beds of gutta percha to minimize noise in operation. He estimated the cost of construction at $15,000,000, with an extra $1,500,000 for lands and buildings.

A plan for a pneumatic tube was presented by an engineer, M. O. Davidson, who proposed to build three routes from City Hall northward. His plan called for circular tunnels 12 to 13 feet in diameter, constructed of brick and cement, with wrought iron tubing where necessary. The cars were to be blown from station to station by huge fans operated from stationary steam engines capable of creating a current of air giving a pressure of three to seven ounces per square inch. The estimated cost for two tracks to 100th street was $4,821,000.

The elevated railroad plan which most commended itself to the Committee, as before stated, was that submitted by Charles T. Harvey. The route was from the Battery up Greenwich street to Ninth Avenue, up Ninth Avenue to a convenient point and thence by the most eligible route to Kingsbridge and Yonkers. He also proposed a route up Broadway to 64th street and thence to Yonkers, and an east side line mainly up Third Avenue to the Harlem River and thence to New Rochelle. All these roads were to be constructed under Mr. Harvey's patents for cable propulsion by stationary steam engines, and became known as "patent" railways. The cars were to be operated on an elevated structure by means of endless wire ropes. These ropes were to be in series, each series covering about 1,500 feet of track, and were to be moved by power furnished by engines placed at intervals along the route. Harvey estimated the cost of the structure at from $250,000 to $500,000 per mile.

Another elevated project which got a good word from the Committee, which, however, was forced to condemn it on account of cost and the time necessary to get title to the required land, was the plan submitted by Gouverneur Morris and Isaac D. Colman. The line was to be built through the center of blocks between Broadway and Third Avenue from Chambers or Chatham street north to the Harlem River on the East Side, with a branch from below 14th street to Ninth Avenue and thence north to 59th street on a course through blocks parallel to Ninth Avenue. It was proposed to acquire a strip of ground 50 feet wide through these blocks for the right of way, and to erect thereon an elevated structure for a four track road and strong enough to carry freight trains and thirty-ton locomotives. The cost of the constuction was estimated at $1,165,000 per mile, but no estimate was made of the cost of real estate for right of way, which, of course, would have been tremendous.

Such were the chief features of the report of the Committee of 1866. It was an important piece of work, as it pointed the way for rapid transit development. The two plans it recommended—for subways and elevated lines—contained the germs which later developed into the existing rapid transit railroads. Its desire to avoid steam as a motive power and its guarded expressions in favor of pneumatic propulsion probably led to the trial later of the Beach Pneumatic railroad. The routes it proposed were better than those subsequently built upon. Its treatment of the steam railroad problem and its expressed opinion that such railroads should be driven off the surface of the streets were such as command general concurrence today.

CHAPTER VII

INCEPTION OF THE ELEVATED RAILROADS.

IN spite of the recommendation for an underground railroad, made by the Special Senate Committee, the next
session of the Legislature, that of 1867, failed to pass a
bill authorizing any such road. Three bills were introduced by as many rival interests, but none of them gained
the approval of both houses. This session, however, did
take an important step in providing rapid transit. It
passed a bill authorizing the construction of the first elevated railroad. In this it acted on the recommendation
made by the Special Senate Committee for a trial of
Charles T. Harvey's scheme. This act, which was
promptly approved by Governor Fenton, gave New York
its elevated railroad system, and much as the type is condemned today it was an important element in the growth
and prosperity of the city.

H. B. Willson and his friends made another fruitless
effort at this session to gain the underground franchise
for which they had been fighting for three years. Their
bill was introduced and a strong effort was made to pass
it, but it was opposed by two others, one backed by the
accomplished lobbyist, Vandenburgh, and the perplexed
Legislators could not decide between them. An effort was
made near the close of the session to combine all three
bills and pass one which would embrace all the rival interests, but this came to naught, and the session closed
without the authorization of any underground road. The
Legislature, it may be said in passing, did pass a bill
granting Jacob Sharp and his associates the right to
build and operate a surface railroad in Broadway, but
this was vetoed by Governor Fenton and its friends were
not strong enough to override the veto. It is highly probable that the passage of this bill was a factor in prevent-
ing the approval of any of the underground measures for
Broadway.

As before stated Harvey at the session of 1866 had obtained the passage of an amendment to the General Railroad law allowing him and his associates to form an incorporation for the purpose of building an elevated railroad to be operated according to his patents by means of cables driven by stationary engines. In July 1866 they acted under this authority and incorporated the West Side and Yonkers Patent Railway company. The capital stock was placed at $5,000,000, and the company was to continue for 999 years. It proposed to build a line 25 miles long, from the Battery by way of Greenwich street and Ninth Avenue and other streets to Kingsbridge and Yonkers.

The directors and stockholders named in the articles were as follows:

William H. Appleton—New York and Riverdale
Chauncey Vibbard—New York
Walter S. Gurnee—New York and Tarrytown
Frank Work—New York
Samuel M. Pettingill—Brooklyn
Moses A. Hoppoch—Hastings
Charles T. Harvey—New York and Tarrytown

The above were named as directors and stockholders and the following as additional stockholders:

John H. Hall—New York
John Perkins—New York
Robert Turner—New York
Isaac Scott—New York
David Crawford, Jr.—New York
John P. Yelverton—New York
F. P. James—New York

The act passed by the Legislature of 1867 authorized the construction by this company of an experimental line one-half mile long in Greenwich street northward from Battery Place. It created a commission of three, two to be appointed by the Governor and one by the Croton Aqueduct Board, to inspect the road on its completion and if approved to certify such approval to the Governor. If approved by him the line was to be extended northward, but if disapproved the part already built was to be removed. If approved the company was given the right to extend the road northward on both sides of Greenwich street and on both sides of Ninth Avenue or streets west of Ninth Avenue to the Harlem River. One year was allowed for the completion of the experimental section.

Fares to be charged by the company were fixed as follows: Five cents for any distance less than two miles; one cent for each additional mile or fraction thereof. The company was allowed at its option to establish a uniform rate of ten cents and to collect the same for five years after the passage of the act.

Compensation to the city was provided for in the following section of the act:

"The said company shall pay a sum not exceeding five per cent. of the net income of said railway from passenger traffic upon Manhattan Island, as aforesaid, into the treasury of the city of New York, in such manner as the Legislature shall hereafter direct, as a compensation to the corporation thereof for the use of the streets thereof."

Harvey's plan of operating the road by means of cables was specified in the act, which said:

"The railway hereby authorized as aforesaid shall be operated exclusively by means of propelling cables attached to stationary engines, placed beneath or beyond the surface of any street through which such railway may pass, and shall be concealed from view so far as the same may be detrimental to the ordinary uses of said street. The structures shall consist of a single track, upon which the cars are to be moved in contrary directions, upon opposite sides of the streets, which track shall not exceed five feet in width between center of rails, and shall be supported by a series of iron columns not exceeding 18 inches in diameter at surface of pavement, or equivalent space (if in elliptical form) which columns shall be placed at intervals of not less than 20 feet (except at street crossings or sidings) along the curbstone line between the sidewalk and carriageway and attached at their upper extremities to the track aforesaid, so that center of the track shall be perpendicular to the center of the columns, and at a distance of not less than 14 feet above the surface of the pavement. Whenever deemed necessary to prevent oscillation of the track aforesaid, a second series of columns may be extended on the building side of the sidewalk at intervals of not less than 20 feet, which shall not be more than 9 inches in diameter at surface of pavement, and shall be so placed as not to obstruct any existing door or window without consent of the owner, and from the upper extremity of which bracers or girders may be extended to the first series of columns mentioned for purposes aforesaid.''

On December 3, 1867 Governor Fenton appointed two Commissioners, as provided in the act, as follows: Freemen J. Fithian, and John H. Morris. To these was added, January 4, 1868, Jacob S. Frear, appointed by the Croton Aqueduct Board, which at the time consisted of Thomas Stephens, Robert C. Darragh and A. W. Craven.

In the meantime Harvey had gone ahead with the construction of the experimental section of the first elevated railroad ever built in New York. It was located in lower Greenwich street and designed to be operated by cables according to Harvey's patented system. It was completed within the one year specified, and in June, 1868, was placed in operation for trial. As may be supposed it was the wonder of the city. Crowds watched its construction, and almost universal skepticism as to its practicability was expressed. Its builders were jeered, and the prediction was made that the structure would never stand the strain of train operation, but would collapse and fall under the weight. Harvey demonstrated to the satisfaction of the Commissioners, however, that he could operate cars over it, and on July 1, 1868, they certified their approval to Governor Fenton, who on the following day gave his formal approval to their report and the railroad. They had inspected the road on June 23, and in their report certified that "it was in practical operation as contemplated by the West Side and Yonkers Patent Railway company," and approved the structure, plan and operation and found "that the same can be operated with safety and dispatch."

There is no evidence in the newspapers of the day that the trial of the first elevated railroad excited popular interest. No ceremonies outside of the necessary official participation marked the event. Nowadays it would be heralded for days in advance and signalized by civic celebration. In 1868 it seems to have been taken as a matter of course. It was on Friday, July 3, of that year when the trial was made, and the following account of it, published in small type under a single line heading, is taken from the New York Times of July 4:

"The trial trip upon the elevated road in Greenwich street having been postponed on Thursday on account of an accident to the machinery came off yesterday at noon and was very satisfactory. The car ran easily from the Battery to Cortlandt street, starting at the rate of five miles an hour and increasing to a speed of ten miles. The company does not pretend with its present machinery to run the cars faster than fifteen miles an hour; but during the next two months will make arrangements for much more rapid motion.

"On the first day of July, 1867, the work was commenced, $100,000 then being pledged for the purpose. Contracts were made and the first column was placed in position on the seventh of October. The machinery was first tried on the 7th of December on the first quarter mile. So well were the directors pleased that they authorized the inventor to order the remainder to Cortlandt street. This was erected in March and April and some improvements introduced. About the first of May the new trial car was placed on the road, and the directors took a ride at the rate of fifteen miles an hour, propelled by an engine out of sight and hearing.

"On the 6th of last June the railway was placed in charge of the Commissioners appointed by the Governor, Messrs. Fithian and Morris, and ex-Senator Frear (of Sullivan county) appointed by the Croton Board for its inspection. During that month Governor Fenton came from Albany and inspected it himself by examining the machinery and taking a ride upon it; also the Croton Board with their Engineer; Mayor Hoffman; the Governor of Minnesota; a deputation from the Common Council of Boston and many eminent engineers and civilians. The opinion was expressed that it was a great mechanical success. On July 1st the Commissioners reported in its favor. The Governor gave it his official approval promptly on the following day. This indorsement vests in the constructing company full powers to proceed with the railway at once from the Battery to Spuyten Duyvil.

"The chief engineer and inventor expresses the opinion that there is no engineering difficulty in the way of having the railway completed to the Hudson River depot at Thirtieth street the present year. Then the passage from Wall street can be made in fifteen minutes! He is desirous of having the whole

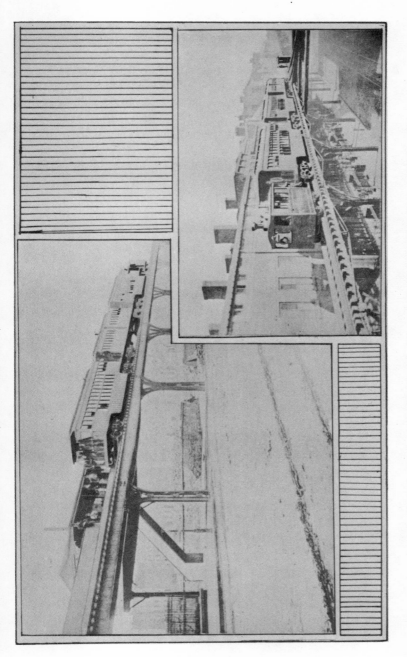

ELEVATED RAILROAD TRAINS DRAWN BY DUMMY ENGINES — ABOUT 1878.

line put under contract at once, that the time of its being thrown open to public use may occur during the terms of the present incumbents of the offices of Governor of the State and Mayor of the City, who have recommended the project and assisted its development as a means of relief to the overcrowded thousands of this city. The inventor will proceed next week to take down the present machinery and substitute some special improvements which he has perfected after testing the working of that already up.''

The financing of this pioneer rapid transit railroad must have been a work of great difficulty considering the skepticism of the time. Mr. Harvey, a year or so before his death in 1913, stated that it was almost impossible to raise money, and that he went to usurious lenders to get the funds to keep it going. The first money, $100,000, was put up by Harvey and his associates in the company, but once the road had received official approval it was possible to borrow on it. As above said, this approval was given on the first and second of July, 1868. On the first of August following the property was mortgaged to George S. Coe and James H. Benedict, trustees, for $750,000 to secure a bond issue of like amount. The bonds were issued in denominations of $500 each, bore 7 per cent interest and were to run 15 years. The mortgage was signed by W. S. Gurnee, president, and Henry W. Taylor, secretary of the company.

This bond issue was floated by two prominent Wall Street houses of the day—Clark, Dodge and Co., of No. 51 Wall street, and Lockwood and Co., of No. 94 Broadway. In the advertisements offering the bonds it was stated that ''Messrs. George S. Coe, president of the American Exchange National Bank, and James H. Benedict, of Lockwood and Co., bankers, are trustees for the bondholders.'' The advertisement was dated at the office of the West Side Elevated Railroad Company, No. 48 Cortlandt street, August 6, 1868. In it the officers of the company were given as follows: W. S. Gurnee, president; William H. Appleton, treasurer; W. H. Taylor, Secretary; and the following directors: William E. Dodge, A. S. Barnes, Samuel D. Babcock, S. M. Pettingill, C. T. Harvey and Robert P. Getty.

The Harvey company, however, never succeeded in getting the elevated railroad further than the experimental stage. It fell into financial difficulties, Harvey was forced out and others reaped the reward which should have been his. H. C. Stryker, in his "Historical Sketches", describes this phase of the Harvey fortunes as follows:

"Financial arrangements followed with a leading banking firm to extend the line to the then terminal of the New York Central railway at Ninth Avenue and Thirtieth street. The cars were placed on the extension and won the approval of the adjoining property owners to the structure as ornamental and to the train service as comparatively noiseless. The stock was in demand at a premium, when 'Black Friday' (Sept. 26, 1869) panic occurred and the bankers raising the funds failed, with the extension to Thirtieth street about half completed to the point where a traffic revenue could be realized.

"In the emergency an offer was made of a loan to complete the extension from the most powerful clique of Wall Street stock operators and accepted, which was upon condition that the stock-voting control should be vested in them as security for the loan until paid. They conceived the idea of having the railway appear for a time as a failure until they could acquire nearly its entire stock ownership at a low valuation and then "boom" the same to high premium prices, make large issues of new stock and realize millions by the "deal." They outlined this scheme to Harvey, and although his share of the profits would have been increased, he declined to participate in the plot because of its perfidy to the original stockholders and its intrinsic dishonesty. The clique determined to carry out the plan, displaced Harvey from his official connection with the railway, forcibly prevented his perfecting details and caused it to appear in temporary disuse and discredit in order to depress its stock market values."

These men did nothing with the property until 1870, when they completed the single track line up Ninth Avenue to Thirtieth street. To do this, however, they encumbered the property with a large debt. On August 1, 1870, the company issued a second mortgage to George S. Coe and Alfred S. Barnes to secure a bond issue of $2,500,000 which was to be used to pay off the previous loan of $750,000 and to raise new funds. Only 200 of these bonds, in denominations of $500 each were issued or printed, and they were numbered 1,501 to 1700, the first 1,500 being reserved for the first mortgage. Of these 200 bonds only 21 were parted with, and they have been paid off. The others are said to be now among the archives of the Manhattan Railway company, the present owner of the elevated railroads in Manhattan and the Bronx.

After the track was completed to Thirtieth street efforts were made to operate it, but the stationary power method proved a failure and the road again lay idle for some months. On November 15, 1870 the property of the West Side and Yonkers Patent Railway company was sold at sheriff's sale and bought in by Francis H. Tows. The property thus conveyed is described as including the road from the Battery to 31st street on Greenwich street and Ninth Avenue, six car bodies and three passenger cars. Tows represented the bondholders, and a committee appointed by them attempted to get the road in running order. One of the acts of the Legislature relating to the company permitted it to substitute locomotives for stationary engines if the Commissioners appointed by the Governor consented. This consent was obtained, and on April 20, 1871 the trustees for the bondholders began running a train of three cars hauled by a dummy engine. Thereafter the road continued in uninterrupted and successful operation.

The bondholders then organized a new company to take over the property. They also interested in it William L. Scott, a wealthy coal dealer of Erie, Pa., whose money and influence put the struggling enterprise on its feet. Mr. Scott was the coal agent of the Pennsylvania Railroad, and counted a wealthy man for those days. The new company was named the New York Elevated Railroad company. Its articles of association were filed October 27, 1871. The capital stock was placed at $10,000,-000, and the following were named as directors: David Dows, Francis H. Tows, Ashbel H. Barney, John D. Mairs, Haney Kennedy, all of New York City; William L. Scott, of Erie, Pa.; Danforth N. Barney and Frederick H. Foster, of Irvington, N. Y.; William L. Wallace, of Tarrytown; George H. Marvin, John H. Cowing, Alfred C. Barnes and George C. Martin, of Brooklyn.

In addition to the directors the stockholders included Edward C. Delavan, of New York; William L. Oakey, of Brooklyn; Charles T. Barney, of New York; William N. Goddard, of Brooklyn; Henry W. Taylor and Augustus Hull, of New York; James R. Cowing, Charles H. Marvin and T. H. Marvin, of Brooklyn; Daniel W. Wyman, of Jersey City; James R. Jessup, of New York and Milton Courtright, of Erie, Pa.

David Dows took 400 shares of the stock; Danforth A. Barney 400; William L. Scott, 600; Alfred C. Barnes, 150; Ashbel H. Barney, 100; Milton H. Courtright, 100 and the others 10 shares each.

The life of the company was placed at 100 years. It

proposed to build altogether 160 miles of road. It named a route from the Battery through the Western part of the city to Westchester county and through the westerly part of that county to Putnam county; also from the Battery through the easterly part of the city and the easterly part of Westchester county to Portchester; also lines in every ward of New York City across town from river to river; also from Yonkers across to New Rochelle and from Tarrytown to Portchester. In addition the company named the route of the West Side and Yonkers Patent Railway company from the Battery up Greenwich street, Ninth Avenue and other streets on the West Side to Kingsbridge and Yonkers. Stock in the New York Elevated Railroad company to the amount of $801,825 was issued for the property and franchises of the Patent Railway company.

From the list of stockholders and directors of the New York Elevated Railroad company it is apparent that Harvey, the originator of the elevated plan, was finally eliminated. With him went the cable method of operating, which never thereafter was tried on an elevated road in New York City. The dummy engines, introduced by the trustees for the bondholders in 1871, continued as the motive power, with slight variations in type, until the elevated roads were electrified 31 years later in 1902.

One reason for the embarrassment of the old company was the litigation in which it became involved. Another was the opposition by the Tweed Ring. After the experimental half mile had been built and accepted by the Governor, lawsuits were brought to prevent the extension of the line to Thirtieth street. While some of these suits were inspired, no doubt, by the horse railroad interests, others were brought by property owners who alleged that the road would injure their holdings. This question of damage to property became a burning issue in the '70's and it required a constitutional amendment and several court decisions to settle it.

After the New York Elevated Railroad Company had taken over the property it obtained the passage of an act by the Legislature, confirming its acquisition of the rights granted to the West Side and Yonkers Patent Railway Company and authorizing it to continue and complete the railroad thereby granted. This act required the New York Elevated Railroad Company to construct and complete at least one track within five years, under the supervision of the Commissioners named by the Governor, who were continued, vacancies in their number to be filled by the Governor. The Commissioners were to receive $10 per day each, to be paid by the company. The supplemental act also authorized the company to charge a 10 cent fare for five miles or less and not exceeding two cents for each additional mile or fraction. This ended the first period of the elevated railroad movement, which thereafter gained great impetus. Another company, the Gilbert, was soon chartered, and the two were firmly established by the Rapid Transit Commission of 1875, as will be told in a subsequent chapter.

The Tweed opposition to the first elevated road is described as follows by H. C. Stryker in his Historical Sketches above quoted, which were indorsed by Charles T. Harvey himself:

"But a new transit possibility had developed from the then political dictator of the city and the state—the most notorious corruptionist of the century—William M. Tweed—having decided to introduce another rapid transit system known as the "Viaduct Plan" for exclusive extension on Manhattan Island. He was then Commissioner of Public Works of the city of New York, with its immense patronage. He was a State Senator and considered the actual representative of the city in Legislative affairs. He had a charter granted for the "New York Railway Company", with a capital of $25,000,-000, of which the city of New York was directed to take five millions at par, the county of Westchester was authorized to be bonded to aid it to any extent the Board of Supervisors might decide, which might be twenty-five millions or more.

"The Board of the Railway company comprised some of the wealthiest capitalists of the city as associate directors with Tweed. A magnificent suite of offices was occupied, and printed plans published showing a grand terminal station facing the City Hall Park, where the city office building is now being erected. The railway was to be built upon elevated masonry arches through blocks instead of streets, and a picture was published of its crossing Broadway on a heavy masonry arch some forty feet high. That its cost per mile would be in millions was certain, and that it would never serve as adequate or convenient transit for the wage-earning masses was no less sure.

"The only rival in sight was the discredited Elevated Railway on Ninth Avenue and Greenwich street, and this Senator Tweed decided to have destroyed forthwith. He introduced a bill in the Senate, March 28, 1871, authorizing him as Commissioner of Public Works to remove it within ninety days, and made his boast that within sixty days after the bill became a law he would have it wholly torn down. The bill passed the Senate two days later by a vote of 20 yeas to 9 nays, and was sent to the Assembly for concurrence, it being known that the Governor would approve it.

"The clique in control of the Elevated Railway were taken by surprise and were hopelessly unprepared to effectually defend it at Albany. Harvey was, however, informed of the emergency, and valuing the public interests above any instincts of personal revenge upon his despoilers, he, as its originator, appealed to Hon. Erastus Corning, then residing at Albany, to save the Railway for friendship's sake, as Mr. Corning had no investment interest whatever in it. The memory of the Canal episode sufficed to cause Mr. Corning to appear in the Assembly chamber to oppose Tweed's bill. An onlooker saw on the afternoon of that fateful day Tweed in one part of the chamber marshalling the New York City members to vote for his destructive measure, while Mr. Corning was seen in another part of the chamber among groups of country members urging them to vote against it. He was considered as the most influential citizen of the State outside of New York City, and the country Assemblymen generally accepted his advice.

"When the vote was taken the bill was defeated by the decisive majority of 74 nays to 34 yeas—the only defeat Dictator Tweed experienced during that session. Conclusive evidence is preserved in State documents proving that the Tweed measure would have passed but for Mr. Corning's interference, and that his only motive was his personal regard for Harvey, coupled with the memory of the latter's engineering achievement before mentioned. But for that memory-inspired victory, the nucleus of the Elevated Railways of New York would have then been destroyed and the system become too discredited to enlist capital for its re-introduction. With Tweed in control, the "Viaduct" system would doubtless have been adopted as the only transit system available. Contracts to build it would have been let with a "rush," New York as well as Westchester county heavily bonded under special laws and a hundred millions probably expended to prove the system a practical failure.

"The Elevated system thus saved passed through several changes of control, but was gradually extended and enlarged until it had a patronage of over a million passengers per diem and for thirty-five years was the only means of rapid transit in the city.''

The ''canal'' incident alluded to in the above was a happening in Harvey's younger days. He was engineer for a company, of which Erastus Corning was president, engaged in constructing the first great ship canal around the falls at the outlet of Lake Superior. The work was being done under a contract with the State of Michigan, and when the time limit was nearly up it was discovered that what was thought to be a sand bar was really a ledge of rock, which the dredge provided for the purpose could not excavate. Harvey saved the day and got the contract finished in the time specified by inventing a machine which broke up the ledge under water so that it could be dredged out with the apparatus provided. The directors gave him a vote of thanks and Corning never forgot the service.

It has been said above that the first elevated road incurred the antagonism of the Tweed Ring. This opposition was described in an article published in the New York Herald of June 5, 1877, favoring the holding of a citizens' meeting to encourage the companies then beset by vexatious legislation. That article said:

''In the days of the Tweed ring the corruptionists went so far as to try to indict the Greenwich Street elevated railroad as a nuisance; they boasted that they would not only tear down the road, but would fine and imprison the enterprising citizens who advanced money to try this important and now entirely successful experiment. Engineers and newspapers were hired to assert that the road would not stand; that it was dangerous to the lives of the passengers; that it would cause constant runaways of horses; that it would destroy business; and attempts were even made at one time to incite mob violence against it. Today the elevated railway is, as far as the track extends, one of the greatest conveniences the city has.''

Harvey, who died in 1913, maintained his interest in rapid transit to the last. In the early part of 1912 he submitted to the Public Service Commission, then engaged in perfecting the Dual System plans, a project for an improved, noiseless elevated railroad and urged its adoption. The plan, however, was not adopted, and soon thereafter Harvey was stricken with his last illness.

CHAPTER VIII

FIRST UNDERGROUND CHARTERS AND FIRST TUNNEL BUILT UNDER BROADWAY.

IN the Legislature of 1868 the scramble for rapid transit charters was resumed. In addition to the former applicants several new names appeared in a multitude of bills introduced. In one of these, which proposed to confer a grant for a road under Broadway to Madison Square and thence to the Harlem River, the names of the incorporators included those of Cornelius Vanderbilt, August Belmont, Horace Greeley, William G. Fargo, Peter B. Sweeney and Jacob Sharpe. The bill did not pass.

The session produced a law, which led to the construction of the first passenger subway in New York City, but this experiment in underground transit, like the first elevated road, ended in failure. This was the so-called Beach tunnel built under Broadway at Murray street, the remnants of which were exhumed in 1912 when the Public Service Commission began work on the new Broadway subway. In the construction of the Beach tunnel a huge practical joke was played on Father Knickerbocker. The law passed by the Legislature of 1868 authorized certain men to form a company and to construct a "pneumatic dispatch" line under Broadway, to consist of two tubes each of 54 inches diameter, through which parcels etc. were to be transmitted by pneumatic power. Without official or public knowledge, however, the company actually built a tunnel nine feet in diameter, carried passengers in it without authority of law and excused the feat on the ground that it had to build one large tunnel to carry the two 54 inch tubes and since it was built desired to demonstrate the practicability of propelling passenger cars by the pneumatic method!

Those authorized in the bill to form a company for the

purpose of building the pneumatic tubes were:

Alfred E. Beach, Robert G. Hatfield, Horace T. Caswell, Nathan Kellogg, Moses S. Beach, Salem H. Wales, R. H. McClellan, Julius H. Pratt, Frederick H. Betts, Charles H. Neill, Thomas Graham, T. G. Ford, John E. Ashe, John Leonard, J. Netto Burns, Charles H. Whiley and Samuel Marsh, Jr.

These men organized the Beach Pneumatic Transit Company, the articles of which were filed August 1, 1868. The capital stock was placed at $5,000,000 and the following were named as directors:

Alfred E. Beach, Horace T. Caswell, Joseph Dixon, Moses S. Beach and Frederick H. Betts.

The Beach Pneumatic Railroad was the invention of Alfred Ely Beach, an engineer and editor of the Scientific American, who was a prominent figure in the life of New York City in the late '60's and early '70's. His son, Frederick C. Beach and his grandson (son of the latter) are today on the editorial staff of the same publication.

In the early 60's pneumatic power was exploited in England, and in 1867 Alfred Ely Beach introduced it to New York. In that year he gave an exhibition of its possibilities at the American Institute, held in Armory Hall in Fourteenth street. There he erected a section of pneumatic tube in the main hall of the exposition, and in it by means of a blower he operated a car large enough to carry passengers. He also exhibited a smaller tube for the dispatch of letters and parcels by the same method. That it was then his intention to apply this principle to the transportation of passengers in the streets of New York City or under them is shown by a pamphlet he published in the fall of 1867. The pamphlet was entitled ''The Pneumatic Dispatch, with Illustrations''. In it he described the demonstration of pneumatic power at the American Institute. Here is a paragraph from it:

> ''The pneumatic system appears to be admirably adapted to the purposes of rapid city transit, since

the ventilation is perfect and the freedom from all jarring and dust is complete. Mr. Beach is indefatigably laboring to accomplish its introduction here, and it is to be hoped his efforts will meet with due encouragement and reward. About 75,000 have already enjoyed the atmospheric ride, and it is expected that more than 100,000 will have passed through the tube before the close of the exhibition, about November 1. As soon as proper Legislative authority can be obtained it is proposed to lay down tubes under the principal streets and under the adjacent rivers, when, it is stated, passengers will be carried from City Hall, New York, to Madison Square in five minutes, Central Park in eight minutes, Harlem and Manhattanville in fourteen minutes, Washington Heights in twenty minutes, Jersey City or Hoboken in five minutes and City Hall, Brooklyn, in three minutes.''

Under the authority conferred by the act of 1868 the company began work in that year, but so quietly was it done that the public remained in ignorance of it for many months. The first public announcement of it was made by the New York Times in January, 1869. This was supplemented by an article in the same paper of February 17, 1869, which said:

"Nearly a month ago the Times exclusively advised the public that a company of English capitalists, who had obtained a charter from the Legislature for that purpose, had commenced to construct a pneumatic disptach tube in the lower part of the city for the conveyance of parcels and letters and, it might be, passengers also. As then published, Mr. Moses Beach, president of the company, hired the basement of the Messrs. Devlin's store, corner of Broadway and Murray street, as a starting point for the line, with the intention of carrying it to the Nassau street post-office. The work of tunneling beneath Broadway then begun has been slowly but steadily progressing and will be pushed forward to completion as rapidly as possible. The details of these operations of the company have been carefully withheld by them from the public, in order to avoid the otherwise inevitable annoyance of injunctions from stage-line proprietors and property owners on the route."

As before stated the company decided to build two tubes at once, and to this end bored one large tunnel, in which it was proposed later to construct the two small tubes. In a pamphlet issued subsequently by the company it is explained:

"It is a portion of this outer tunnel which has been erected; and as it proved to be strong enough and large enough for the transit of passengers, the company laid down therein a railway track and provided a passenger car for the purpose of temporarily illustrating by an actual demonstration the feasibility of placing a railway under Broadway without disturbance of the street surface or injury to adjacent property."

The tunnel was 312 feet long and started on a curve from the west curb line of Broadway at Warren street and extended down the middle of Broadway to a point a little beyond the south line of Murray street. It was 21 feet beneath the surface, was painted white and lighted with gas. It consisted of a circular tube 9 feet in diameter, built of iron plates for about 60 feet on the curved portion and of brick masonry for the rest of the distance. It had been bored by means of a metallic shield, invented by Alfred Ely Beach, and this was the first application of the shield method of tunneling in America. This shield was pushed forward by means of hydraulic jacks as fast as the earth in front of it was excavated, when the bore behind it was immediately filled with a lining of brick masonry or iron plating. The work was carried on without opening the surface of Broadway, and few persons who walked over it daily knew what was going on beneath their feet.

Early in 1870 the tunnel was opened to the public and experimental operation was carried on. A circular car to fit the inner diameter of the tube was provided, large enough to hold twenty passengers. A huge blower or fan was installed at the end of the tube and the car was blown forward by force of the air. In February, 1870, a trial trip was made with the Mayor and other notables, and thereafter hundreds of citizens enjoyed the "atmospheric ride". Many persons now living recall the experience.

Thereafter no attempt was made to build the dispatch tubes, as the company bent every effort to get a franchise for a passenger railroad. The Legislature of 1871 passed such a bill, but it was vetoed by Governor Hoffman. The Legislature of 1872 repassed the measure, but it again encountered the gubernatorial veto. In 1873 Governor John A. Dix succeeded Hoffman, and he approved a similar bill passed by the Legislature of that year. In this bill the company was authorized to build an underground road and to operate it with steam locomotives, the pneumatic method not having proved a success. By this time (1873) the new elevated railroad was already in successful operation, and the Beach company failed to raise the capital necessary to build the road. The franchise slumbered for a number of years and finally passed into the possession of the New York Parcel Dispatch Company.

The name and objects of the Beach company were changed by amendatory acts passed at different times. The act of 1873 gave the company the right to build and operate an underground railroad from Bowling Green up

Broadway to Madison Square and thence up Madison
Avenue to the Harlem River; also from Madison Square
up Broadway to Central Park and Eighth Avenue. The
act of 1874 changed the name to the Broadway Underground Railway Company. In January, 1885, by order
of the Supreme Court, the name was changed to the New
York Arcade Railway Company, and by a Legislative act
of 1897 to the New York Parcel Dispatch Company,
which is the present title.

As may be inferred from the foregoing, the company
passed through much litigation. In 1870, when the
knowledge of the construction of the tunnel under Broadway became public, the City of New York brought suit
for an injunction on constitutional grounds. The courts
upheld the act, refusing to grant an injunction. Many
years later, when it was known as the New York Arcade
Railway Company, it lost a much more important suit.
This was the case of Astor and others against the New
York Arcade Railway Company. The plaintiffs attacked
the rights of the company to build a railroad for *passenger* transportation, and the courts held the act of 1873,
which conferred such rights, unconstitutional by reason
of a defective title. The original act of 1868, however,
was upheld, and the company now claims only such rights
as were granted by it—namely the rights to build and
operate underground tubes for the transmission of letters, packages and merchandise.

The act of 1897 confirmed these rights, but limited
their exercise to such streets as are not required for rapid
transit roads unless the Board of Rapid Transit Railroad
Commissioners give their consent. This board was succeeded by the Public Service Commission, and in 1909
the New York Parcel Dispatch Company applied to that
Commission for its consent to the building of tubes for
the transportation of letters, packages and merchandise,
or for a freight subway as it was called, on such streets
as the Commission should designate. No action was ever

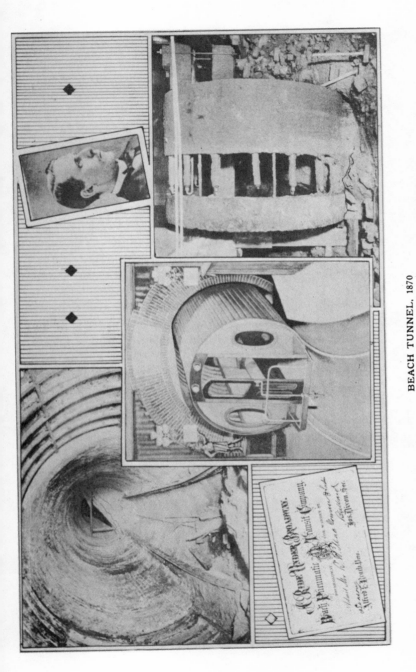

BEACH TUNNEL. 1870

1. Interior After Years of Disuse; 2. Alfred Ely Beach, Inventor and Builder; 3. Ticket Issued in 1870; 4. Car Propelled by Air; 5. Shield Found in Tunnel in 1912.

taken on the application. Three years later, when the Commission awarded the contract for the construction of the new Brooklyn subway in lower Broadway, the company, through its attorneys, Krauthoff, Harmon and Mathewson, filed this protest:

"NEW YORK CITY, February 19, 1912.

"To the New York Public Service Commission of the First District, to William R. Willcox, John E. Eustis, Milo R. Maltbie, J. Sergeant Cram, William McCarroll, and all whom it may concern:

"Notice is hereby given that the tunnel under Broadway from Warren Street southward about two hundred and ninety-four (294) feet in the Borough of Manhattan, City, County and State of New York, is the property of the New York Parcel Dispatch Company, that anyone molesting or interfering therewith will be proceeded against as a trespasser and that the rights of the owner will be enforced in the courts.

(Signed)   NEW YORK PARCEL DISPATCH COMPANY
By Eugene W. Austin, President."

No attention was paid to the protest. The Commission had awarded the contract before it was received, and the contractor proceeded with the work, which involved the unearthing and destruction of the old tunnel. Parts of the old car, the rails and the boring shield were found, although the wooden parts were rotted away with their forty-two years entombment under Broadway. The metallic parts of the boring shield were fairly well preserved. The Commission offered the relic to Mr. Frederick C. Beach, editor of the Scientific American and son of the inventor. Mr. Beach looked over the shield, found that it could be restored and had it removed. He presented it to Cornell University as an interesting engineering relic. The University accepted it, took it to Ithaca and placed it on exhibition in the museum of Sibley College, where it can be seen today.

When opened the old tunnel was found to be in good condition. The brick walls had withstood leakage, and the air in the tube was dry and warm. The remaining wood work of the car was brittle with dry rot, and some of it fell apart when removed. Enough of it was saved to assemble in the office of the Public Service Commission almost the complete end of the car.

To return to the Legislative session of 1868, when as before stated a number of rapid transit bills were introduced. In the past most of the opposition to underground grants had arisen because such rights were sought in Broadway, the leading thoroughfare of the city, the property owners in which discountenanced any kind of a railroad therein. In 1868 a group of new applicants, believing in following the line of least resistance, asked for an underground grant in other streets. The result proved their wisdom, for the Legislature passed their bill, which was duly approved by Governor Fenton—the same Governor who in 1865 vetoed the Willson underground bill for the Broadway route. The act of 1868, approved April 18, incorporated the New York City Central Underground Railroad Company, with a capital stock of $10,000,000 and the following incorporators:

W. Butler Duncan	William B. Ogden
George Griswold	James Boorman Johnston
George D. Cragin	James M. Brown
William E. Dodge	Henry F. Vail
Lewis B. Brown	Edwin Dodge
S. W. Hopkins	Edward K. Bell
J. S. Thayer	Clarence S. Brown
Henry E. Davis	Julius F. Cheesboro
W. W. Huntington	D. M. Hildreth
J. S. Schultz	H. W. Slocum
Horace Deming	John Phillips
Everett H. Kimbark	Bryan Lawrence

Joseph Dixon

Henry Marshall

Royal N. Torrey

William Johnson

William C. Squier

Edward C. Byrne

Benjamin Weed

Samuel K. Jewett

Issac Bell

Eugene Bissell

Edwin J. McKee

Thomas Canary

Bernard Kelly

John Fitch

Henry Smith

Edward Coles

Ezra Clark Jr.

John T. Conover

These men were authorized to construct and operate an underground railroad in the following route: Beginning at Broadway and Park Place in front of the old City Hall and curving to City Hall Place, thence to Pearl Street, to Mulberry Street, to Bleecker Street, to Lafayette Place, to Astor Place, to Eighth Street and "easterly of St. Ann's church on Eighth Street" to Fourth Avenue, to Union Square, to 17th Street, private property, to 23d Street and Madison Square to 26th Street and Madison Avenue, up Madison Avenue to the Harlem River, and easterly and westerly along the Harlem River, connecting with the Harlem Bridge at Third Avenue.

North of 99th Street an elevated or surface road was permitted. South of that street the road was to be a subway, built deep enough to avoid interference with the water mains of the Croton Board. The fare was fixed at 6 cents for any distance under three miles and two cents for each additional mile or fraction. The road was to connect with the Harlem Railroad at 42d Street, and up to that point was to be finished in two years. The company was required to deposit $300,000 with the Controller of the City, to be forfeited if the road was not completed in that time. Five years more were allowed for the completion of the road to the Harlem River. It was to be operated in connection with the Harlem Railroad so that there should be "a steam road from one end of the Island to the other." This quotation is from the New York Times of April 18, 1868, which stated that among the incorporators were Edward Dodge, of Jay Cooke and Co.; Henry F. Vail, of the Bank of Commerce and James M. Brown and Clarence Brown, of Brown Brothers.

The New York City Central company failed to deposit $300,000 with the Controller as provided in its charter, and went back to the next Legislature, that of 1869, for an amendment of the act. By an amendatory act, passed May 11, 1869, new directors were added and the time to do the work was extended. The new directors were Marshall O. Roberts, William A. Whitbeck and Origen Vandenburgh. The company was given two years in which to begin and five years in which to complete the work. After this act took effect the company retained three engineers, W. W. Evans, E. S. Chesbrough and George S. Greene, to make surveys. They did so and made a report to William B. Ogden, president of the company, in October, 1869. They estimated the cost of building and equipping the line, from the Battery to the Harlem River, at $17,625,301. From the traffic expected they estimated the gross earnings at $7,200,000 a year, of which $214,560 was to come from freight. They expected to carry 70,000,000 passengers a year. Operating expenses were estimated at $3,000,000, leaving $4,200,000 for interest and dividends. It was proposed to use locomotives with coke as fuel, and to have trains of from five to eight cars, each car to seat 40 passengers.

The two years in which the company was to begin work expired in May, 1871, and just before the limit some actual construction was done. According to the first report of the company, dated December 1, 1871, excavations were made in May at Madison Avenue and 96th Street and a cut was opened "to a proper point to begin a heading of the tunnel southwardly." It was also stated that a section of tunnel abutment wall was built on the route thirty feet deep between Bond and Great Jones streets. While this was enough to save the franchise, it proved of little moment, for the directors got to quarreling and no more work was done. After the year 1872 the company became embarrassed and in 1874 Origen Vandenburgh, one of the directors, sued and got judgment against it for about $95,000. This judgment was affirmed by a decree in 1876, when the property was sold under foreclosure, the total of Vandenburgh's claim then being $102,977.93. This indebtedness, it was said, was incurred during the years 1869, 1870 and 1871. Vandenburgh bought in the property, had its franchise amended by an act passed by the Legislature of 1880 and organized the New York Underground Railway company, which took over what was left of the old company. Vandenburgh was the man who began fighting for an underground franchise in 1865 after he had parted from Hugh B. Willson, whose original plan for a subway he supported in 1864.

A glimpse of the troubles of the New York City Central Underground company is given in a letter signed by W. W. Evans and published in the New York Herald early in February, 1875. Evans was chairman of the board of three engineers who reported on the scheme in 1869. In this letter he said:

"I might here state that a contract drawn by Mr. Ogden to build this railway was made and executed with a gentleman from London, and that this railway would have been built and in use at the present day but for three reasons: One was that Mr. Ogden was called to the West and was away for some months; another was that some of the members of the Board of Directors got a 'crotchet' in their heads that the contract had enormous profits in it and should be quashed, also that others wished 'a finger in this pie'; the third reason for the failure of this company and the contract was that Tweed was then 'the King' and nothing could be done without his assent and concurrence."

Other underground charters beside the New York City Central Underground and the Beach Pneumatic were granted by the Legislatures of those times, but for various reasons the roads so authorized were never built. Among them was the franchise of the New York City Rapid Transit Company, granted by an act of the Legislature of 1872. This act authorized Cornelius Vanderbilt (the Commodore) and such other persons as he should associate with him to organize this company, with a capital stock of $12,000,000 and to build and operate a two-track tunnel railroad from the City Hall Park to Fifty-ninth street, with a connection with the Vanderbilt railroad system. The bill as first introduced covered a part of the route already granted to the New York City Central Underground company, but when Governor Hoffman during the session vetoed the second Beach tunnel bill because it did the same thing, Vanderbilt, in the last days of the session, had the measure amended so that a conflict with the Central Underground route was avoided. As amended the bill passed both houses and was approved by the Governor on May 22, 1872. The route as fixed was from the East Side of Broadway at City Hall Park eastward to Chatham or Centre Street, to Park Street, to Mott Street, to the Bowery, to Third Avenue, to Fourth Avenue and up Fourth Avenue to "a point between 48th Street and 59th Street."

While the bill was pending the Legislature passed another Vanderbilt measure, authorizing the separation of grades on the New York Central north of 42nd Street.

The charter of the Central Underground company also covered an East Side route, the line north of 23rd Street running up Madison Avenue to the Harlem River. While the Vanderbilt bill was pending in the Legislature, Oliver W. Barnes, president of the Central Underground company, publicly charged Vanderbilt with trying to steal the route of the latter. In a signed statement published in the New York Times of April 30, 1872, Barnes said the

Vanderbilt bill was introduced at about the same time that news of the combination between the Hudson River and Harlem railroads for a line to Montreal was published, and that this line depended on the Central Underground route for access to New York City.

In the statement Barnes also declared that his company had only recently thrown off the control of the Tweed Ring, whose influence had prevented it from beginning work. The avowed purpose of the Ring, he said was to allow the charter to expire by lapse of time ''in order that they might profit by other and competing schemes.'' When Tweed was Commissioner of Public Works in 1871 the Central Underground company applied to him for the necessary permit to open the streets for the beginning of work. The request was ''met with a flat refusal and the threatening statement that the company should never put spade in the earth of Manhattan Island.''

Before the Tweed Ring got control of the company, Barnes said, every effort was made to get Vanderbilt interested. His son-in-law was a director in the company, and he was offered every inducement to build the road. His only reply, according to Barnes, was: ''No, I shall be underground a d——d sight sooner than this thing.''

As before stated, however, the Vanderbilt bill was amended so that the route would not conflict with the Central Underground charter and became a law. The Commodore's plans must have changed soon after its passage, for the New York City Rapid Transit Company did not build. All that was done was to get the engineer of the Harlem Railroad Company, Mr. Buckhout, to make surveys, plans and estimates for the line. In 1877 Allan Campbell, Commissioner of Public Works of the City of New York, in a report to the Mayor on the feasibility of building a rapid transit road from 42d street down town by private enterprise, wrote:

''In regard to the Vanderbilt underground road,

no reports or estimates were published, though surveys, plans and estimates were made by Mr. Buckhout, the engineer of the Harlem Railroad company. These documents cannot at present be found, but the information obtained by me when the work was under consideration, at which time I had several interviews with Commodore Vanderbilt upon the subject, will suffice for our present purpose."

Campbell then quoted the following figures, which he said had been prepared for Commodore Vanderbilt by "responsible and experienced contractors":

Construction work..............	$6,000,000
Private property...............	1,000,000
Rolling stock and engineering....	1,250,000
10% for contingencies..........	850,000
	$9,100,000

Campbell said the estimate for the same distance made by Chesbrough and Greene for the Central Underground company, was more than $10,000,000. He also cited the fact that the law provided for openings every 20 feet in the Vanderbilt tunnel.

Among other early charters for underground roads was one passed by the Legislature of 1868 to incorporate the New York and Brooklyn Iron Tubular Tunnel Company. This act authorized Silas C. Herring, George Hazewell and others to form a company with $5,000,000 capital to "erect an iron tubular tunnel" across the bed of the East River from a point between Wall and Jackson streets, New York, to a point between Montague street and Hudson Avenue, Brooklyn. The act failed to specify what the tunnel was to be used for, and in 1869 it was amended to authorize the company to transport passengers and freight through it. The amendment changed the name of the company to the New York Tunnel com-

pany and allowed the company two years to begin and
seven years to complete the work. Nothing ever came of
this ambitious scheme, which was the forerunner of the
present sub-river tunnels built a quarter of a century
later.

It was the Legislature of 1871 which passed the charter for the Tweed viaduct railroad. This act authorized
Peter B. Sweeney, William M. Tweed Jr., Jose F. Navarro, James G. Bennett Jr., August Belmont, Horace
Greeley, James B. Swain and others to incorporate the
New York Railway company with $25,000,000 capital and
to build and operate a steam railroad through blocks between Broadway and Chatham Street from Chambers
Street north, up the East Side between Third Avenue
and the East River to Harlem and up the West Side west
of Sixth Avenue to Spuyten Duyvil near Kingsbridge.
The fare was to be 15 cents from Chambers Street to
Harlem and 20 cents to Kingsbridge. Tweed's downfall
came so soon after the passage of this act that nothing
was done with the franchise, which lapsed by time limi-
tation. This was the franchise that called for the investment of $5,000,000 by the City of New York.

On May 25, 1871, the incorporators met in the City
Hall, New York, and elected directors. The meeting was
held in the Governors' Room, and among those present
were Peter B. Sweeney, Hugh Smith, Forbes Holland,
J. J. Sewell, Leopold Eidlitz, James P. Burnett, R. B.
Connolly, William R. Travers, William M. Tweed Jr.,
Sheppard Knapp—the first ten of the incorporators, and
Senator Cauldwell, James Sweeney, Oswald Ottendorfer,
Justice Shandley, James Irving, Alderman Cowan "and
many other well known Democratic politicians"

It was a cause for wonder at the time how Tweed
managed to get prominent men not identified with politics to join with him in this scheme, but he succeeded in
convincing many that the only way to get rapid transit
was through a company which had his support, and men

like A. T. Stewart, August Belmont, Horace Greeley and John Jacob Astor took stock in the enterprise and allowed themselves to be named and advertised as directors. The new directors met in June to take subscriptions to the capital stock of the company, for the act provided that no steps toward construction could be taken until at least $1,000,000 had been subscribed. Most of the directors took 500 shares each.

But Tweed's downfall was approaching, and he was soon deserted by his respectable associates. In November all the directors of the company resigned, and the board was reorganized with the Tweed men left out. John Taylor Johnston was elected president and the following men composed the new board of directors:

A. T. Stewart, Sydney Dillon, August Belmont, Charles A. Lamont, James F. D. Lanier, Franklin Osgood, William Butler Duncan, Oswald Ottendorfer, Charles L. Tiffany, William R. Travers, William B. Ogden, John Jacob Astor, Abraham S. Hewitt, Levi P. Morton, S. D. Babcock, William P. Blodgett, James B. Colgate, Jose F. Navarro, Edward B. Westley, John Taylor Johnston, Andrew H. Green, William H. Appleton and Joseph Seligman.

This was a board to command the confidence of the financial world, but even with such men interested the viaduct scheme was found to be too expensive to justify the large investment involved, and no serious effort was made to carry it out. The project languished and the franchise lapsed. It was impracticable from the start, for it contemplated the purchase of a wide right of way through blocks of property so valuable that a road built thereon could not possibly get enough traffic to pay the interest on the investment.

The collapse of the Viaduct Railway stimulated interest in the underground projects, forgotten during its exploitation by Tweed. Vandenburgh tried to inject new life into the Central Underground company by proposing

a consolidation of that concern with the reorganized Viaduct company, but nothing came of the move, and in a
few months Vandenburgh was busy at Albany trying to
save the Central Underground franchise from being
wiped out by the grant to the Vanderbilt company (the
New York City Rapid Transit Company) by the Legislature of 1872.

Forty years later, namely in 1912, when the Metropolitan Street Railway Company was being reorganized
after passing through the hands of receivers, the new
company was named the New York Railways Company,
the plural of "Railway" being used because the name of
Tweed's company, the New York Railway Company, still
stood on the list of chartered corporations.

Perhaps the oddest of all the schemes for rapid transit which got the ear of the Legislature was that contemplated by the charter of the Metropolitan Transit
Company, granted by act of 1872. This was the project
of James B. Swain, once State Engineer. It was known
as the "two-tier" railroad, but in reality was a three deck
highway. Instead of using the streets, Swain proposed
to buy a right of way through blocks, and in this right
of way build three railroads, one over the other. The
lowest level was to be a subway for freight, the next a
slightly depressed road for passenger traffic and the
third was to be an elevated structure from which passenger cars would hang suspended and be drawn by
horses driven on the roadway below. Aside from its
fantastic nature, the cost of right of way and construction would have been prohibitive, yet in those days Swain,
a good engineer, was enthusiastic over the plan and enlisted sufficient support to get his bill through the Legislature. The route was to be from Bowling Green to Morris
Street and through blocks west of Sixth Avenue to 37th
street, thence over to Seventh Avenue and through blocks
west of it to 42d Street, with a branch to the Grand Central station, then up to 58th Street and Broadway and

then west of Ninth Avenue to 175th Street and the Harlem River. In spite of the costly nature of the scheme, the capital stock authorized was only $5,000,000.

Swain never raised the capital to build the road, but he worked at it for several years. In February, 1875, his company issued a statement soliciting subscriptions to $2,000,000 of the stock and $1,000,000 of the bonds, in which it was said:

> "All the preliminary steps required by the statute have been taken, and the construction of said railroad has been commenced sufficient to comply with the charter, Peter Cooper, the venerable philanthropist, laying the corner stone of the structure Dec. 24, 1874."

Another tubular tunnel act was passed by the Legislature of 1873. It authorized Drake DeKay and others to form a company and build and operate a tubular tunnel from Staten Island to New Jersey under the waters of the Kill von Kull or Staten Island Sound. It allowed the directors to use any motive power found desirable and to charge any rate of fare, but when the profits exceeded 12 per cent. the fare was to be reduced. The amount of capital stock authorized was $300,000. Nothing ever came of the scheme.

CHAPTER IX

The Gilbert Elevated Railroad and the Rapid Transit Commission of 1875.

SHORTLY after the New York Elevated Railroad Company had taken over the Harvey elevated road in 1871 a rival interest appeared in the rapid transit field. This was the Gilbert Elevated Railway Company, chartered by act of the Legislature of June 17, 1872. Like Harvey's, this was a patent railway. The inventor and patentee was Dr. Rufus H. Gilbert, a veteran of the Civil War, who on taking up a peaceful avocation shortly after the close of the war devoted himself to perfecting a design for an elevated railroad. Like Harvey, too, he got a franchise and started his road, only to lose all interest in it to the men associated with him and see its profits go to others.

After six years of effort Dr. Gilbert succeeded in getting the Legislature of 1872 to pass an act incorporating the Gilbert Elevated Railway Company, with a capital stock of $3,500,000, to build and operate a railroad according to the plans of "Gilbert's Improved Elevated Railway." The incorporators named in the act were:

George B. Grinnell	B. W. Van Voorhis
Elisha A. Packer	Rufus H. Gilbert
William Foster Jr.	Henry J. Davidson
Burnett Forbes	M. O. Davidson
J. E. Southworth	Howell W. Bickley·
Isaac P. Martin	P. Lorillard
H. D. Clapp	J. C. Williams
B. J. Dillon	Henry S. Winans

The route was not fixed in the act, but a Board of Commissioners was named to select one. This Board, named in the act, consisted of Henry G. Stebbins, Major General Quincy A. Gilmore, Sheppard Knapp, Chester

A. Arthur, many years later President of the United
States, and General John A. Dix, afterward Governor of
New York.

The plan of "Gilbert's Improved Elevated Railway"
provided for tubular iron roadways suspended above the
streets by Gothic arches springing from the curb lines.
Through these tubular roads cars were to be propelled
by atmospheric or other motive power. The company
was to build a road from the Harlem River southward
through the city according to the route to be fixed by the
Board of Commissioners. It was to complete the road
as far north as 42d Street in one and a half years, to 86th
Street in two and a half years and to the Harlem River
in three years. An amendatory act passed in 1873 prohibited the use of Broadway south of 34th Street.

Here is the route selected by the Board of Commis-
sioners: From Kingsbridge on the Harlem River down
River Street, Eighth Avenue, 110th Street, Ninth Ave-
nue, Fifty-third Street, Sixth Avenue, Amity Street,
South Fifth Avenue, West Broadway, College Place,
Murray Street, Church Street, New Church Street to Mor-
ris Street; thence through private property and Bowling
Green to Beaver Street; thence by Beaver and Pearl
Streets, the New Bowery, Division Street, Allen Street,
First Avenue, Twenty-third street, Second Avenue and
River Street to the first named line at River Street and
Eighth Avenue; also a connecting line along Chambers
Street and Chatham Street and a branch on Sixth Avenue
from 53d to 59th Street.

In 1874 the Legislature passed an act confirming the
route and extending the time of construction for three
years. The panic of 1873 and the financial depression
following it, together with the impossible method of construction prescribed, prevented the company from getting the capital to build the line. Accordingly an appeal
was made to the Legislature of 1875 for relief. This was
obtained by the famous act of 1875, creating the first

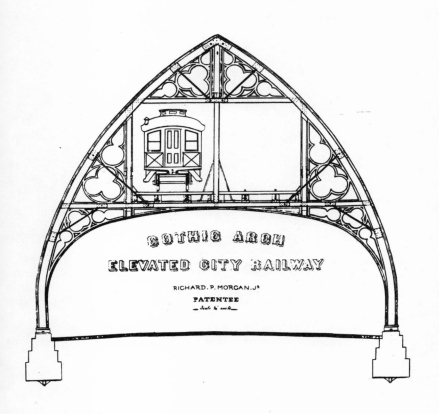

**ONE OF THE DESIGNS FOR GILBERT
ELEVATED RAILROAD, 1872.**

Rapid Transit Commission. This act confirmed the company in its routes and authorized it to use a simple method of construction. It was approved by the Governor, who was Samuel J. Tilden.

The elevated railroad system in Manhattan and the Bronx as it exists today owes its existence to the Board of Commissioners of Rapid Transit formed under this act, which not only provided for the building of the Gilbert road, but also laid down "connecting" routes for the New York Elevated Railroad Company, the connections being longer than the original lines. The act, which was denominated a general act in deference to a recently adopted amendment to the State constitution forbidding the enactment of special legislation, in reality applied only to New York City. In general it provided that, whenever fifty or more householders in a county or city should make application that there was need of a steam railway in such county or city, the Board of Supervisors or the Mayor, as the case might be, should appoint five commissioners, who were thereby empowered to fix the routes over which such steam railroads should be built, and to fix routes for the connection of any existing steam elevated railroad with ferries and other railroads.

In June 1875 two petitions from householders were presented to the Mayor of New York City, then W. H. Wickham. One declared that need existed for another steam railroad in the city, and the other that the existing line of the New York Elevated Railroad Company, in Greenwich Street and Ninth Avenue, needed connections with other steam railroads and with the ferries. Among those who signed the first petition was Theodore Roosevelt, of No. 6 West Fifty-seventh Street, New York. On July 1 Mayor Wickham appointed the following five Commissioners:

Joseph Seligman, of No. 26 West 34th Street.
Lewis B. Brown, of No. 257 West 45th Street.

Cornelius H. Delamater, of No. 424 West 20th Street.
Jordan L. Mott, of Third Avenue near East 133d Street.
Charles J. Canda, of No. 208 West 14th Street.

The Commission met on July 6 in the Mayor's office. Mayor Wickham was present and informed the Commissioners that fifty householders, as provided by the act, had petitioned him that there was need of a rapid transit steam railway in New York and asking that commissioners be appointed. Later the Commission organized by electing Mr. Seligman chairman. Burton N. Harrison acted as Secretary. It immediately advertised in the newspapers for rapid transit plans, to be submitted by August 1. Various plans were submitted, and the Commission held many conferences with those who presented them.

Many opinions were obtained from counsel on the interpretation of the act under which the Commission was proceeding. Among them was one which led to the "connection" of the Ninth Avenue elevated line with the Grand Central station and the ferries by doubling the Battery and running up the East Side. The law forbade the laying out of a route in Broadway south of 34th Street, and the Commission asked counsel whether this provision inhibited the crossing of Broadway. Counsel held that such crossing was prohibited, but that the New York Elevated Railroad could be "connected" with South Ferry and the Grand Central station by an extension "turning" Broadway at its southern end and continuing up the East Side to Forty-second Street and beyond to the northern ferries.

On September 2, 1875, the Commission adopted resolutions fixing the routes for the New York Elevated and the Gilbert Elevated roads. The resolution for the former read in part as follows:

"Resolved: That, in pursuance of the powers and

authority conferred upon us by Chapter 606 of the Laws of 1875, we do hereby fix and determine the route or routes by which the New York Elevated railroad, an elevated steam railway now and at the time said law was enacted in actual operation, may connect with other steam railways or the depots thereof and with steam ferries as follows'':

Here the route of the Third Avenue elevated was recited in full, "turning" Broadway as suggested by counsel. A similar resolution was adopted on the same day, fixing the routes for the Gilbert Elevated road, as given above. On the next day, September 3, the Commission voted down a resolution to fix a route for the plan of J. B. and J. M. Cornell by a vote of three to two, Delamater and Mott for, and Seligman, Brown and Canda against. This was the only project outside of the New York and Gilbert Elevated schemes which came to a vote. The Commission refused to consider any underground projects on the advice of counsel that "to attempt to authorize the construction of a road to be built entirely or mainly under the surface would be a proceeding of such doubtful legality that we cannot advise it."

Rates of fare were prescribed for both elevated lines. From the Battery to Fifty-ninth Street the fare was to be 10 cents; from the Battery to Harlem not to exceed 15 cents and to Highbridge not to exceed 17 cents; for five miles 10 cents and each additional mile 2 cents. The resolutions also provided for "Commission trains", to be operated from 5:30 to 7:30 o'clock in the morning and from 5 to 7 o'clock in the evening, on which the fares should be half the above, namely 5 cents from the Battery to Fifty-ninth Street, 7 cents to Harlem and 8 cents to Highbridge.

By railroad men the so-called "rush hours" in New York are known as "commission hours," because of the fact that "commission trains" as provided for by the

Commission of 1875 were operated at a cheaper fare in those hours.

As the act authorized the Commission to organize a company to build a road in case no company carried out the plans approved, the Commission in October caused the organization of the Manhattan Railway Company, with a capital stock of $2,000,000, all of which was subscribed for. The incorporators included men interested in both the New York and Gilbert Elevated companies. The directors, elected under supervision of the Commission, November 10, 1875, were:

Cornelius K. Garrison   George M. Pullman
Horace Porter   Jose F. Navarro
Milton Courtright   William L. Scott
John F. Tracy   David Dows
                    John Ross

The articles of association for the Manhattan Railway company recited at length the resolutions adopted by the Commission in fixing the routes for the two elevated systems, as well as the resolutions in which the Commission specified the plans on which the roads should be built. These contained directions for placing the elevated pillars to support the elevated structure and complete specifications for the work and the materials to be used. The company was given till May, 1877, to complete the roads to Fifty-ninth Street and till June, 1878, to the Harlem River, on the West Side of the city, and till December, 1877 and December, 1878, respectively those portions on the East Side.

The schedule of fares adopted by the Commission was also included in the articles. An interesting feature of this schedule was that it provided that passengers in non-rush hours who could not get a seat in the trains could travel free. Provision also was made for ''saloon or drawing room'' cars, for a seat in which the company might charge an extra fare. The articles declared specifically that the Manhattan company should not build the roads authorized to be built by the Gilbert Elevated or the New York Elevated company unless the latter failed to construct its road in the time allowed.

The Board of Directors met on November 12, 1875, and elected David Dows president and Horace Porter secretary of the Manhattan company.

At the request of the New York Elevated company the Commission on December 2, 1875, fixed more definitely the route across the Battery, by which the "connection" with ferries and the Grand Central station was to be made. This action gave the company specific rights across Battery Park. After approving and filing the bonds given by the two elevated companies, the Commission finished its work and on December 11, 1875, adjourned "subject to the call of the president or of any two of the Commissioners." Its last act was to draft and send to Mayor William H. Wickham a farewell letter, in which it said:

"We have every reason to expect that Rapid Transit will now be afforded to the city."

The effect of the Commission's action was soon seen. Each of the companies made the requisite financial arrangements and began construction, which was pressed as fast as circumstances would allow. Obstacles of various kinds were encountered, not the least of which were injunction suits brought by property owners. These, however, were fought successfully, and in 1877 final decision in favor of the roads was handed down by the Court of Appeals. The New York Elevated company completed its line up Ninth Avenue to Fifty-ninth Street and began operating it in 1876; its line from Battery Place to South Ferry in 1877; the Third Avenue line from South Ferry to 42d Street in August, 1878, and to 129th Street in December, 1878. In 1880 the Second

Avenue line reached 67th Street and the Ninth Avenue line Harlem.

Work on the Gilbert Elevated company's lines began in 1876, but was stopped by legal proceedings brought by property owners and the surface railroad companies, culminating in the injunction which was finally dissolved by the Court of Appeals decision in November, 1877. Construction was then pushed rapidly, and the line from Morris Street to Fifty-ninth Street (the Sixth Avenue road) was completed in April and placed in operation in June, 1878. In the same month by court order the name of the Gilbert company was changed to the Metropolitan Elevated Railway company. Financial difficulties beset the company, and differences arose among its directors. As a result the Manhattan Railway Company, organized by the Rapid Transit Commission of 1875 for just such an emergency, stepped in, leased both roads and took control of the work on the Gilbert road in September, 1879, and completed construction to the Harlem River. It was in May, 1879, that both old companies, the New York and the Metropolitan, made a contract with the Manhattan Railway Company, for the lease of the property and rights of the former. The lease took effect as of January 31, 1879.

This lease was made the subject of special inquiry by the Railroad Committee of the New York Assembly in an investigation of railroads held in 1879. It was spread upon the minutes and men prominent in both the New York and the Gilbert companies were examined as to its terms and conditions. It was testified that the Manhattan Railway Company had $13,000,000 in capital stock, half of which was issued to each company in return for stock in the old companies. The lease was to run 999 years and the rental was fixed at ten per cent. on the stock of each of the old companies, which was $6,500,000 each. It was also brought out in the testimony that the New York Elevated company was obligated to pay to the

ELEVATED RAILROAD.

(As it will be cor. 6th Avenue and 23d Street.)

**HORRORS OF ELEVATED RAILROAD OPERATION
AS SEEN BY ITS OPPONENTS.**

City of New York five per cent. of its net earnings, and the Metropolitan, or Gilbert company, two per cent of its dividends.

According to the testimony the original elevated roads cost about $700,000 to $800,000 per mile of double tracked structure and the cars about $3,100 to $3,500 apiece. Jose F. Navarro was the leading promoter of the Gilbert road. He testified that he had obtained his stock at various prices, some as low as twenty cents a share and some as high as par value. Before the charters were upheld by the Court decision of 1877 he said it was difficult to interest capitalists in the project. After he persuaded Commodore Garrison and George M. Pullman to take stock, it was easier to interest others. William H. Vanderbilt had been approached, but he would have nothing to do with the project, because he believed that people never would consent to walk up and down stairs to and from the railroad. Navarro said his road had increased the assessed value of city property $100,000,000 and in five years more would increase it $500,000,000.

Benjamin Brewster, a stockholder in the New York Elevated company, which took over the old Harvey road, testified as to the reasons for the merger of the two companies in the lease to the Manhattan Railway company. Both old companies, he said, were compelled to use the same tracks in Pearl street from Beaver street to Chatham Square, and in Ninth Avenue from 53d street to 110th street. This involved grade crossings for the trains of each and meant dangerous operation. His company had appealed to the Assembly for the right to build crossings, but had been told that it was a matter the companies must settle between themselves. The only way they could settle it was by getting together and forming one operating company; hence the lease.

Both Navarro and Brewster were examined as to the rates of fare, which then were ten cents on each road, with five cents in the "commission" hours, so called because the Rapid Transit Commission stipulated for a five cent fare for workers going to and coming from work. Each declared that a uniform five cent fare would be too low. Navarro said his company was entitled to charge 26 cents to Harlem and 12 cents to Central Park, but voluntarily had reduced the rates to ten cents, which he thought low enough. Brewster said his company was entitled to charge ten cents from Battery to Fifty-ninth street and two cents a mile additional, not exceeding fifteen cents to Harlem River. He also said the New York Elevated stock was then (1879) worth $165 and had been as high as $200.

Brewster was asked about certain letters published in the daily press, crediting Samuel J. Tilden and Cyrus W. Field with having made $1,000,000, out of an investment of about $200,000 in New York Elevated stock. He said he imagined that came from the fortunate period when Mr. Field and Mr. Tilden went into the enterprise. It was practically broken down and elevated roads were in bad odor; that was before the Court of Appeals had affirmed the validity of the elevated road legislation.

With the extension of the elevated roads to the Harlem River, their business expanded by leaps and bounds. In 1878, before either line had reached Harlem, the total number of passengers carried on both roads was 9,236,-670. In December of that year the Third Avenue line reached 129th street, and the passengers carried in 1879 jumped to 45,945,401. In 1880 the Ninth Avenue line reached Harlem and the Second Avenue line reached 67th street. The figures for that year increased to 60,831,757. As this immense business of course meant large profits, it is small wonder the stock of the elevated roads was in demand.

By this time the success of the elevated system of city travel was established. That it was so is due almost entirely to the act of 1875 and the proceedings of the Rapid Transit Commission acting under it. In a report made to a sub-committee of the committee appointed by the Assembly in 1879 to investigate railroad conditions in New York City, E. Sweet, an engineer, wrote:

"The Rapid Transit act of 1875 and the proceedings of the Commission appointed under it insured a certain and rapid solution of the quick transit question in New York City by fixing so small a number of routes as to make them valuable, and by making the enjoyment of these routes by the companies on which they were conferred dependent upon immediate development. They created for both the Metropolitan and the New York Elevated companies the possibility of the success they have now realized."

The evolution of the elevated railroad from the crude conception of Harvey in 1866 to the successful operation of 1879 was attended by revolutions within the companies themselves. It has been told how Harvey, the inventor, lost the rewards which his work merited and was eliminated from the reorganization of his company. A similar fate overtook Dr. Rufus H. Gilbert, the inventor or projector of the Gilbert or Metropolitan railroad. Gilbert, like Harvey, had a crude idea. His plan contemplated the construction of a huge iron tube through which he proposed to propel cars by pneumatic power. The law granting the rights for this railroad had to be amended so as to permit the building of a simple structure carrying an open track which could be operated by locomotive engines before the project became practicable. Like Harvey, also, Gilbert lacked the financial ability to successfully organize his scheme. In his efforts to enlist capital he gave away the control of the company, and his final elimination without the reward to which he was entitled followed its reorganization. Others reaped what he sowed. One version of his unfortunate experience was given in a speech made by Isaac Hayes, a member of

Assembly, at a meeting held in Chickering Hall on June 21, 1877, as a protest against allowing the Gilbert Elevated company to inflict damage on private property without compensating the owners. In that speech Mr. Hayes said:

"Things in the Gilbert company appear to be rather mixed. They don't seem to deal any more fairly by each other than they do by the property owners whom they threaten with calamity nor the public who 'demand' the building of the road. I judge this from reading the title of a suit now pending in the U. S. Supreme Court which runs thus: 'Rufus H. Gilbert, plaintiff, against J. T. Navarro, William Foster Jr., the Gilbert Elevated Railway Company, the New York Loan and Improvement Company and the Edgemoor Iron Company, defendants.'

"Now all of these parties to the suit have been more or less interested directly in this combination to destroy South Fifth Avenue, Amity Street and Sixth Avenue. I will tell you how, to begin at the beginning. Dr. Gilbert, who has been apparently most grievously wronged, conceived the idea of a rapid transit road to be built of iron. He had seen plenty of shot and shell during the war, and iron was a favorite with him. He worked away over that idea for six long years, and finally in 1872 he secured a charter from the Legislature. Then he meets William Foster Jr., and they together make up a company. They create directors and issue stock. Foster Jr. takes some thousands of these shares to sell, but he doesn't sell them. But he falls in with Mr. Navarro, who has some knowledge of a company with a charter, called the 'New York Loan and Improvement Company'. And now others step in, and a little ring is formed, and this little ring manage to get possession of all the stock of the Gilbert Elevated

Railway Company, the Doctor's included, and Dr.
Gilbert, who had obtained the franchise, after six
years finds himself out in the cold. But he pockets
a promise of ever so many shares of the New York
Loan and Improvement Company in lieu of his own,
and is content. To be sure, he never got the stock,
as he swears, hence the suit. Well, this Improvement
company undertook to construct the road. * * *
The Gilbert Elevated Railway Company * * *
never did have any money, as one would think, or
they would hardly have gone over body and soul
through the agency of Foster Jr. and Navarro to
the Improvement company. And now the said Improvement company, finding itself in this sad predica-
ment of impecuniosity, sublet their contract with the
Railway company to the Edgemoor Iron Company,
of the State of Delaware.''

Mr. Sweet in the report above quoted said that the
New York Loan and Improvement Company financed the
Gilbert project, making a contract in 1876 with the Railway company to build and equip the line for $500,000 in
stock, $750,000 in first mortgage bonds and $750,000 in
second mortgage bonds for each completed mile of double
track road.

While the Rapid Transit Commission of 1875 undoubtedly did much for the New York Elevated Railroad,
it must not be inferred that it did everything for it. That
company was on its feet and part of its road was in successful operation at the time the Commission was created.
Its report dated January 20, 1875, shows that it was then
running cars from Greenwich Street up Ninth Avenue
as far as 34th Street, and an immediate extension to 59th
Street was recommended. By this report it was shown
that the company had expended more than $1,300,000 in
building and equipping the road. Its receipts from passenger fares for the year were $82,945, and this was for

only 313 days, the road not having been operated on Sundays. Its trains were composed of two cars or three cars, and the average daily receipts were $265. Owing to a lack of turnouts, it took 35 minutes to make the trip from 34th Street to the Battery and return, and among the recommendations of the report were more turnouts and the immediate extension of the line to 59th Street. Another recommendation was that the guage of the track be reduced from five feet to four feet, eight and one-half inches, the standard of the steam railroads. On the lower part of the road the rails had been laid on longitudinal timbers, while above 30th Street they were laid on iron cross-ties. The report recommended the substitution of wooden cross-ties as better and less expensive. All these changes were made in time.

That the company was apprehensive of the results of pending legislation (the Rapid Transit Act of 1875) is shown by the following closing paragraph:

"This company, as the pioneer in the experiment of elevated rapid transit in this city, and in consideration of the long struggle it has had and the large expenditure it has made in demonstrating its success, is, I think, entitled to, and will, I trust, receive proper consideration from the State authorities and from the authorities and people of this city in the movement now going on for a general system of elevated rapid transit for the city."

The report was signed by Milton Courtright, then president of the New York Elevated Railroad Company.

James Grant Wilson's History of New York says the Greenwich street elevated road, while the germ of real rapid transit, was "the butt of good natured ridicule till it was sold out by the sheriff in 1871. Its new management made a strong effort to push it northward, but legal obstacles beset them on all sides, thrown in their way by the strenuous opposition of the horse railroads and of property owners.''

The "terrors" of the elevated railroad are pictured in an old print, which is reproduced on another page. This print was found in a pamphlet published in 1877 describing a meeting of the "antis" in Chickering Hall on June 21 of that year. This meeting was held to "protest against the destruction of property by elevated railroads without compensation to owners." Henry M. Taber was elected chairman, and there was a large list of vice-presidents, headed by Smith Ely Jr. The resolutions adopted included the following:

"Resolved, that we will aid by our means and influence any legitimate and adequate method for rapid transit, believing that a necessity exists for a speedy, safe and comprehensive system of communication between the two extremities of the city; but in doing so we utterly repudiate the idea that the property of one man is to be sacrificed to put money into the pockets of another. We believe that the citizens of New York can afford to act honestly and pay fairly for what the city needs; and we believe that the so-called elevated railroads are a sham and a snare, the tendency of which is to defeat the real object in view.''

How the opposition to the elevated roads viewed the Rapid Transit act of 1875 is shown by an address delivered at this meeting by Robert H. Strahan, chairman of the Judiciary Committee of the Assembly of 1877. A part of Strahan's speech follows:

"Let it be understood, then, that by certain amendments to the constitution of this State, which went into effect on the first of January 1875, all special legislation as to street railroads was prohibited. It was necessary to the success of the two projects in question (the Gilbert elevated and the New York elevated) that this prohibition be got around in some way. To do it an act purporting to be a General Rapid Transit act was passed. This was also in 1875. This was a very remarkable piece of legislation. It purported to be a general act, applicable to the whole State, this to avoid the constitutional objection as to special legislation; but it was in fact of the most special character. It was intended for the exclusive benefit of these two companies—the Gilbert Elevated and the New York Elevated companies.

"This 'general' act authorized the appointment of five commissioners, to whom were given powers of legislation and administration. This commission of five was authorized in the first place to determine upon the necessity of these railways in any county or city; they were given exclusive power to locate these railways over, across or under any of the streets or avenues of the cities of this State. They were given power also to adopt plans of construction and conditions of construction, and they had power to prepare articles and to organize companies. If a corporation be formed by enactment of this commission to build these railways, certain powers were given to it by this act, among which was the power of eminent domain—that is, the right to take private property.

"Such a Commission of Five was appointed by the Mayor of the City of New York for this city and county, and they were clothed with these general powers."

The speaker then pointed out that, if the commission should *happen* to locate a route coincident with the route of an existing corporation, that corporation might build its route *according to the plans of the Commission*. This

While drying upon the house-top, clothes will get the benefit of smoke and cinders.

Passengers will, no doubt, often be treated to a bath, on arriving at the Battery.

Individuals may also be dropped at the wrong place by the conductor.

Passengers will find it to their advantage to carry hooks along with them in case the train jumps the track.

People will have to stand from under when the engineer cleans out the fire-box.

While waiting for the train, travelers can amuse themselves reading the Rapid Transit Signs.

Another Chapter on Rapid Transit.

Art Printing Establishment, 39 Broad Street, N. Y.

DODGER ISSUED BY OPPONENTS OF CON-
STRUCTION OF SIXTH AVENUE
ELEVATED RAILROAD.

provision, the Gilbert corporation claimed, exempted it from building the kind of a structure required by its charter, and accordingly "it is now endeavoring to build the cheap and unsightly and unheard of structure which is intended as its road."

Another provision of the law empowered the Commission, in case there was an elevated railroad already in operation, to lay out and give it what was called "connecting" routes with other railroads or ferries. That meant the New York Elevated company, the speaker said, and "this peculiar phraseology enables it to encircle the whole island. It was the only corporation in the whole world which had an elevated railway, or part of one, in operation. Now, that is all there is of this great GENERAL rapid transit law. That Commission, clothed with these general powers, is dead; it cannot again be called into life. It has left nothing to show for its work except just what it did for the Gilbert company and for the New York Elevated company. By this peculiar legislation and the operation of the Commission appointed under it, these two private corporations have got possession, now and forever apparently, of the whole field of rapid transit operations in the whole city of New York."

This period, namely, from 1870 to 1877, was made notable by other transit improvements. Up to 1871 the Hudson River Railroad, the New York and New Haven Railroad and the New York and Harlem Railroad had their terminals in the center of the up-town district—the Hudson River company at 30th Street and Ninth Avenue, and the other two at Madison and Fourth Avenues, Twenty-sixth and Twenty-seventh streets. In 1871 the first Grand Central station at 42d Street and Park Avenue was opened, and all three roads terminated there. In 1875 the work of separating grades north of the station was completed, and for 4½ miles the railroad ran through tunnel, open cut and on a stone viaduct above the street surface from 42d Street to the Harlem River.

This work cost $6,000,000 and was paid half by the city and half by the railroads. The train service was increased, and rapid transit to Harlem by this route was realized.

In ten years after Harvey started his experimental line in 1867 the elevated railroads were carrying 3,000,000 passengers a year, and their practicability and success were thoroughly demonstrated. In 1877 they attracted the attention of Cyrus W. Field, the great financier who had built the Atlantic cable. He decided to invest in the new railroads and purchased control of the entire system, embarking his whole fortune in the undertaking. It was under the stimulating influence of his genius and capital that they were completed and made into a really important transportation system.

CHAPTER X

ERA OF PUBLIC OWNERSHIP OPENS AND MAKES POSSIBLE NEW YORK'S FIRST SUBWAY.

IN the preceding pages the origin and development of Rapid Transit have been traced for the fifteen years between 1865, when the first rapid transit bill was passed by the Legislature, and 1880, when the completion of the elevated railroads to Harlem and the increased business thereby obtained demonstrated the complete success of passenger transportation on overhead structures built above the street surface. This period might well be termed the Era of Private Ownership, for all transportation enterprises then undertaken were based upon the absolute ownership, control and operation of such facilities, even though dependent on public grants for their rights of way, by private capital.

The next fifteen years, namely from 1880 to 1895, may be as properly called the Era of Public Ownership, for during that time the perpetual and gratuitous franchise was abolished and the right of the public to build, pay for, own and if necessary operate street railroads was successfully asserted. It was in 1891 that the present Rapid Transit Act was enacted and soon thereafter amended so as to permit cities to use their own capital in construction, and in 1894 on a referendum vote the people of New York City decided by a substantial majority in favor of public ownership. But before entering upon a description of this momentous change in public policy it may be well to trace briefly the struggle to effect it.

Following the introduction of horse-drawn street cars on metallic rails in 1832 the possibility of profit-making in the transportation of large numbers of passengers for a small per capita fare appealed to the moneyed men of the day and in consequence to the politicians, who found themselves in position to confer the needed rights in the public streets. As the city controlled such thoroughfares for other purposes, it was taken as a matter of course that the Common Council was the authority to confer upon a private corporation the right to lay and operate street railroads. The first street railway franchises were granted in this way, the city granting the charters for the Sixth Avenue, Eighth Avenue, Second Avenue, Third Avenue and Ninth Avenue surface lines. In a report on the subject made by the Committee on Political Reform of the Union League Club in January, 1873, this language was used:

"The immense values thus given away by a simple resolution of the Common Council opened up visions of sudden wealth to members. Rings were formed, candidates nominated and elected simply for their readiness to plunder the city.

"The Broadway franchise for only two miles was valued by the company who thought they had secured it at $1,500,000. Unseemly contests for possession between rival companies occurred in the streets. The defeated and disappointed companies appealed to the courts. It was then found that the City had not the legal right thus to give away to corporations, to use for private gain, the public streets purchased and graded with money obtained from the people by taxation and assessment. In 1854 the Legislature, by an act that appeared to be for a different purpose, yet by a clause skillfully thrust into the third section, confirmed and made valid the grants theretofore obtained from the City.

"The courts having decided that the City officials could not donate to their friends the City streets and squares, the whole business of giving to these corporations the public property of the City was then transferred to Albany. The Legislature at once became surrounded and besieged annually by an army called the Railroad Lobby. Members were chosen for their subserviency to this interest. Such proceedings were had that street after street was given away, when on the point of donating the Broadway franchise Mr. A. T. Stewart checked the evil by offering to pay the City for this grant two millions of dollars. This was justice, for there was no plunder either for the Lobby or the Legislature in this offer; and the grant was refused. Finally the demand of the citizens for protection against the rapacity of these corporations was recognized, and the Twenty-third street franchise was sold at public auction. The extension of the Dry Dock, East Broadway and Battery road was granted on condition that five per cent. of the proceeds of the cars run thereon should be paid annually to the City. The word 'net' having been inserted before 'proceeds', the company, though doing a lucrative business, paid nothing for five years, till overhauled by a member of this Committee last spring, when they paid up for the five years the sums due the City. The extension of the Second Avenue road was granted last winter on condition that they pay to the City the value of the franchise for the extension.

"After long struggle against the Lobby, the Reformers have at last got the principle of payment to the City for the franchises recognized. It now remains to fix a just rule of value for franchises that may be hereafter granted".

Even after this principle was recognized the idea that only private capital could properly engage in the construction of such facilities prevailed. Municipal ownership was a theory held by some advanced thinkers, doubtless looked upon as visionary radicals in those days. However, its advocates eventually got a hearing. In

1873, the same year in which the Union League committee made the report just quoted from, a bill was introduced in the Legislature by a Mr. Opdyke to authorize a board of City officers to build and turn over to a City department to operate a rapid transit railroad. This measure, which was introduced in January, was endorsed in February at a meeting of the Rapid Transit Association in New York city, at which General Sigel delivered an address. As far as research discloses, this is the first recognition of municipal ownership in legislation or attempted legislation. The time, however, invited such a move. Samuel J. Tilden, reformer, had been elected Governor in 1872, and the Legislature of 1873, elected with him, had a membership more or less sympathetic to reform ideas. Indeed, it was Tilden's influence which brought about the important legislation resulting in the formation of the Rapid Transit Commission of 1875.

In the same month, February 1873, a mass meeting was held in Cooper Institute, New York, at which Abram S. Hewitt, afterwards Mayor, made an address in favor of City-owned rapid transit lines. Resolutions were adopted favoring a City-built and City-operated line, and a Committee of One Hundred was appointed to go to Albany to support the Opdyke bill. This bill authorized the Governor and Senate to appoint six commissioners, who, with the Mayor and two heads of City departments, was to constitute a commission with power to survey and build a rapid transit railroad. The fare was to be seven cents, and the interest on the bonds issued by the City for construction was to be paid out of earnings and the fare reduced if the earnings would permit. The Chairman of the Committee of One Hundred was Rudolph A. Witthaus. It did valiant work, and mass meetings were held in various parts of the city to aid the cause, but the time was not yet ripe, and the Opdyke bill failed to pass. It undoubtedly had a marked effect on the public mind and unquestionably led the Legislature of 1875 to the consideration and passage of the bill authorizing the Mayor to appoint the first Rapid Transit Commission, which confirmed and amplified the rights of the new elevated roads.

The Legislature of 1874 considered the subject, but took no remedial action. In March the Assembly Committee on Railroads reported against the creation of a rapid transit commission, on the ground that no commission could build a road unless the City would pay for it, and this was not desired.

Public sentiment as voiced by the press, also, was still hostile to public ownership. The Times in an editorial published on April 1, 1874, said:

> "Much as we have found to condemn in the action of the Assembly Railroad Committee, we thoroughly approve of their determination to sanction no scheme which provides for the expenditure of City money in the construction of local railroads."

In March 1875 the Committee on Rapid Transit of the Board of Aldermen reported a recommendation that private capital be given the first chance to build a rapid transit line, and if that failed the City should undertake the work. A minority report favored City ownership, but the Board adopted the majority report.

Early in the year 1875 the Chamber of Commerce held a meeting at which subscriptions were taken to start a rapid transit fund. A Committee of Fifty was named to solicit further subscriptions, and the subscribers organized the New York Rapid Transit Association to further the construction of a road. Gouverneur Morris was chairman and C. H. Roosevelt secretary of this meeting. During the early part of the same year a committee of the American Society of Civil Engineers made a report recommending the construction of elevated roads to supply the rapid transit needs of the city.

Mayor Wickham in his annual message in January 1875 mentioned the subject and stated that the need of rapid transit had been partially supplied by the New York Central improvement from 42d street to the Harlem River. This was the tunnel and viaduct carrying four tracks which was paid for half by the City and half by the company. The City's share was $3,200,000. It is difficult now to appraise a state of public sentiment which frowned upon using public money to build a road to be owned by the public, but condoned the outright gift of $3,200,000 to a corporation for improving its own property. Of course, in this case the City gained something in the elimination of many grade crossings, and the principle of contributing toward the cost of such work is still recognized as sound, but such a disposition of public funds in those days seems a contradiction of the evidently prevalent opposition to public ownership.

In the same message Mayor Wickham congratulated the city on the rapid transit assured by the Central improvement. He said:

> "As provided by the law authorizing the improvement, two of the tracks are to be devoted exclusively to rapid transit within the city."

A later enactment relieved the company of this obligation.

The first elevated railroad was built in the absence of any law to compensate owners of property along the line. In 1872 a constitutional amendment was adopted requiring the consents of property owners as a prerequisite to railroad construction, to the extent of at least one half in value of the abutting property. This requirement was embodied in the Rapid Transit act of 1875, which provided that in lieu of such consents the railroad must get a favorable decision from three commissioners to be appointed by General Term of the Supreme Court, such decision to be reported to and confirmed by that court. This bill was known as the Husted bill, it having been introduced in the Senate by General Husted, who worked indefatigably for the cause of rapid transit both in and out of the Legislature. Governor Tilden also supported the measure, which was also known as "the Governor's bill". The appointment of commissioners under this bill by Mayor Wickham and the important work they did have been noted in a previous chapter.

The extension of the two elevated railroads under the plan adopted by the Rapid Transit Commission of 1875 allayed for a time the agitation for rapid transit. Many thought the problem solved, and the next ten years were barren of any important movements looking to new construction aside from that of the elevated roads. By the end of the 80's, however, the elevated lines had become congested and it became apparent that additional rapid transit roads must be provided.

In 1888 Mayor Abram S. Hewitt, whom many regard as the father of modern rapid transit and who had urged public ownership as early as 1873, sent to the Common Council a message, in which he advocated the use of the credit of the City for the construction of a road to be owned by the City but which could be leased to a private company for operation. His plan, which was practically that later incorporated in the Rapid Transit act of 1894, provided for construction by a contracting company, which should lease the road for operation for a term of years, give a sufficient bond, pay for the equipment of the line but give the City a lien on such equipment and guarantee to pay the City annual interest and one per cent. for a sinking fund on the bonds issued for construction.

The Common Council did not approve the plan, but Mr. Hewitt and the Chamber of Commerce had drafted a bill embodying it, and this bill was introduced in the Legislature of 1888. It failed for reasons which Mr. Hewitt himself thus described:

"The prejudice against the scheme was so great, however, that it was difficult to find any member of the Legislature who would be responsible for the

introduction of a bill, which was opposed not only
by the Common Council of the City, but by the political organization which controlled the politics of the
City. The Mayor appeared, however, before the
Committee of the Legislature and made a very elaborate argument as to the necessity for increased rapid
transit facilities and of the mode under which he
proposed to secure them at an early date. The Committee, however, declined to report the bill back to
the Senate, and so far as that session was concerned
the proposition entirely failed.''

Hugh J. Grant, a Tammany man, was inaugurated
Mayor in January, 1889, and with his inaugural message
took up the question. Sentiment for public ownership,
however, apparently had not crystallized in the preceding
decade, for Mayor Grant, while urging the construction of
new lines, declared that they must be built, equipped and
operated by private capital. Here is an extract from his
message:

"It may be proper, however, to state that, in the
construction of a rapid transit road, it will be necessary to rely upon private enterprise. We might indeed prefer that the road be constructed at the public
expense and when completed leased for a term of
years to the highest bidder, upon conditions which
would carefully provide for the comfort of the citizens and for a suitable return to the public treasury,
but in view of the limit to which the borrowing
capacity of the City is now restricted, this scheme
would be impracticable. Private capital must, therefore, furnish the means for the construction of the
road, but the public authorities must be vigilant to
guard the right of the citizens to the enjoyment of a
fair proportion of the benefits that will flow from its
operation.''

The tone of this message shows what a change had taken place in public sentiment in the preceding decade. While preference for construction by private capital is shown, the advantage of limited term franchises is recognized and the duty of public officers to see that the public shall share in the profits of the undertaking is affirmed. The day of perpetual franchises granted without compensation to the municipality was gone forever.

Mayor Grant in March 1889 had drafted a bill to amend the Rapid Transit law, which he sent to Albany. This bill gave the Mayor power to appoint a rapid transit commission without waiting for a petition from taxpayers, as required by the original act. Owing to political opposition, however, this bill failed of passage. The Mayor, with considerable acumen, appealed to the Legislature to give to the City of New York the right to name the men to act as Commissioners. This invocation of the home rule principle eventually proved successful. In 1890 a hostile Senate again killed his bill, but in 1891 the bill was reintroduced and passed both houses. Meanwhile, in December 1890, in order to get action Mayor Grant, on the petition of taxpayers, appointed a commission under the Act of 1875. The men he named were William Steinway, John H. Starin, Samuel Spencer, Eugene L. Bushe and John C. Inman. How this action was brought about was told by the late John D. Crimmins. In a statement published in the Evening Post on October 24, 1913, Mr. Crimmins said:

"In 1889 on the assumption of office by Mayor Grant I made known to him the importance of taking up the rapid transit situation. I personally circulated the petition and knew every signer, had the signatures acknowledged and brought the petition to Presiding Justice Van Brunt of the Appellate Division of the Supreme Court who prepared and administered the required oath. I may mention here that Mr. George S. Lespinasse was enlisted with me in this movement, securing and witnessing signatures. I brought the completed petition to Mayor Grant, who instructed me to find the men who would serve. I received more refusals than consents. I made the offer to James McCreary, Charles Stewart Smith and others. Mr. Smith was later a member of the Board of Rapid Transit Commissioners. The Commissioners appointed by Mayor Grant, were required first to adopt the routes and general plan of construction of a rapid transit railroad, and then to obtain the necessary consents for its construction from the local authorities and the property holders affected. That was the beginning of the work of the Rapid Transit Commission, the results of which we see today.''

The Commission named by Mayor Grant met and organized on January 6, 1891, electing William Steinway chairman. On January 9 following the Commission met again and decided to proceed under the existing law, although a bill for a new act was pending. The Commissioners, however, seemed to have felt assured that the bill if passed would not upset what they might do. Accordingly they issued a public call for plans and suggestions.

Before the end of the month of January the Legislature passed the Stewart rapid transit bill and on the last day of the month it was signed by Governor David B. Hill. William F. Sheehan, later prominent as a traction lawyer in New York City, was Speaker of the Assembly and by his rulings assisted the final passage of the bill in that house.

This was the Rapid Transit Act of 1891, which with numerous amendments still stands on the statute books. It created the Board of Rapid Transit Commissioners and named as the first Commissioners the five men appointed in December 1890 by Mayor Grant. The act authorized the board to lay out routes and adopt plans for a rapid transit railroad, either supra- or subterranean, and to put up the franchise to build and operate at public auction. It also required the consents of the local authorities and of the abutting property owners to the extent of one half in value of the property affected.

The Commission on February 9, 1891, reorganized under the new law, electing William Steinway, President, John H. Starin Vice President and Eugene L. Bushe Secretary. Its work went right along unaffected by the reorganization, and it proceeded to consider plans, hear arguments and receive suggestions.

The law itself, as shown by the provision for the auction of the right to build and operate, contemplated private ownership, but the advocates of public ownership soon made themselves heard. One of the first if not the first was Jacob H. Schiff, the banker, who appeared before the new Commission on March 13 and made an argument for the use of City funds to defray the cost of construction. Mr. Schiff's theory was that an underground railroad would be a very expensive undertaking and it was doubtful whether its operation would pay a sufficient return on the money invested to make it an attractive investment for private capital. The City, however, could borrow money at three per cent., a much lower rate than private capital could command, and therefore could better afford such an investment.

Another phase of the problem to which the Commission devoted considerable attention was the question of motive power. It was the desire of all interested that an underground road should be built if practicable, and the kind of motive power to be used was a most important consideration. The experience of the London underground with steam, in spite of smoke-consuming devices, had not been satisfactory, and the best engineering thought of the day in the United States was averse to employing it for an underground road in New York, where from the nature of things there must be long stretches of tunnels without open spaces such as relieve the London tube. Electricity had been recently applied to street car propulsion, and it was favored for the new underground road if built. At the same meeting at which Mr. Schiff urged public construction, Mr. Frank J. Sprague, afterwards famous as an electrical engineer, appeared and advocated the use of electricity.

The Commission appointed William E. Worthen as its Chief Engineer, and later William Barclay Parsons Deputy Chief Engineer. During the summer it came to a decision to build an underground road and announced its preference for a route running up Broadway and the extension of Broadway then known as the Boulevard. Worthen and Parsons reported plans for an underground road, and in October, 1891, the Commission adopted and submitted them to the Common Council for approval. On October 28 that body approved the routes and plans and gave its consent as the local authority to the construction of the underground road. The Mayor's approval was added on October 31.

In the Commission's report to the Common Council there is evidence of much valuable work done in a short time. Its engineers had made borings to determine the depth and character of the rock along the proposed route, had investigated the trend and extent of traffic and studied the problem of treating the sewer and water pipes, the several possible methods of construction and other matters necessary to the intelligent undertaking of a work of such importance. The Commission decided to build the road as close to the surface of the streets as possible, so as to make access to the stations easy for passengers, but was in doubt whether to construct the four tracks contemplated on one level or to make a double deck subway with local tracks on the upper and express tracks on the lower level. Its engineers, therefore, were instructed to make alternative plans showing both methods, but the Commission in its report plainly showed a preference for the one level construction.

On the subject of motive power the report said:

"While the Board is convinced that electricity as a motive power is available for the purposes of the railway recommended by this report, it is not deemed wise at the present time to exclude other forms of power answering the essential conditions of speed and non-combustion in the tunnel, or to attempt to direct the exact method of application of such power as shall finally be adopted."

The report was accompanied by reports from four consulting engineers to whom the plans prepared by Worthen and Parsons were submitted. These engineers were Octave Chanute, of Chicago; Joseph M. Wilson, of Philadelphia; Theodore Cooper, of New York and John Bogart, State Engineer of New York.

In the plans submitted by Mr. Worthen and Mr. Parsons there was a notable difference. Worthen proposed four tracks on a level built near the surface, but below the level of gas and water and sewer pipes, so that the latter might be left undisturbed. Parsons suggested a double-deck subway on each side of the street, the space between to be made into a pipe gallery under the center of the street in which all pipes removed in construction should be placed, such gallery to contain all pipes laid in the future. Some years later, when Parsons became Chief Engineer of the Board which built the first subway, it is interesting to note that the Worthen plan for four tracks on one level was adopted.

Following the approval of the project by the municipal authorities the Commission had the detail plans made and advertised for bids for the franchise. Bids were solicited in the fall of the year 1892. Only one bid was

received, that of Col. W. N. Amory, who offered $1,000
for the rights. His bid was rejected. It was openly
hinted that the opposition of the elevated railroads, then
in the control of Jay Gould, was responsible for the failure to sell the franchise. Gould, of course, did not want
a competitive transit line in the city, and certainly was
powerful enough, financially and politically, to interpose
obstacles. Later the Steinway Commission tried to get
the elevated roads to build extensions, but this effort also
proved abortive.

William Barclay Parsons, in a conversation in
1913, declared that the Steinway Commission was a Tammany board and that the elevated railroads, which did
not want the competition of an underground road, were
all powerful in shaping its work.

After the failure to sell the franchise, Mr. Parsons
said, a strange thing happened in the Steinway Commission. "All the employes of the Board, myself included,"
said Mr. Parsons, "were dismissed, and in thirty days
all were reappointed except me. The Board then offered
the elevated railroads rights for important extensions.
Having failed to enlist capital for an underground road,
the Board did what was expected of it and made elaborate
plans for extending the elevated railroads. Then another
strange event happened. The elevated railroad interests,
then dominated by Jay Gould, and Russell Sage, refused
to build the extensions offered. They felt so secure in
their monopoly that they actually scorned the gift the
Board would make them. That ended the Board of 1891.
Having failed to build either subway or elevated lines
there was nothing more for it to do. The Legislature of
1894 abolished the body and created a new Rapid Transit
Commission, of which Alexander E. Orr was made chairman. This was the board which built the first subway
and I became its chief engineer."

There could be no more fitting close to this chapter
than the following extract from an address delivered by

Abram S. Hewitt on October 3, 1901, upon receiving from the New York Chamber of Commerce a gold medal bestowed in recognition of his long and effective work for rapid transit:

"In the meantime (after the failure of the plan to obtain construction by private capital by the 1891 board) the difficulties of the situation became more and more manifest, until at length a proposition was made to the Chamber of Commerce of the State of New York by a well known and responsible banking house in this city to undertake the construction of the underground system, provided the City of New York would loan its credit to the corporation undertaking the work to an amount not exceeding thirty millions of dollars. This proposition was referred to a committee of the Chamber, who, despairing of any other solution of the question, reported at a meeting of the Chamber in favor of the proposition. It was my privilege to point out in the discussion which followed that such a loan of credit would be contrary to the Constitution of the State of New York, and that it was not expedient to submit to the people any proposition under which the public credit could be utilized for private enterprises. The importance of vesting ownership in the City was insisted upon, and after full discussion my contention was unanimously approved by the Chamber of Commerce, and a new committee, of which I was a member, was constituted to formulate a bill to be presented to the Legislature under which the suggestions made by the Mayor in 1888 were to be incorporated in the proposed legislation.

"Taking the original bill as a basis, and with the aid of the late Henry R. Beekman, who as Corporation Counsel had drawn the original bill, a new bill was prepared and reported to the Chamber of Commerce for its approval. Having received a unanimous vote in its favor, the committee caused it to be submitted to the Legislature, where, after full discussion and some amendments, one of which required a referendum to the people, the bill was enacted into a law on the 22nd of May, 1894. Under its provisions the work is to be done as proposed by the Mayor in 1888 by the issue of bonds under contract open to public competition, providing for an adequate bond for the completion of the work and for the investment of a large amount of capital, estimated between seven and ten millions of dollars, for rolling stock, real estate and appliances, all of which are held by the City as security for the fulfillment of the lease by the lessee."

CHAPTER XI

PUBLIC OWNERSHIP ASSURED—THE RAPID TRANSIT ACT
AND COMMISSION OF 1894.

THE failure of the Steinway Commission to bring about
the construction of new rapid transit lines spurred
the people of New York City to further efforts. Led by
Mayor Hewitt and the Chamber of Commerce, the citizens appealed to the Legislature of 1894 for some sort of
legislation which would bring about the long desired
result. The act passed in accordance with the plan of
Mayor Hewitt, May 22, 1894, accomplished what previous
acts had failed to achieve mainly if not entirely because
of the provision for public ownership. This made possible the use of the city's credit in providing the millions
needed to bring the great project to fruition.

"The great object aimed at", said Mr. Hewitt in the
address before quoted, "was to secure the early completion of the work, its continued ownership by the city
and its reversion at the end of fifty years to the city, free
and clear of all encumbrances of every kind and nature
whatever."

While this feature was new, the statute in form was
but an amendment of the act of 1891, which, though it
failed of its immediate purpose, nevertheless was the first
practicable legislation since the act of 1875. This was
recognized by the board created in 1894, and in its first
published report it gave credit to the important work
done by its predecessor under the act of 1891.

Governor Flower signed the bill of 1894 on the day of
its enactment, namely May 22, and it went into effect
immediately. By its terms a new board, known as the
Board of Rapid Transit Railroad Commissioners, was
substituted for that appointed under the act of 1891. The
act itself provided that the new board should consist of
the Mayor and the Controller of New York City and the

president of the New York Chamber of Commerce as *ex officio* members, and of Messrs. William Steinway, Seth Low, John Claflin, Alexander E. Orr and John H. Starin. These men were all prominent business men of New York and Brooklyn, and commanded the confidence and respect of the community. Seth Low later became Mayor of Greater New York.

The provisions of the act of 1891 authorizing the board to grant additional franchises to existing railroads (namely the elevated lines) was retained unmodified in the new statute. In brief the new board was authorized to lay out routes for rapid transit lines, to cause such lines to be constructed if the constitutional consents of abutting property owners and of the local authorities were obtained, to adopt the plans made by the old board or to make new ones, and prior to undertaking construction but after adopting plans and getting consents to submit to the qualified electors of the city at the next general election "the question whether such railway or railways shall be constructed by the city and at the public expense." In the event of a negative vote on the referendum, the board was authorized to sell the franchise to build and operate the railway to some private corporation as provided in the act of 1891.

After adopting the routes and plans and getting the necessary consents the board was authorized, in case of an affirmative vote on the referendum, to advertise for proposals and to enter into a contract with some person or corporation to build the road for the city and at its expense. The contractor was to be required to operate the railroad as the lessee of the city for a term not less than thirty-five nor more than fifty years, and at an annual rental sufficient to pay the interest upon the bonds issued by the city for construction and one per cent. in addition as a sinking fund to retire such bonds at maturity.

It was also provided that the contractor should fur-

BOARD OF RAPID TRANSIT RAILROAD
COMMISSIONERS — 1904

1. Mayor George B. McClellan;   2. John Claflin;   3. Morris K. Jessup;
   4. Chairman Alexander E. Orr: 5. John H. Starin;   6. Woodbury
Langdon;   7. Charles Stuart Smith;   8. Comptroller Edward M. Grout.

nish the equipment for the road at his own expense, but that the city should have a lien on such equipment. A bond to guarantee faithful performance of the contract, in an amount to be fixed by the board, was prescribed, and the contractor was to be obliged to deposit with the Controller the amount of $1,000,000, to be returned to the depositor upon the completion and equipment of the road. The board was invested with the duty of supervising the construction and operation of the road.

No time was lost by the new board in setting to work. It met for the first time on June 8, 1894, and organized, electing Alexander E. Orr, as president. No higher encomium could be passed on Mr. Orr than to cite the fact that he remained president until the board had successfully performed its gigantic task and was replaced by the Public Service Commission in 1907. In other words for thirteen years Mr. Orr devoted himself to the service of the public and masterfully piloted the board through innumerable difficulties to triumphant success.

At the time of his election as president Mr. Orr was also president of the New York Chamber of Commerce. He therefore resigned the individual appointment conferred on him by the act, and Mr. John H. Inman, one of the members of the Steinway Commission, was elected to fill the vacancy, the statute permitting the board to recruit its membership. At subsequent meetings John H. Starin was elected vice-president, Henry R. Beekman and Albert B. Boardman were chosen counsel and William Barclay Parsons chief engineer.

Early in its deliberations the new board reached the conclusion that the only way of meeting the transit situation was to build underground railroads, and this decision as soon as announced met the approval of a public wearied with the inadequacy of the service supplied by the elevated railroads and of the presence of their unsightly structures in the streets of the city. It also decided that the plans made by the Steinway Commission

must be changed in some respects if the cost of the
proposed railroad was to be kept within the limit fixed
by the statute, $50,000,000, but as the act permitted modi-
fications of such plans the new board contented itself
with a tentative approval of the old plans and routes as
a basis for submitting to the voters the question whether
the new road should be constructed and owned by the
city. This course was adopted on advice of counsel.

This action was taken on July 17, and before the election in the ensuing November the board issued an address
to the people, in which the intention was declared of considering the question of routes and plans *de novo* should
the electors decide for municipal ownership. At the same
time it sent Mr. Parsons, its chief engineer, to foreign
lands to study the systems of rapid transit employed in
certain cities on the continent of Europe and in Great
Britain. Mr. Parsons' report was published later under
the title, "Report on Rapid Transit in Foreign Cities."

The proposed referendum was held on November 6,
1894 at the general election, and the climax of the Era of
Public Ownership was reached in an overwhelming majority in favor of municipal construction. The total vote
was 184,035, of which 132,647 were for and 42,916 against
municipal construction and ownership of the new roads,
there having been cast 399 ballots which were declared
defective and not counted.

Having received the mandate of the people, the board
proceeded to push the difficult work of selecting the final
routes and perfecting the detail plans, which already had
received much consideration. At the election a new
Mayor, William L. Strong, had been chosen to succeed
Thomas F. Gilroy. The Controller, Ashbel P. Fitch, was
continued in office, so that the only change in the composition of the board with the coming of the new year, 1895,
was the substitution of Mayor Strong for Mayor Gilroy
as one of the *ex officio* members. One of its counsel, however, Henry R. Beekman, had been elected Justice of the

Supreme Court, and upon his retirement the board named
Parsons, Shepard and Ogden to serve with Tracy, Boardman and Platt as counsel. This brought to the service
of the public the brilliant mind of the late Edward M.
Shepard, to whose able work much of the later success of
the board was due.

There was such great divergence of opinion as to the
best route to be adopted that the board decided (December 26, 1894) to submit the recommendations of its own
engineer to a special board of experts. As such a board
President Orr appointed Abram S. Hewitt, Thomas C.
Clarke, Charles Sooysmith, Octave Chanute and Professor William H. Burr, of Columbia University. These
men at once began their investigations, and on January
29, 1895, submitted their report.

This report approved the estimates made by Mr.
Parsons that an underground road could be built to the
northerly city line within the $50,000,000 limit and that
the subway for four tracks should be made fifty feet wide
instead of forty-four as fixed by the Steinway Commission.

On the question of route the experts suggested a line
from the City Hall northward through Elm Street, Lafayette Place and Fourth Avenue to Fourteenth Street,
instead of the line up Broadway favored by the Commission. It was estimated that such a change, by avoiding
the expensive construction in lower Broadway, would
save $3,700,000. The Commission had considered such a
change itself, but did not make it at this time. On May
9, 1895, the board adopted a resolution fixing the route
for the new line and transmitted it to the Common Council. Briefly sketched, this route was as follows:

From a loop at Battery Park up Broadway to Fifty-
ninth street and up the Boulevard (Broadway extended)
to about 124th street; thence by viaduct over the Boulevard to about 134th street; thence under the Boulevard
and Eleventh Avenue to about 185th street. There was

to be a loop at City Hall, connecting with a line from Park
Row to a junction with the Broadway line at Fulton
street.

Also a line diverging from the Broadway route at
Fourteenth street, running under Union Square to Fourth
Avenue and up Fourth and Park Avenues to about 98th
street; thence by viaduct over Park Avenue to the Har-
lem River, across the Harlem by bridge and up Walton
Avenue to about 146th street.

In the resolution it was specified that the line should
be a four track road from Park Place on the South to
135th street on the North on the West Side, and from
Union Square to Forty-second street on the East side;
elsewhere there were to be only two tracks. All tracks
were to be constructed on one level at standard guage,
with a width of 12 feet and one half for each track. The
whole line was to be a subway except for the viaducts on
the West Side between 124th and 134th streets and on the
East Side north of 98th Street. The tube was to be at
least twelve feet in height in the clear, and the roof as
near the surface of the street as possible. Along Broadway from Park Place to 34th street all water and sewer
pipes and other sub-surface structures were to be placed
in pipe galleries built as part of the subway work.

The right to construct pipe galleries was conferred
on the board by an amendment to the Rapid Transit Act
passed at its solicitation by the Legislature of 1895. This
amendment also provided that the City should extinguish
all easements of abutting property owners whose property might be affected by the building of the road and
authorized the expenditure of $5,000,000 additional for
that purpose. Litigation over such rights had been the
source of much trouble and expense in the construction
of the elevated railroads. The board also was given
power to grant franchises for the extension of existing
railroads by a vote of six of its members, instead of the
unanimous vote previously required, but only on condi-

tion that the recipients of such grant should make proper compensation to the City and that this compensation should be subject to adjustment at the end of periods to be fixed by the board, such period not to exceed thirty-five years.

Not being able to obtain the requisite number of consents of property owners along the proposed route, the board in the fall of 1895 made application to the Appellate Division of the Supreme Court for the appointment of commissioners and a determination by the Court in lieu of such consents. The matter came up on the request of the board for the Court to name the newspapers in which such application should be published. To the surprise of all the Court refused to consider the matter at all, and entered an order to that effect on October 7, 1895. The board at once appealed, and the decision was reversed by the Court of Appeals on October 22 following. The Supreme Court then named Frederic R. Coudert, George Sherman and William H. Gelshenen as Commissioners to take testimony and report whether the proposed rapid transit railroad ought to be constructed. After a long contest, with the Rapid Transit board and advocates of subways on one hand and property owners who opposed the project on the other, the commissioners, on March 6, 1896, reported unanimously in favor of the new road. On the argument, the Appellate Division unanimously refused to confirm the report of its commissioners. This decision was rendered on May 22, 1896, and the board gave careful and respectful consideration to the reasons advanced by the Court for its decision.

These reasons in brief were: that the proposed road when constructed would not furnish a complete system of transit from one end of the city to the other; that it was doubtful whether any large part of the road could be built within the limit of the funds then at the city's disposal, and that it was certain that the expenditure of such a large amount for rapid transit would deprive the city of the financial ability to engage in any other public work and possibly might impair its credit for years. The board deduced from this decision that the Court would not consent to any route under Broadway or to an underground road on any other route unless it extended practically from one end of the city to the other and it was conclusively shown that the total cost would be much less than $50,000,000.

The effect of such a decision on the mind of a public clamoring for additional rapid transit facilities may be imagined. Public meetings were held, resolutions adopted, the press urged some action and the board received letters from many prominent citizens advocating a continuance of the work. The board therefore set about devising a scheme which would meet the approval of the court. Routes and plans were reconsidered, and by the end of the year 1896 the board had determined to adopt the Elm Street route in place of the Broadway line south of Forty-second street. The decision was not formally made, however, until the next year.

In the meanwhile the board had been fighting for its very life in another litigation, which attacked the constitutionality of the Rapid Transit Act. This was caused by an action brought by the Sun Printing and Publishing Association and others as taxpayers, seeking to enjoin the city from expending its funds for a rapid transit subway on the ground that the act of 1894 was unconstitutional. On February 20, 1896, Justice Truax in Special Term of the Supreme Court upheld the constitutionality of the act, and his decision later was affirmed by the Appellate Division in July, 1896, and by the Court of Appeals in March, 1897. During this trying year of 1896, when the board was fighting for its life in the Sun case and struggling with the court to get legal authority to build a subway, the rapid transit situation was further complicated by an attempt of the Manhattan Railway company, probably made to head off the threatened sub-

way, to obtain rights for extensions of the elevated railroads. This application was made on June 11 and after
conferences with the board was modified on July 15. The
company asked for franchises for thirty miles of new
routes besides additional facilities upon existing routes.
It did not pledge itself, however, to build such extensions
within any period of time, made no offer of rental to the
city for such privileges and limited its application by a
condition that it must receive immunity from claims for
damages on account of construction.

The board on August 6, 1896, rejected this application,
pointing out in its answer that the board had no power
under the law to grant to a private corporation immunity
from damage claims, that the statute required a company
to pay rental to the city for extensions and that a grant
not limited as to time would be tantamount to giving an
option for rapid transit extensions which the company
could build or not, and if it did not build the very existence of the grant would prevent relief from any other
quarter. The board then requested the company to
amend its offer to overcome these difficulties, but no further application was received. A year and a half later,
however, when it became apparent that the city was
actually going to build a rapid transit railroad, the company filed another application, of which notice will be
taken further on.

During the year 1896 Seth Low resigned from the
board and John H. Inman and William Steinway died.
The vacancies were filled by the board, which elected
Woodbury Langdon to succeed Low, Geo. L. Rives to
succeed Inman and Charles Stewart Smith to succeed
Steinway.

With the coming of the year 1897 the board was ready
to change the proposed route to meet the views of the
Appellate Division, namely that the road should extend
from one end of the city to the other and must be built
at a cost much less than $50,000,000. Accordingly, after

receiving a report from Engineer Parsons, the board on
January 14, 1897, adopted a revised route and general
plan, under which the proposed road would run up Elm
street and Fourth Avenue from City Hall and connect
with the Broadway route by a cross-town line through
Forty-second street. The modified route began at the
intersection of Broadway and Park Row, ran thence
under Elm street, Lafayette Place and private property
to Fourth Avenue, up Fourth and Park Avenues to Forty-
second street, west under Forty-second street to Broadway, and up Broadway and the Boulevard to 124th street,
thence by viaduct over the Boulevard to 134th street,
thence under the Boulevard and Eleventh Avenue to a
point north of 190th street, over private property, Ell-
wood street and Broadway to Riverside Avenue and over
Riverside Avenue to a point near Kingsbridge station of
the New York and Putnam railroad.

The route also provided for a loop at City Hall and
for an extension from the main line near 103d street
under Lenox Avenue to and under the Harlem River and
under 149th street to Westchester Avenue and thence
over Westchester Avenue by viaduct to Southern Boulevard, over Southern Boulevard to Boston Road and over
Boston Road to Bronx Park.

It was provided that the road should have four tracks
from City Hall to 103d street and two tracks elsewhere,
and that all tracks should be built on one level. The
resolution also contained this clause: "The general mode
of operation shall be by electricity or some other power
not requiring combustion within the tunnels or on the
viaducts, and the motors shall be capable of moving
trains at a speed of not less than forty miles per hour
for long distances, exclusive of stops."

The modified route was later approved by the court
and was followed in the construction of the road. This
change in the route is responsible for the zig-zag line
of the first subway. The Rapid Transit Commission,

therefore, cannot be charged with this peculiar alignment. The board originally favored a straight line up
Broadway, but the court objected to the expense and the
Elm street route was substituted to save a few millions
of dollars. In consequence the first subway is an East
Side line below and a West Side line above Forty-second
street. This initial mistake proved costly to the City in
later years when the building of extensions of the subway was undertaken, for the zig-zag line compelled the
laying out of a new route on the same plan or the building of north and south wings to the existing road, which
of course meant operation by the company which leased
the first subway. It is difficult to estimate the time consumed in adjusting the new lines to this situation, but it
is safe to say that rapid transit relief was delayed some
years in consequence.

At the time, however, the Elm street route was generally approved, for it was felt that it would meet the
main objection advanced by the Appellate Division. The
people wanted rapid transit, and it mattered very little
to them whether the new road ran straight up and down
the island or zig-zag across town. In a report published
after the subway was completed, the Rapid Transit Commission spoke as follows of the Elm street route:

"The scheme thus adopted complied, it was
hoped, with the requirements of the Appellate Division. In the first place the road was estimated to
cost about $35,000,000, and that this estimate was
correct time has conclusively proved. In the second
place it ran from the City Hall—or near the souther-
ly end of Manhattan Island,—to Kingsbridge as the
terminus of one branch and to the Bronx Park as
the terminus of the other. At Kingsbridge a physical connection with the New York Central lines to
Yonkers and beyond was easy. At the Bronx Park
the northerly limits of the city were nearly reached;

and if the court had insisted on a further extension here, it would have cost little, comparatively, to extend the road still further by an elevated structure through the Park.

"The necessity of avoiding Broadway below Thirty-fourth street so as to meet the views of the court compelled the use of Fourth Avenue and Elm street for the main stem, and the introduction of an awkward alignment from Fourth Avenue to the Westward along Forty-second street to Broadway."

In the modified route no provision was made for the extension of the subway south from City Hall, the board being unwilling to plan an extension down Broadway in view of the dicta of the court. When this became known the property owners along Broadway filed with the board a petition for such a route signed by a majority in value of the abutting property. Accordingly on April 1, 1897, the board adopted a resolution providing for a two track extension of the subway down Broadway to Battery Place, with a loop under Battery Park, Whitehall street and State street.

The city authorities promptly gave their consents to the route above City Hall, but the board was unsuccessful in obtaining the consents of the property owners for that part of the line. Therefore it determined to pursue the alternative course and applied to the Appellate Division for the appointment of commissioners to inquire and report whether such a railroad ought to be constructed in the public interest. In July, 1897, the court appointed Arthur D. Williams, John Sabine Smith and George W. Young as such commissioners. Again opposing interests made a fight against the proposition, but the commissioners on November 6, 1897, submitted a unanimous report in its favor.

In a short time, namely on December 17, 1897, the Appellate Division confirmed the report of its commissioners, but coupled its approval with the condition that the Rapid Transit Commission should stipulate that upon awarding any contract for construction and operation of the railroad, "the penalty of the bond specified in Section 34 of the Rapid Transit Act will be fixed at not less than $15,000,000." In the language of the court this was done to give "some assurance that the powers of the Rapid Transit Commissioners in respect to security should be exercised so as to protect the interests of the city in a substantial manner."

Such an approval was tantamount to disapproval in the minds of those conversant with the situation, for the requirement of a bond in such an amount as $15,000,000 to run for the whole period of the lease of the road, as required by section 34, was about equivalent to a prohibition of any lease. Nevertheless the board endeavored to comply with the wishes of the court and appointed a committee to inquire whether such a bond could be obtained.

While this committee was at work another serious problem confronted the board, which seemed fated to encounter a new obstacle as soon as an old one had been solved. This was the financial condition of the city after its enlargement to take in Brooklyn, Queens and Richmond boroughs. This consolidation took effect January 1, 1898, when Robert A. Van Wyck became Mayor and Bird S. Coler Controller. Under the statute these new officers became ex officio members of the Rapid Transit board, taking the places respectively of William L. Strong and Ashbel P. Fitch. As Greater New York had to assume the indebtedness of all the communities it absorbed, it was feared that the added burden would bring the debt of the city so close to the constitutional limit of ten per cent. of the assessed value of its real estate as to prohibit the issue of bonds in amounts large enough to defray the cost of the proposed rapid transit railroad. The danger, however, was more apparent than real. It was found that property in the old city had been assessed much lower than the property in the communities absorbed, and as the law provided for assessment at actual value, the assessment of the old city was soon raised to somewhere near an equality with that in the annexed boroughs, thereby expanding the debt-incurring power of the city as a whole to such an extent that no difficulty was anticipated in financing the new road.

Another effect of the consolidation and one not anticipated was the hostile sentiment developed in Kings, Queens and Richmond boroughs against the proposed rapid transit road. As laid out the road ran entirely within New York county, or in the boroughs of Manhattan and the Bronx. By the consolidation, however, the property in the other boroughs must be taxed to defray a portion of the cost. Objection at once was made against using the general credit of the city to pay for an improvement confined to two boroughs, and for a time the members of the board feared that this sentiment would defeat the project. The press supported the board, as did many broad-minded citizens having property in the other boroughs, and it was pointed out that the road would be used by residents of all boroughs and undoubtedly would be extended to Brooklyn, Queens and Richmond in the course of time. Opposition gradually lessened and the board soon was able to proceed with the project, but during the first part of the year 1898 there is no doubt that its members felt discouraged and apprehensive of the failure of the enterprise.

The opportunity was seized by the Manhattan Railway company to create another diversion. It made public a statement that it would enlarge its system of elevated railroads just as soon as it could get the rights from the board or from the Legislature. On January 31 it filed with the board an application for the right to make certain extensions of the existing elevated roads, mainly by lengthening the lines to the north, but made no offer

STAFF OF BOARD OF RAPID TRANSIT
RAILROAD COMMISSIONERS

A. B. Boardman, Counsel;   2. William Barclay Parsons, Chief Engineer;
    3. Edward M. Shepard, Counsel;   4. Georg L. Rives, Counsel.

of rental to the city. The board referred the matter to a special committee and its chief engineer, who held several conferences with Jay Gould, Russell Sage and others interested in the elevated company. The committee reported on March 17, 1898, to the effect that the northern extensions asked for by the company would not give the additional facilities demanded unless additional tracks were built on the southern portions of the lines, where the two tracks existing were already badly overcrowded. The committee accordingly recommended that seven certificates for new rights should be prepared and offered to the company, which would provide for substantially everything asked for and in addition the extra tracks needed to enlarge the capacity of the whole system.

The lines covered by the proposed seven franchises had been approved by the board's engineer and submitted to the elevated company. The latter, while admitting the practicability of the routes from an engineering standpoint, declined in the absence of accurate figures as to cost to commit itself to their construction, and also asked for further time in which to determine what if any rental it would be able to pay the city for the new rights. To save time, therefore, the committee recommended that the seven certificates be prepared for tender to the company and that during the time taken in their preparation the officers of the latter could deliberate upon and decide the questions as to cost of construction and the amount of rental to be paid to the city.

"Every day is adding to the difficulties of the situation" said the report. "So long as the Manhattan application is pending, the consideration of other plans looking to a solution of the rapid transit problem is necessarily deferred."

The report was adopted, the seven franchises were prepared and formally tendered to the company by the board on April 7, 1898. The company, however, did not accept them, and the board pursued its work to bring about the construction of the proposed subway. Indeed its work in this regard had never been intermitted. While the Manhattan proposal was pending and before it was submitted, the board sought the aid of men of wealth and influence to consider the building and operation of the road. Conferences were held with the leading transportation men of the city, including Cornelius Vanderbilt and Chauncey M. Depew, of the New York Central system; Charles P. Clark, of the New York, New Haven and Hartford company and William C. Whitney and others interested in the Metropolitan Street Railway company. None of them would take any active part in the project. Could any of them have foreseen the enormous profits later made out of the operation of the first subway by the Interborough Rapid Transit company, there would have been a different reception accorded the advances of the board in 1898.

On January 13, 1898, the board received the report of its committee appointed to inquire into the possibility of obtaining a bond of $15,000,000, as required by the court. The committee found that it would be next to impossible to get a contractor who would be able or willing to give such a large bond, and accordingly recommended that the court be requested to limit its requirement to a bond for construction and equipment and to leave to the board the fixing of the amount of the bond to be given to protect the city in regard to the payment of rental and satisfactory operation of the road. The board followed this recommendation and on January 17, 1898, instructed its counsel to apply to the court for a modification of its order.

The application was duly made and the Appellate Division granted it to the extent of modifying its previous order so that, while insisting on a bond of $15,000,-000, it consented that the liability of the sureties as to $14,000,000 thereof should terminate on the completion and equipment of the railroad, limiting the permanent bond to $1,000,000. While this was still a severe restriction in the opinion of the board, it was not prohibitive, and the board accordingly entered into the stipulation required by the court.

After all these difficulties had been surmounted the board should have had plain sailing, but its usual adverse luck still prevailed and a formidable but unlooked for obstacle arose. The law required that any contract prepared by the board for the construction and operation of the railroad must be approved as to form by the Corporation Counsel, the legal advisor of the city government. This official was John Whalen, appointed by Van Wyck, the new Mayor. The proposed contract was adopted by the board on March 31, 1898, and submitted to the Corporation Counsel on April 7 following. He was asked to give it his attention and report at once. Instead of acting promptly he held the contract for nearly a year and a half without acting, and in September 1899 returned it to the board with suggestions for several amendments. His reason for holding it so long was that it was the practice of the Law Department never to approve a contract which could not legally be made.

This delay by the city administration, which if it reflected the sentiment of the people would have cordially supported the Rapid Transit board, brought matters to a standstill, and the year 1899 opened with the Commissioners marking time and longingly awaiting the action of the Corporation Counsel. The situation was intolerable, and the board determined to appeal to the new Legislature just convened. A memorial to that body was prepared by the board and sent to Albany, and its publication and discussion eventually cleared the atmosphere. In this memorial the board set forth the whole rapid transit situation, called attention to the debt limit restriction and the doubts of the city authorities that a sufficient margin existed to justify undertaking city construction of the rapid transit railroad; suggested a possible way out by authorizing New York county instead of the city to issue bonds for its construction; and in view of the possibility of not getting enough public funds to construct the line suggested that the board be empowered to resort to private capital and given the broadest powers to make the franchise attractive and arouse competition.

Hardly had this memorial been transmitted when certain men interested in the Metropolitan Street Railway company, who a year before had refused to consider building and operating the rapid transit road for the city, informed the board that if a new company to be formed by them were granted a perpetual franchise they would construct a road according to the plans of the board, complete the west side branch to Fort George within three years and the remainder of the road within two years after the corporation should earn five per cent. on the cost of building the first section. They offered to pay the city five per cent. of the gross receipts annually, provided the company first took out of earnings five per cent. net upon the cost of construction.

This offer was seriously considered by the board, which, while favoring public ownership, believed that rapid transit by aid of private capital was better than no rapid transit at all. Accordingly it unanimously approved a resolution offered by Mayor Van Wyck on March 29, 1899, declaring "that it is in the public interest that, in addition to the powers already possessed by the board, the Legislature should grant to the board the power to contract for the construction and operation of the rapid transit railroad by private capital."

Something might have been achieved along these lines if the friends of the Metropolitan Street Railway had not overplayed their hand. A bill was introduced in the Legislature to confer on the board the power to grant a perpetual franchise to a private corporation. The press and the public instantly took alarm. The bill was taken as an attempt on the part of the Metropolitan to "grab" a valuable franchise for the underground railroad and was bitterly denounced. Agitation continued and attained such proportions that the bill failed, and the Metropolitan coterie who had approached the board withdrew its offer, stating that the opposition which had developed had created such a situation that "success in the enterprise would be impossible."

The Legislature, however, passed the bill amending the rapid transit act, which had been submitted by the board, but amended it so materially that it would seriously hamper any negotiations which the board might undertake to enlist the aid of private capital in the construction of the railroad. Mayor Van Wyck refused to accept it for the city, and so the legislative session ended without any rapid transit relief. The board, therefore, began prodding the city authorities for action, as public construction was now the only course open.

Meanwhile a new member had entered the board in the person of Morris K. Jesup, who was elected president of the Chamber of Commerce in May, 1899, and thereby became a member of the board, succeeding Alexander E. Orr, the president. But John Claflin resigned at the first meeting thereafter, and the board elected Mr. Orr to succeed him, so that there was no break in Mr. Orr's service. Another election was held, and Mr. Orr was re-elected as president on May 29, 1899, Mr. Starin, the vice-president, having acted as president during the interim, namely from May 11 to May 29. About the same time Lewis L. Delafield, the secretary of the board, resigned and Bion L. Burrows was elected to succeed him.

The first gun in the board's assault on the city authorities was in the form of a letter to Mayor Van Wyck, dated May 19, 1899. It opened with the inquiry as to the extent "to which the municipal authorities will feel able to promote construction by the city of the proposed rapid transit railroad." It then set forth briefly the various steps taken to date by the board, including the submission of the draft contract to the Corporation Counsel for his approval on April 7, 1898, adding significantly "but no communication has as yet been received from him, whether of approval or disapproval."

Municipal construction under the law as it stood was declared by the board to be entirely feasible, "provided the municipal authorities will co-operate with the board." Further progress, however, was impossible until the Corporation Counsel should give his approval to the form of the contract as required by law.

The debt limit situation was discussed in the letter, and it was stated that the board believed the provisions concerning it in the contract were sufficient, but that if the Corporation Counsel deemed them insufficient he should advise the board to that effect so that the contract might be amended. In conclusion the letter said:

> "The board begs to repeat that its power to carry out the purpose for which it was created now depends practically, first upon the permission of the Corporation Counsel to make any contract, and, second, upon the assent of the Board of Estimate to a postponement of the making of other contracts involving large municipal debt until a rapid transit contract actually made shall assure the carrying out of that great public measure. The board, therefore, respectfully asks your Honor, and through you the other municipal authorities, whether in these two respects it may be aided to secure prompt and actual construction of the rapid transit road by the city."

This letter placed the responsibility for further delay squarely on the city administration and focused public attention on Mayor Van Wyck. There was no other difficulty in the way. A new assessment had been made in July raising the valuation of the real estate of the city more than $420,000,000, and thus adding $42,000,000 to the borrowing capacity under the debt limit. In addition a constitutional amendment was to come before the people for adoption in the ensuing election exempting from charging against the Greater City an indebtedness of about $30,000,000 carried by the separate counties when taken into the consolidation. This amendment, which was approved by the people, still further added to the city's borrowing capacity.

Through the spring and into the summer the City Hall remained silent. The board waited respectfully for a reply until July 13, when it addressed another letter, this time to the Board of Estimate, again reviewing the situation. Attention was called to the fact that the margin below the debt limit was fully $40,000,000, that no contract could be made till the Corporation Counsel acted, that a rapid transit debt could not be created till after the contract was executed and that meanwhile other debts might be incurred which would so lessen the borrowing capacity of the city as to prevent any rapid transit construction and thus defeat the will of the people as registered in the vote on the referendum in 1894. The board, therefore, expressly asked that no further debt be authorized in an amount sufficient to reduce the borrowing margin below the estimated cost of the proposed road until there should have been reasonable opportunity for the letting of the contract.

This evoked a response on September 20, when the Corporation Counsel transmitted to the board his views on the draft contract, as before mentioned. In this letter he stated that the city was now in a position to undertake the work and he had already conferred with the counsel for the board with a view "to expediting the business." The Corporation Counsel made eight points against the contract, to which the board replied. His first point was that the Law Department of the city should have charge of all proceedings for the condemnation of land. The board tersely responded that the law itself expressly provided that the Corporation Counsel should have charge of such proceedings.

His second point was that the contract ought to provide for the transportation of light parcels and packages. Again the board countered by quoting another provision of the act which authorized the use of the railroad for that purpose.

It is unnecessary to refer to most of the other points. The best suggestion made was that the contract be amended by making special reference to the Labor law, although it already contained a provision requiring compliance with all laws. The board agreed to this suggestion and subsequently incorporated a special provision on the Labor law.

The board then revised its form of contract and again transmitted it for approval to the Corporation Counsel on October 6, 1899. The most important amendment was a provision to limit the initial work to that part of the road extending from Brooklyn Bridge to 59th street and giving the city the option to require the contractor to complete the rest of the line within certain specified periods. By thus limiting the initial expenditure it was thought that all question as to obtaining the funds necessary would be avoided. Conferences followed with the Corporation Counsel, and the amended form of contract was approved by him on October 11, 1899, about a year and six months after it had been submitted to him.

Once having decided to co-operate with the board in providing new rapid transit facilities, it must be said that the city authorities gave generous assistance. The Corporation Counsel joined counsel for the board in making application to the Appellate Division for a modification of the stipulation previously entered into by the board on the matter of the bond to be required of the contractor. This, it will be remembered, was for a $1,000,000 continuing bond and for a bond of $14,000,000 during the progress of the work. The joint application was made on

October 20, 1899, and was argued on October 30. It proved successful, for the court on November 10 gave a decision ordering a modification of the stipulation so as to reduce the amount of the bond to $5,000,000. Thus the year 1899 ended with all the legal difficulties cleared away, all other obstacles surmounted and the path open for the advertisement and award of the great contract.

CHAPTER XII

IT was on June 8, 1894, that the Board of Rapid Transit
Railroad Commissioners created by the act of that
year held its first meeting. A period of five years and a
half, therefore, had been consumed in the preparatory
and preliminary work. The actual work necessary could
have been done in a year, but pioneer labors always take
more time than similar labors after the pathway has been
blazed. For none of the delay can the Rapid Transit
Commission be blamed; it was due entirely to legal obstacles and municipal tardiness.

But "all's well that ends well", and both the commission and the public forgot the troubles of the past in
the joy of starting the final work which was to bring
about the beginning of actual construction. But joy was
not unconfined by apprehension lest there might be difficulty in finding a contractor with money enough and courage enough to undertake the work. For be it remembered
that underground transportation of passengers was then
an untried experiment in New York City. True, London
had for some years successfully operated a subterranean
road, but the conditions there were vastly different from
those in New York, and skeptics were many and vociferous. A bit of encouragement came from Boston, where
a subway had been completed and was working well. But
here again the cry was that conditions were totally dis-
similar and that what might succeed in Boston might fail
in New York.

There was a difference of opinion even among engineers and men experienced in the transportation business. Among the former there were some who scouted
the idea of a subway underneath the heavily traveled
streets of New York, with their tall and costly buildings

erected on either side of the route. Nothing could prevent such buildings from settling or falling into the cut, it was claimed. Well known railroad men, including Chauncey M. Depew, were doubtful of the success of the railroad even if constructed. Human beings, they declared, liked the open air and would not readily burrow into the ground unless compelled to do so. Mr. Depew said that the great majority of passengers would avoid the underground road if there were any other way of traveling. We now know that such views were mistaken ones, but at the time they were held by many and voiced to such an extent that a respectable minority of the public questioned the practicability of the project.

As was told in the last chapter, several men eminent in the railroad world had been approached by the board and urged to take a hand in the work, but all without exception refused. None had faith enough in the project or courage enough in pioneer endeavor to make the venture, entailing as it did an expenditure of millions even though the cost of construction should be defrayed by the municipality. But there were two men in New York, who had the qualities demanded by the crisis—one with nerve and immense financial resources, and the other with nerve and the capital of actual experience in underground construction—namely, August Belmont, a banker and John B. McDonald, a contractor. The public had called for volunteers and they responded. And they were not alone, for Andrew Onderdonk, another experienced contractor, also volunteered, but fortune favored McDonald and he, backed by the Belmont money and influence, undertook the work.

Immediately after the court had reduced the amount of the bond to be required of the contractor, the board prepared an invitation to contractors and published it as required by law. It was inserted in six daily newspapers twice a week for three successive weeks, and the date of opening bids was fixed for January 15, 1900.

During the period of advertising the newspapers were filled with speculations as to the possible bidders, and there were not wanting the pessimists who predicted that there would be no bids at all. When the fifteenth of January came, however, two proposals in the form prescribed by the board were received, one from John B. McDonald and the other from Andrew Onderdonk. Mr. McDonald offered to build the whole road for $35,000,000; Onderdonk for $39,300,000. Onderdonk in addition agreed to pay the city five per cent. on the first million dollars of revenue in excess of $5,000,000 a year and two and a half per cent. on each additional million up to a maximum of 15 per cent. Both bidders agreed to the statutory rental, namely interest on the bonds issued by the city for construction and one per cent. additional for a sinking fund.

The board after referring both bids to a committee and in accordance with the recommendations thereof, decided to award the contract to McDonald. The latter promptly made arrangements with August Belmont for the necessary financial backing. After the decision had been made negotiations were entered into with McDonald and with August Belmont and Company, and it was agreed that the latter should organize a new company to enter into a contract with McDonald to promote the work, to furnish the security to be given by him and to finance the undertaking. This company was incorporated later as the Rapid Transit Subway Construction company.

It was also agreed that the Rapid Transit Commission should apply to the Appellate Division for a further modification of the requirements as to bonds; first to annul the provision as to the construction bond requiring sureties to qualify in double the amount of the liability and to reduce the minimum amount to be taken by each surety from $500,000 to $250,000; second that McDonald should furnish the continuing bond in amount of $1,000.-000, with sureties qualifying in double that amount and

FINANCIER AND BUILDER OF FIRST SUBWAY
1. August Belmont;   2. John B. McDonald.

at the same time deposit with the Controller securities of the value of $1,000,000, which ultimately were to be substituted for the bond for that amount; third, that the Rapid Transit Subway Construction company become surety on McDonald's bond for $4,000,000; fourth, that McDonald deposit $1,000,000 in cash as required by the contract and assign to the city his beneficial interest in the bonds to be required of sub-contractors; fifth, that McDonald cause an additional $1,000,000 to be deposited by January 1, 1901, to be held as additional security for the sureties on the construction bond.

The Appellate Division promptly approved this plan when it was presented, and the board, after approving the various bonds, executed the contract on February 21, 1900, the various deposits of cash and securities being made on the same day.

This contract, now known as Contract No. 1, provided both for construction of the road and its proper equipment and operation under a lease to run for fifty years and to be renewable for twenty-five years on readjustment of the rental. McDonald was both contractor and lessee, but the city through the board was to exercise constant supervision over construction, even to the inspection and approval of materials and work. The contractor was bound to begin construction within thirty days after the execution of the contract and to complete the entire road within four years and a half.

While the city agreed to pay McDonald $35,000,000 for the work, it was obligated also to purchase the real estate required for terminals and stations. The contractor was required to construct such terminals as work aside from that covered by the $35,000,000, and was to be paid therefor cost plus ten per cent. up to a limit of $1,750,000; the city also was to provide land necessary for stations to the extent of $1,000,000, but if the needed property cost more than such amount the excess should be paid by the contractor.

Cars and other equipment were to be provided by the contractor at his own expense, but were to be purchased by the city at the end of the lease at a price to be agreed upon or if not agreed upon to be fixed by arbitration. When the construction work was two-thirds finished the contractor was to begin supplying the equipment, which was to be delivered complete three months before the completion of the road or any part of it ready for operation.

For the lease the contractor bound himself to pay to the city as rental each year an amount equal to the interest paid by the city on its bonds issued for construction, plus one per cent. a year for a sinking fund to retire such bonds at maturity, except that, if the profits from operation fell short of five per cent., payment of the sinking fund for five years would be suspended and reduced to one half of one per cent. for the next five years provided the profits continued to fall below five per cent.

Motive power, it was specified, should be either electricity or compressed air, but if in future any method of generating or transmitting power superior to electricity and involving no injury to the purity of the air in the tunnels or cars shall become practicable, the contractor should have the right to adopt such method, if approved by the board, on two months' notice.

Such in brief were the terms of the contract which gave New York city her first subway. It was an epoch in municipal history, for it embodied the right of the people to build and if need be operate their own transportation lines. In spite of precedent, in spite of prejudice and in spite of the opposition of private interests engaged in transportation, not however without a severe struggle, the people had asserted and maintained this right, and the rapid transit contract of 1900 exercised it for the first time and thereby sealed the doom of private exploitation of city franchises. Credit for the achievement is due to the long line of public spirited men who championed public ownership from the early days of the '70's, but in the end chiefly to the broad-minded members of the Orr Rapid Transit Commission, who with exceptional courage and a perseverance that knew no flagging kept hammering away at legal and political obstacles until the goal was gained.

The impartial historian would be false to his duty if he neglected to credit August Belmont with the important work he did in assuring the construction of the first subway. He had the broad and penetrating vision which other financiers of that day lacked. He saw the dawning of the day of public ownership, he realized the need of additional rapid transit facilities and he felt that unless some one came to the assistance of the city in this emergency not only would rapid transit relief be delayed but the cause of public ownership would be set back and the existing monopoly of urban transportation would be perpetuated. Mr. Belmont for years had been interested in the subject. He had been in the promotion and organization of the Brooklyn elevated railroads, and the limitations of such agencies in crowded streets had impressed him strongly with the desirability of underground railroads. So when John B. McDonald bid for and obtained the rapid transit contract in January 1900, Belmont was ready to lend a willing ear to his request for financial assistance. Mr. Belmont himself in June, 1914, gave his own view of the situation. The conversation took place in his private office. Mr. Belmont talked for an hour or more, and his expressions in substance were as follows:

> "With all due respect to McDonald, Freedman and others, the subway would not have been built if I had not taken hold of the work. McDonald had a contract with the city, but he could not get the money to finance the work. He had verbal assurances from surety companies that he could get the necessary

help when he needed it, but after he got the contract this help was not forthcoming.

"Andrew Freedman brought McDonald to me first. I had been interested in rapid transit for many years—was in the Kings County elevated, and I believed that with electric traction an underground road would pay. I went over the matter with Mc-Donald, and he showed me figures from other contractors, agreeing to build the subway for a price well within the amount he was to get from the city. I then took hold of it and agreed to find the money necessary to carry out the contract.

"McDonald under his contract had to deposit $150,000 with the Controller. I helped him to make that payment. Just how much I paid I do not now remember. Then there was another payment of $1,000,000. I paid that, knowing that I had no legal security to protect me. It was necessary to get an assignment from McDonald, and pending the transfer of the lease and the formation of an operating company, all I had to secure me was a paper signed by McDonald—I think it was filed with the Controller—to pay over to me his receipts from the city; and during that time he collected every dollar from the city and turned it over to me. Had he not done so I would have had great difficulty in establishing legally my right to the money.

"Of course, I relied on McDonald's integrity, but if anything had happened to him I would have been in a dangerous position. My lawyers told me I was taking a great risk. Mr. Shepard, then of counsel for the Rapid Transit Commission, and my own lawyer tried to work out a plan which would absolutely protect me, but it could not be done. Finally I told them I would take the risk, and I did. If I had not, the subway would not have been built—at least not at that time. The result justified my action, and everything came out all right in the end, but I confess I was uneasy for a time.

"Then the matter of getting an operating company caused me considerable annoyance. McDonald had agreed to assign the operating lease to a company to be formed by me, but it was necessary to get a charter for such a company from the Legislature. At that time the old street car interests were all powerful with the Legislature, and when I tried to get a charter I found the door closed. Apparently nothing I could do was able to get that charter through the Legislature. Finally, after trying in every possible way to get action, I resolved to go straight to a man who was all powerful, or at least most influential with the powers that were, and I did. I went to that man, told him just what I was trying to do, what the project meant for New York and how certain influences were trying to prevent me from carrying it out. He promised his help and gave it, and a short time later we got our charter."

This description so well fitted the late Senator Thomas C. Platt, at that time known as the "boss" of the Republican party in New York state, that Mr. Belmont was asked if the man he referred to was Senator Platt.

"I will not say who it was", Mr. Belmont replied, "as it is immaterial now. But meanwhile I had tried other means. When I found that it would be difficult if not impossible to get a charter from the Legislature, I looked about to see if I could get one ready-made. Every street car company with an operating franchise was owned or controlled by the old traction interests, but after a search I found a little company up in the Bronx which had a perfectly valid charter to operate a street railroad. That was the City Island railroad. It wasn't much of a road, but I bought it and fully intended to operate the subway under its franchise if I couldn't get one of my own."

Mr. Belmont was asked what led him to go into the
rapid transit project. He replied:

"I lived on Long Island for many years. As I
have said I was interested in the Kings County elevated, and I realized that the elevated roads, while
they had served a most useful purpose, must be
superseded or supplemented by fast, electric underground roads. And by the way, that Brooklyn extension of the first subway was my idea. I always
believed in it. You know what I mean: the original
contract, Contract No. 1, ended at the City Hall.
The extension down Broadway and under the river
to Brooklyn was built under a separate contract.
Mr. Bryan, then president of the Interborough company, and others of our people were opposed to it.
But I believed in it and insisted that we should bid
for it and bid low enough to get it.

"Well, after Contract No. 1 was signed, giving
us a lease for fifty years, the Citizens' Union got
busy and there was a great agitation for a shorter
lease for the Brooklyn extension, Contract No. 2.
They wanted it cut down to twenty-five years. I
remember very well the hearing on the subject before the Rapid Transit Commission. There were
present Mr. Orr, the chairman, Mr. Grout, the Controller, and you will recall the other members. Grout
luckily made the suggestion that the new lease be
made for thirty-five years. I recall that Mr. Baldwin, president of the Long Island railroad, was
sitting beside me. When Grout made that suggestion I saw instantly what a good thing it would be
for us to have two leases expiring at different times
—but that's been changed now by the Dual System
contracts—so I leaned over to Baldwin and said:
'That suits me. Now, I'm going to get up and oppose it, and if I do they'll adopt it.' I did. I made
a speech opposing the thirty-five year lease and

pointing out how much better it would be for the city to have both leases expire at the same time. What I said had the effect I expected, and they adopted the thirty-five year lease.

"The result justified my expectations. The Brooklyn extension has been a most profitable one. And now they're talking a good deal about the Dual System contracts—how much better they are than the old contracts, especially as to the preferential payments. Why, that idea came from Brooklyn. It was the only way the Brooklyn company could get out of a bad situation and insure a continuation of its present profits. When Shonts, president of the Interborough company, found out that the city was willing to give it to the Brooklyn company, he said 'if it's good enough for them it's good enough for us', and forthwith put it in his proposition. That's how we got the preferential payment."

On the witness stand in a lawsuit (Venner vs. Belmont et al.) later in the year 1914 Mr. Belmont repeated the statement made in the above as to the influential man to whom he appealed for help to get his charter from the Legislature. When asked the name of this man he at first refused to give it, but on direction of the court finally answered the question. He then said it was William C. Whitney, who at the time was one of the principal owners of the Metropolitan Street Railway system, which operated the surface car lines in Manhattan.

Belmont's partner in the subway enterprise, John B. McDonald, was a man almost as well known in the contracting field as was Mr. Belmont in finance. Of powerful frame and much shrewd ability, he was well fitted for the arduous life of the contractor and had unusual success before he came to New York. He built the Baltimore & Ohio Railroad tunnels at Baltimore, a celebrated piece of work for those days, and it was his experience there gained in underground construction that led him to become a bidder for New York's first subway.

On March 24, 1900, ground was broken in front of the City Hall for the new subway, although actual construction lagged for several months while the Rapid Transit Commission was recruiting its engineering staff and the contractor was planning his work, subletting it in sections and organizing his own force. Working drawings also had to be made by the commission's engineers, and this took some time, so that it was well on in the year before construction was fairly under way.

Under the supervision of McDonald the work was done by the Rapid Transit Subway Construction company, organized by Belmont for the purpose. This concern was capitalized for $6,000,000, all of which was issued in common stock, to which Belmont and those he interested in the project subscribed. Among the latter was Cornelius Vanderbilt, son of the "Commodore" of the same name and one of the officers of the New York Central Railroad. Others included General James Jourdan, of Brooklyn, Adrian Iselin, William A. Read, Gardiner M. Lane and George W. Young. Its first officers were:

President, August Belmont; treasurer, Walter G. Oakman; secretary, Frederick Evans.

During the year 1900 the board devoted considerable time to making needed modifications of the plans and contract, as well as the route. The route was changed so as to run the west side line from Fort George to Kingsbridge by way of Naegle Avenue, Amsterdam Avenue and Kingsbridge Road instead of by the route first approved. The contract was changed so as to permit of the construction of local stations 450 feet long, and the loop at City Hall was reduced so as to run entirely between the City Hall and the Post Office instead of passing completely around the latter. Cornelius Vanderbilt is credited with the invention of the loop idea.

CONSTRUCTION OF FIRST SUBWAY

Lifting by Force of the Tide   Old Bridge Over Harlem Ship Canal.

The subject of an extension of the proposed subway
to Brooklyn engaged the attention of the Rapid Transit
Commission as soon as the contract with McDonald for
the Manhattan and Bronx lines was executed. Immediately thereafter the board instructed its chief engineer
to investigate and report upon the cost of such an extension, to run from City Hall south to South Ferry and
thence by tunnel under the East River to Brooklyn.
Property owners, as before stated, had petitioned for
the extension down Broadway.

In the meantime the board sought to have its powers
as to Greater New York clearly defined. Both the rapid
transit act of 1894 and the vote of the people on municipal ownership antedated the consolidation of New York,
Brooklyn and the other neighboring communities into the
larger city. It was a question whether an act authorizing the construction of a rapid transit road in the old
city, comprising only Manhattan and the Bronx, applied
to the consolidated city embracing as well Brooklyn,
Queens and Richmond. So the Legislature was asked
to pass and did enact an amendment to the law, extending
the powers of the board to all parts of the Greater City.
This act became effective April 23, 1900.

Early in the same year a large and important delegation from Kings County appeared before the board to
urge the construction of a Brooklyn extension. During
the month of May several public hearings were held on
the subject. The question of the best route to be followed was discussed, and two lines were proposed. One
was an extension of the Manhattan line from Broadway
to Whitehall street, thence under the East River to
Joralemon street, Brooklyn, and up Joralemon street,
Fulton street and Flatbush Avenue to Atlantic Avenue.
The other followed the same route in Manhattan but entered Brooklyn by way of Hamilton Avenue and ran
thence towards South Brooklyn and Bay Ridge. Study
of this situation occupied the rest of the year.

Another important problem which engaged the attention of the board during the last three months of 1900 was the possibility of making a physical connection at the Grand Central station in Forty-second street between the new rapid transit road and the tracks of the New York Central and New Haven steam railroad lines. It was believed that the public would be better served if the trains of the rapid transit road could operate over those tracks northward into the suburban communities reached by the two railroads. Acting under the instructions of the board, its president, Mr. Orr, and its chief engineer, Mr. Parsons, took up the question with Mr. W. K. Vanderbilt, Mr. Callaway, then president, and Mr. Wilgus, then chief engineer of the New York Central. The Central authorities insisted that, if a connection were made, the rapid transit road must not at any point be on Grand Central station property. This condition was regarded by the board as prohibitory, and after considerable correspondence Mr. Callaway refused to yield, stating that their plans were "when an electric or air motor can be had to run our trains any considerable distance, to tunnel underneath the depot and use the space there for our own suburban service." Many years later the idea thus suggested by Mr. Callaway was carried out.

The decision to omit pipe galleries also was reached in the latter part of the year 1900. Construction of such galleries was actually commenced on the Elm street route, but both the contractor and the Departments of Sewers and Water Supply of the City objected to them, and the board, on McDonald's agreement to stand the cost of abandoning the work, agreed to its indefinite suspension. The pipe gallery as an adjunct to subways was revived in later years, and some contracts including them were awarded, but every time the city departments objected and eventually the matter was dropped.

The year 1900 also saw the passage of an amendment to the rapid transit act, proposed by the board, which enlarged its powers in respect of the condemnation of land. Under the original act the city was limited to the condemnation of the right or easement for the passage of the rapid transit line. By this amendment the city was given power to condemn the fee of property so that, if it became necessary to tear down buildings, the board could take the title to the property, remove the buildings and later sell the property subject to the easement for the subway.

CHAPTER XIII

THE FIRST SUBWAY COMPLETED AND PLACED IN OPERATION.

On January 24, 1901, the Rapid Transit board adopted the route and general plan for the Brooklyn extension of the subway. This was done in less than a year after the execution of the contract with McDonald for the construction of the Manhattan-Bronx subway. The line as approved extended from City Hall down Broadway to the Battery and thence by tunnel under the East River to Joralemon street, Brooklyn, up Joralemon street to Fulton street near Borough Hall, thence under Fulton street to Flatbush Avenue and under Flatbush Avenue to Atlantic Avenue, near the Brooklyn station of the Long Island Railroad.

The resolution approving the route was transmitted to the Municipal Assembly on February 2, 1901, accompanied by a letter in which the board set forth its reasons for the choice. In this letter the board said:

"The board is aware that the route now proposed does not afford a complete solution of the rapid transit problem in Brooklyn. It is, however, beyond doubt, the best route for the first rapid transit connection between the boroughs. It reaches two great distributing points in Brooklyn, Borough Hall Park and the Long Island Railroad station. The new road can thence be conveniently extended as the financial means of the city will permit, to any and every important district in Brooklyn. It is to the interest of the city that the rapid transit connection now proposed between the boroughs should be promptly constructed rather than that the city and especially the Borough of Brooklyn should be made to wait several years for the initiation of a system more nearly complete."

After public hearings the Municipal Assembly on May 21, 1901, approved the new route, the Mayor gave his approval on June 1 and the Park Board its consent on July 11. This completed the consents of the local authorities, and the Rapid Transit board, having failed to get the statutory consents of property owners, applied to the Appellate Division, First and Second Departments, for the appointment of commissioners and a determination in lieu of such consents. The First Department tribunal appointed Theron G. Strong, Thomas C. T. Crain and Henry W. Gray as its commissioners, while the Second Department named William Cullen Bryant, Richard H. Laimbeer and Frederick R. Kellogg in similar capacity. To expedite proceedings both sets of Commissioners sat together to take testimony, and on December 26 and 27 respectively reported favorably on the route. Thereupon the board proceeded with the preparation of detail plans preliminary to the letting of the construction contract. The reports were confirmed by orders of the respective Appellate Divisions on January 30 and January 17, 1902.

A sub-committee consisting of Mr. Orr and Mr. Charles Stewart Smith was appointed to draft the contract for the Brooklyn extension. This committee reported on May 23, 1902, submitting a draft following the general lines of Contract No. 1 for the Manhattan-Bronx road. It was provided, however, that the bidder should name in his bid what connections he would make with other railroads or rapid transit lines for a single fare of five cents. This was undoubtedly to provide an opportunity for the Belmont company, which was building the Manhattan-Bronx line, to bid for the Brooklyn extension, so that both roads might be operated as one and for a single fare between the boroughs. The contractor was required to deposit $1,000,000 in cash or securities, to give a bond in the same amount, to deposit with the board all bonds of sub-contractors, and to provide at his own expense all of the equipment of the road on which the city was to have first lien. The work was to be done and the road ready for operation in two years after the execution of the contract. A new provision not in Contract No. 1 was that no advertisements were to be allowed in the stations except by special permission from the board.

After a public hearing the board adopted the form of contract substantially as submitted by the committee, the only changes of consequence being the length of the leasing term, which was fixed at thirty-five instead of fifty years and the extension of the period for construction from two to three years. The contract was approved June 12, 1902, and the board immediately advertised for bids, to be opened July 21. On that day three proposals were received as follows:

From John L. Wells, of counsel for and representing the Brooklyn Rapid Transit Company, who offered to build the road for $8,000,000—$7,000,000 for construction and $1,000,000 for terminals. For connections at a single fare Mr. Wells offered a series of rides over various lines of the Brooklyn Rapid Transit Company extending to Fort Hamilton on the south, Kings Highway on the roads to Coney Island, East New York and interior points.

From the Rapid Transit Subway Construction Company, offering to build the road for $3,000,000 for construction and $1,000,000 for terminals. For connections at a single fare the company offered through rides from the Brooklyn extension over the lines of the Manhattan-Bronx subway to be operated by the Interborough Rapid Transit Company, except if the contractor made any agreement with a connecting line to carry a passenger for less than five cents such passenger coming from the Brooklyn line should not be carried beyond Fifty-ninth street for the less fare. This bid was accompanied by a letter from John B. McDonald stating that in the event of its acceptance he would agree to build an extension of the Manhattan subway from Forty-second street south in

Broadway to Union Square for $100,000 provided he was awarded the contract prior to July 1, 1903.

From the Rapid Transit Subway Construction Company, offering to build the road for $2,000,000 for construction and $1,000,000 for terminals, with the same provisions for connecting trips at a single fare as in the other bid by the same company. McDonald's offer to build the Broadway extension in Manhattan, however, was not embraced in this bid.

The last bid, namely $2,000,000 for construction and $1,000,000 for terminals, being the lowest, was accepted by the Commission on July 24, 1902, when the contract was awarded to the Rapid Transit Subway Constrution Company. It was executed on the 11th day of September following. Thus on account of the Belmont company's eagerness to acquire the Brooklyn extension, the city got for the sum of $3,000,000 a piece of railroad and tunnel construction which the Commission's engineers estimated could not be done for less than $6,000,000. As a matter of fact it cost much more than that. Construction of the road was formally begun in front of No. 17 State Street, Manhattan, on November 8, 1902.

During the year 1902 the Pennsylvania Railroad Company obtained its franchise to construct its tunnel and terminal system in Manhattan, so as to bring its trains into the heart of New York City. Its first appeal was to the Legislature, where a bill was introduced to confer the required rights. The Rapid Transit board successfully asserted the rights of the city to control underground railroad construction in its streets, and obtained the passage of an amendment to Section 32 of the Rapid Transit Act making it the duty of the board to grant such franchises, with the result that the Pennsylvania Company received its franchise from the board only after a complete study had been made of the project and the route and terms had been fixed satisfactorily from the viewpoint of the city.

Under the same amendment the board also acted on the application of the New York and Jersey Railroad Company for a tunnel under the New York half of the Hudson River to Morton Street and to Christopher Street in Manhattan. This franchise was granted by the board on July 10, 1902, and with subsequent modifications made possible the construction of the McAdoo system of tubes now operated by the Hudson and Manhattan Railroad Company.

The success in placing the contract for the Brooklyn extension led the board to consider the plan for another tunnel to Brooklyn to connect with the Brooklyn Rapid Transit system and thus to give the people of both boroughs the benefit of the connections on the Brooklyn side offered in the bid submitted by that company. Accordingly on July 24 Mr. Orr offered and the board adopted a resolution directing its chief engineer to submit route and general plan for a rapid transit railroad which would "as directly as practicable connect the general region of the City Hall Park, in the Borough of Manhattan, with the general region of Borough Hall Park, or some other equally convenient passenger transportation center, in the Borough of Brooklyn."

Prior to this time the board on May 9 had instructed its chief engineer to prepare and submit to the board a comprehensive scheme or plan of rapid transit for the whole city, looking to the needs of the future as well as to the present. In his letter to Mr. Parsons conveying these instructions Mr. Orr said:

"The far-reaching plan I have suggested could not, of course, be carried out at once, or perhaps, completely carried out for many years. But if such a plan be now wisely prepared and the streets of New York be dedicated to tunnel railroad purposes with a proper regard to the long, and no doubt splendid future of the city, two things may be reasonably

OLD AND NEW METHODS OF BUILDING
SUBWAYS

Upper Broadway During Construction of First
Subway;   2. Lower Broadway During Con-
struction of Brooklyn Extension, Showing
Decked Roadway.

expected: First that rapid transit construction will proceed upon the lines so laid down as rapidly as the means of the city and the amount of private capital ready for rapid transit investment will permit. And, second, that relatively unimportant franchises will not be granted in such way or special routes be so devised as to prevent or obstruct a permanent and sufficient programme.''

Later we shall see the result of this foresight on the part of Mr. Orr and his fellow commissioners.

It was about this time that an important change took place in the composition of the city government and therefore in the personnel of the Rapid Transit Commission. In the campaign of 1901 for the election of officers of the Greater City, Tammany Hall met with a crushing defeat. Seth Low, the candidate of the fusion forces, was elected Mayor with all his associates on the city ticket, the fusionists also capturing a small majority of the Board of Aldermen. At the end of the year, therefore, Mayor Van Wyck and Controller Bird S. Coler retired and were succeeded on January 1, 1902 by Mayor Low and Controller Edward M. Grout, who became ex officio members of the Rapid Transit Commission.

Another change in the board's membership took place at the close of the year 1901. George L. Rives resigned on December 27 and John Claflin was elected in his place. Mr. Claflin was named in the act of 1894 as one of the original members, but had resigned in 1899. Mayor Low also had been one of the original members, but had resigned in 1896. The opening of the year 1902 saw them both back in the board, much to the gratification of the other members. Mr. Rives later was appointed one of the board's counsel on the retirement of Edward M. Shepard.

Construction work on the Manhattan-Bronx rapid transit road proceeded rapidly after the signing of the contract with McDonald. At the end of the year 1902 the board reported that $23,464,000 had been expended, out of the estimated total of $35,000,000. It was necessary here and there to alter the plans, and in some cases the route, but these were minor changes and did not affect the general lay-out of the line. The work was unattended with serious interruptions or accidents until January 27, 1902, when an explosion of dynamite in the contractor's shanty at Forty-first street and Park Avenue near the Murray Hill hotel killed five persons and injured many others. The explosion shook down the plaster in the Murray Hill hotel, broke all the windows in houses in the vicinity and in some buildings 600 feet distant. No serious damage was done to buildings or to the subway structure. This accident led to the appointment by Mayor Low of a Municipal Explosives Commission, which revised the city regulations governing the storage and use of high explosives in the city limits.

On March 20 and 21 slides of rock occurred in the deep tunnel for the subway on the eastern side of Park Avenue between Thirty-seventh and Thirty-eighth streets. No lives were lost here, but the accident caused some delay and gave the contractor much trouble.

Pursuant to the act of the Legislature of 1902 Belmont and his associates were enabled to form a corporation for the construction and operation of the municipally-owned rapid transit railroad. This was done in April, 1902, when they incorporated the Interborough Rapid Transit Company for the purpose. The original capital of this company was placed at $25,000,000 divided into 250,000 shares of the par value of $100 each, all of the stock to be common stock. The incorporators, each of whom subscribed for ten shares of stock, were: William H. Baldwin Jr., Charles T. Barney, August Belmont, Andrew Freedman, James Jourdan, John B. McDonald, Delancey Nicoll, Walter G. Oakman, John Peirce, William A. Read, Cornelius Vanderbilt, George W. Wickersham,

George W. Young, all of New York City; E. P. Bryan, of Yonkers, N. Y.; and Gardiner M. Lane, of Boston, Mass. Of these all but Nicoll and Wickersham were named as directors. The capital stock subsequently was increased to $35,000,000.

It was provided in the articles of incorporation that the directors might annually appoint an executive committee composed of seven of the directors, who should exercise all the powers of the board of directors except when the board is in session. The certificate of incorporation was filed with the Secretary of State on May 6, 1902, and the company paid a tax of $12,500 for the privilege of organizing.

The type of cars to be used in the subway when completed gave the Interborough company much concern. Finally two cars were built to illustrate various details of manufacture. The car chosen was to be a wooden frame on a steel bottom, with sides sheathed with copper and the electrical machinery encased in fireproof casing. The length was about 51 feet and the width eight feet eleven and seven-eighths inches. This was four feet longer and four inches wider than the cars used on the Manhattan elevated lines. While the question of multiple doors was considered, the company decided to adhere to the usual plan with platforms and end doors. Contracts were placed for five hundred of these cars during the year.

At the close of the year 1902 the Rapid Transit Commission had 322 men on its engineering payroll. The executive officers of this department were: William Barclay Parsons, Chief Engineer; Geo. S. Rice, Deputy Chief Engineer; Albert Carr, Engineer First Division; Alfred Craven, Engineer Second Division; Beverly R. Value, Engineer Third Division; Eugene Klapp, Engineer Fourth Division; Calvin W. Hendrick, Engineer Sewer Division; St. John Clarke, General Inspector of Designs; W. A. Aiken, General Inspector of Materials; M. J. Farrell, Private Secretary.

The construction work was divided into five divisions, each being placed in charge of a Division Engineer. The First Division covered the work from City Hall north to 41st street and Park Avenue; the Second Division, from Forty-first street north to 104th street and Broadway; the Third Division, from 104th street to the portal of the tunnel at Fort George on the west side, and to the portal of the tunnel at Westchester Avenue on the east side; the Fourth Division, all of the viaduct or elevated railroad work north of the last two mentioned points and the viaduct over Manhattan valley between 125th and 135th streets; the Fifth or Sewer Division, all reconstruction of sewers in streets off the line of the road.

The above divisions were strictly engineering divisions; for construction purposes the work was further divided into sections and each section was awarded to a sub-contractor by the Rapid Transit Subway Construction company.

In all there were seventeen contract sections and as many different sub-contracts, but as some contractors got more than one section the number of sub-contractors was only twelve. They were: The Degnon-McLean Contracting Company, the Holbrook. Cabot and Daly Contracting Company, Ira A. Shaler, Naughton and Company, William Bradley, Farrell and Hopper, McMullen and McBean, J. C. Rogers, the Terry and Tench Construction Company, E. P. Roberts, John Shields, and L. B. McCabe and Brother. The Degnon-McLean Company, which had the two contracts extending from City Hall to Great Jones and Centre streets, was the first to begin work, which was started on March 24, 1900. Nine other contracts were begun in that year, and the remainder in 1901 and 1902.

The furnishing of materials of construction was also committed to sub-contractors, of whom the leading ones were the American Bridge Company for steel, John Fox and Company for cast iron, the United Building Material

Company for cement and the Sicilian Asphalt Paving Company for asphalt, waterproofing and felt. All sub-contractors were placed under heavy bonds.

As the contract with the city made it the duty of the contractor to supply all the equipment, including power houses, the Rapid Transit Subway Construction Company purchased a site for the main power house between 58th and 59th streets and Eleventh and Twelfth Avenues and there erected a complete electricity generating plant with a total energy of 90,000 horse power. Property also was purchased for the necessary sub-stations, of which there are eight located in various parts of the territory reached by the road.

In the days since the subway traffic reached a million passengers a day, the statement has been made frequently that it was designed to carry only 400,000 a day. Efforts to verify this statement have failed. George S. Rice, who was Deputy Chief Engineer under Mr. Parsons, asserted that the engineers used no upset figure in calculating the capacity of the line, or rather did not plan a road to carry any estimated number of passengers, but planned to give it as great a carrying capacity as the limitations of the line would permit. There must have been some reason, however, for limiting the length of station platforms, for at first these were built to accommodate seven-car express trains and five car local trains. As the traffic grew the operating company managed to run eight-car express by allowing the front and rear cars to extend past the ends of the station platforms, but later on all platforms had to be lengthened.

Careful studies of the existing traffic were made, how-ever, by the Commission's engineers, the results of which are set down in the various annual reports of the board. In the present year (1917) when the last year's travel on all the street railroads was more than 1,800,000,000, it is interesting to note that in 1902, when the subway was under construction, it was about 937,000,000. In

other words since the first subway was built the street
railroad traffic in fifteen years has about doubled!

By the end of the year 1903 the work was about 90
per cent. completed and the city's expenditure on account
of it aggregated more than $30,000,000. In the report for
that year the board said the work would have been still
further advanced were it not for delays caused by labor
strikes both on the road and at the power house.

On January 1, 1903 the Interborough Rapid Transit
Company, which was to operate the subway, leased the
Manhattan Elevated Railway, then controlled by the
Gould interests, for 999 years, the lease taking effect
April 1, 1903. The lessee agreed to pay as rental seven
per cent. on the capital stock of the lessor, which was
$60,000,000. This placed the Interborough company in
control of practically all rapid transit lines in Manhattan and the Bronx, for the Manhattan company operated
all the elevated railroads in those two boroughs. These
lines were the Ninth Avenue, the Sixth Avenue, the Third
Avenue and the Second Avenue lines, embracing all the
elevated roads built by both the New York Elevated and
the Metropolitan Elevated (Gilbert) companies.

Although labor strikes continued during the year 1904
the construction work progressed steadily, and on October 27 of that year operation of the finished portion of
the road began. This extended from the City Hall on the
south to 145th street and Broadway, on the West side
branch, and the occasion was signalized by appropriate
ceremonies. The first train over the road started from
City Hall station and was operated by Mayor George B.
McClellan, who had succeeded Seth Low in the city's
chief magistracy as the result of the election of 1903.
Mayor McClellan stationed himself in the motorman's
closet and manipulated the electric controller during the
journey northward.

The ceremonies were held in the Aldermanic chamber
of the City Hall prior to the starting of the train. At

one o'clock the Mayor led a procession into the chamber. He walked with Archbishop John Farley, now a Cardinal of the Roman Catholic church, and following them came Charles V. Fornes, president of the Board of Aldermen, with Coadjutor Bishop David H. Greer, of the Episcopal church; Alexander E. Orr, president of the Board of Rapid Transit Railroad Commissioners, with Rev. M. J. Lavelle, rector of St. Patrick's cathedral; John H. Starin, Vice President of the Rapid Transit board, with the former Mayor, Robert A. Van Wyck; Controller Edward M. Grout; Deputy Controllers J. W. Stevenson and N. Taylor Phillips; Morris K. Jesup, Woodbury Langdon, John Claflin and Charles Stewart Smith, members of the Rapid Transit board; August Belmont, the financier and John B. McDonald, the builder of the subway; William Barclay Parsons, chief engineer, Edward M. Shepard, Albert B. Boardman and George L. Rives, counsel; George S. Rice, deputy chief engineer and H. A. D. Hollmann, auditor of the board.

President Fornes called the assemblage to order and asked Bishop Greer to offer prayer. After the prayer Mr. Fornes yielded the chair to Mayor McClellan, who made an address, in which he emphasized the importance of the occasion and said that without rapid transit Greater New York would be little more than a geographical expression.

Addresses were then made by Mr. Orr, Mr. Starin, Mr. McDonald, and Mr. Belmont. These addresses are published in full in the annual report of the board for 1904. At their conclusion benediction was pronounced by Archbishop Farley, the Mayor declared the new subway open and received from Mr. Belmont an ornamented controller in a mahogany case with which to start the first train. The ceremonies ended at twenty-four minutes past two o'clock and ten minutes later the first train bearing all the above named officials and many invited guests whirled out of the City Hall station under the guiding hand of Mayor McClellan.

The people took kindly to the new mode of transportation, and within a few days after the opening the subway began to show signs of crowding during the rush hours. There never was a break in the increasing tide of travel and the traffic it has built up is one of the wonders in the world of railroading. Nothing approaching it had ever been recorded.

On December 1, 1904, William Barclay Parsons resigned as Chief Engineer of the Rapid Transit Board. The great work which he had called into being was nearly finished—the greater part of it in successful operation— and he desired to resume private practice in his profession. Later he became and still is consulting engineer for the Interborough Rapid Transit Company. The first New York subway stands as a monument to his skill and courage as an engineer. In a conversation in July, 1913, Mr. Parsons said:

"I was thirty-five years of age when I became Chief Engineer of the Rapid Transit Commission. When I look back now I am glad I was not older. I doubt if I could now undertake or would undertake such a work under similar conditions. But I had the enthusiasm of youth and inexperience. Had I fully realized all that was ahead of me, I do not think I could have attempted the work. As it was I was treated as a visionary. Some of my friends spoke pityingly of my wasting time on what they considered a dream. They said I could go ahead making plans, but never could build a practical, underground railroad. This skepticism was so prevalent that it seriously handicapped the work."

Mr. Parsons, who had been an engineer for the Erie railroad, began business in New York City toward the end of the year 1885. He soon became connected with the New

York District Railway Company, an offshoot of the old Arcade Railway, which held the old Beach Pneumatic franchise for an underground road in Broadway. The directors of the Arcade Railway quarreled among themselves, and the dissatisfied element organized the New York District Railway. August Belmont was a stockholder in this enterprise and Mr. Parsons became its chief engineer.

"The New York District Railway," said Mr. Parsons, "was important in its way, for it settled the fundamental law governing the building of a rapid transit railroad. The State constitution provided that no such line could be built without the consents of the local authorities and of a certain proportion of the property owners along the line. Holding that the old Beach franchise was not for a railroad but for a tube 54 inches in diameter, the District Railway applied to the Board of Aldermen of New York City for a franchise for a railroad subway in Broadway. Dominated by Tammany and the elevated railroad interests, the Board of Aldermen refused to make the grant, and the District Railway appealed to the courts. The company contended that the refusal of the local authorities justified it under the Rapid Transit act and the constitution in asking the court for a determination in lieu of their consent. The case was fought to the Court of Appeals, which decided that the consent of the City was vital and that the court determination could serve only in lieu of the consent of property owners. And that is the law today. This decision, rendered in 1886, ended the efforts of the Arcade Railway and the District Railway to build a subway in Broadway."

In December, 1904, George S. Rice was promoted to be Chief Engineer of the Rapid Transit board to succeed Mr. Parsons. This and other changes in the staff made the executive force of the engineering department of the board in 1905 as follows:

Chief Engineer, George S. Rice; Deputy Chief Engi-

neer, Alfred Craven; Engineer First Division, George
Hallett Clark; Second Division, John H. Myers; Third
and Fourth Divisions, C. V. V. Powers; Fifth Division,
Frederick C. Noble; Sewer Division, Amos L. Schaeffer;
General Inspector of Designs, Sverre Dahm; General
Inspector of Materials, W. A. Aiken; General Inspector
of Stations, D. L. Turner; Secretary to Chief, M. J. Farrell; Official Photographer, Pierre P. Pullis. The other
staff officers of the board were Bion L. Burrows, Secretary, and H. A. D. Hollmann, Auditor.

Mr. Rice remained Chief Engineer, Burrows Secretary and Hollmann Auditor until the board was abolished
in 1907 and immediately after the Public Service Commission was created Mr. Rice and Mr. Hollman and most
of the engineers mentioned joined its staff and continued
their former work. Mr. Burrows went into private business and promoted an unsuccessful installation of a type
of mono-rail railroad in the Bronx. He died in 1916.

Other parts of the first subway were opened to traffic
as follows: Broadway, 145th to 157th street, November
5, 1904; Lenox Avenue branch, Broadway and Ninety-
sixth street to 145th street, November 20, 1904; and from
149th street and Third Avenue along Westchester Avenue and Boston Road to the terminus at 180th street,
November 26, 1904. The intervening link from 145th
street under the Harlem River to Westchester Avenue
was opened later and the remainder of the Broadway line,
157th street to Kingsbridge, in March, 1906.

Exceptionally rapid progress was made on the Manhattan part of the Brooklyn extension, which was completed and ready for operation in about two years after
the commencement of work. The line from the Brooklyn
Bridge station at City Hall to the Battery was opened in
1905. This section was built under the direct supervision
of Albert Carr, Division Engineer for the Rapid Transit
board. The rest of the line, including the river tunnel,
was built under the direction of Robert Ridgway, also

a Division Engineer for the board. Mr. Ridgway later
supervised the construction of a part of the Catskill
aqueduct for the City and then returned to rapid transit
work under the Public Service Commission, with whom
he became Engineer in Charge of Subway Construction.

CHAPTER XIV

WHEN the first subway was begun the street railway interests of New York City were controlled by two separate and distinct companies, the Manhattan Elevated Railway Company and the Metropolitan Street Railway Company. The former was owned principally by the Gould and Sage interests. It operated the elevated lines in Manhattan and the Bronx. These consisted of the Ninth Avenue line, running up and down the West Side of the city from the Battery to 155th street and Eighth Avenue; the Sixth Avenue line, running from the Battery mainly up Sixth Avenue to 53d street and through 53d street to a junction with the Ninth Avenue line; the Third Avenue line running from the Battery mainly up Third Avenue to and across the Harlem River to Fordham; and the Second Avenue line running from the Battery mainly up Second Avenue to 129th street and a junction with the Third Avenue line. As told in a previous chapter all these lines were leased by the Interborough Rapid Transit Company, the operator of the subway.

The Metropolitan Street Railway system embraced practically all the surface car lines in Manhattan and the Bronx. It was controlled by Thomas F. Ryan and the late William C. Whitney, formerly Secretary of the Navy in the cabinet of President Cleveland. They and their associates had consolidated several surface car properties into one system by means of leases or outright purchases until they finally controlled all the main north and south and crosstown lines. They believed in free transfers as a means of stimulating traffic, and with each new line acquired the transfer privilege was extended until it covered the whole island.

The consolidation was accompanied by much watering of securities and the making of some extravagant leases. Expenditures were made on a grand scale for electrification of tracks, new equipment, etc., and the earnings did not increase sufficiently to provide needed revenue.

Before the subway was completed it was apparent to men in the business that it would prove a great traffic getter, and with the elevated lines paying well the Belmont consolidation promised to become a most successful one. It was probable that for a time the street surface lines would lose traffic when the subway opened, and they were in no condition to surrender any. In such circumstances, therefore, the astute managers of the Metropolitan system, formed a bold plan to meet the situation. The plan was to get the Rapid Transit Commission to give the Metropolitan company a franchise for a competing subway, or at least for the company to apply for such a franchise. With such a grant the Metropolitan would be in a position not only to sell out to Belmont but to make him buy or merge.

The scheme was a masterly one and it was masterfully carried on. Ryan's company entered upon an energetic campaign to influence public sentiment and through it the Rapid Transit Commission. This campaign was an epoch in the transit history of New York. To carry it on Ryan detailed one of his ablest lieutenants, Lemuel E. Quigg, a well educated, clever man who had begun life as a newspaper reporter, gone into politics, been elected to Congress where he served one term, become an ally and lieutenant of Thomas C. Platt, the Republican leader and under him had acted as president of the Republican County Committee of New York County. Later Quigg studied law and became a member of the bar.

Ryan's first open move was made in December, 1903, nearly ten months before the subway was opened for traffic. He informed the Rapid Transit Commission that, if it would lay out routes for another north and south rapid transit railroad, independent of the one under construction, and so devised as to supplement the surface car lines, his company would be a bidder for the franchise, provided the terms exacted by the city would not be too onerous. The news, which quickly got into the newspapers, caused a tremendous sensation. Rapid transit certainly was "looking up". Here it was only four years ago that none of the transportation managers wanted to have anything to do with a city-owned rapid transit line, and nobody but Belmont could be found to finance one, and he was blamed by many for his adventurous leap into strange waters. And now, before the first city-owned subway was completed, here were the rich and influential traction kings of the Metropolitan system actually petitioning for a chance to build and operate another and competing road.

The city gasped. So did Belmont. The press raved about it, and all New York could talk of nothing else for months. The Rapid Transit Commission openly exulted and in its report for 1903 congratulated the city upon the alluring prospect. The commission, however, was not content with verbal promises. It politely requested Mr. Ryan and his associates to put their offer in writing. This they promptly did, and on February 25, 1904 Ryan and H. H. Vreeland, then president of the Metropolitan company, submitted their written proposals. Mr. Vreeland's letter contained the formal proposal; Mr. Ryan's his endorsement thereof.

In brief the proposal was that the board should lay out a route beginning at about 138th street and Third Avenue in the Bronx and extending thence southward under the Harlem River to Lexington Avenue, down Lexington Avenue to Fifteenth street, under Fifteenth street and Union Square to Broadway, down Broadway to Chambers street, through Chambers street to William street and down William street, through Hanover Square, Coenties Slip and South street to the Battery; thence

turning through the Battery to Greenwich street, up
Greenwich street, West Broadway and Hudson street to
Eighth Avenue, up Eighth Avenue to Thirty-fourth
street, and through Thirty-fourth street to a junction
with the line in Lexington Avenue.

Under the proper terms the Metropolitan company
agreed to build such a line for the city and to operate it
under lease in connection with its surface lines, to and
from which it proposed to give free transfers for a uniform rate of five cents a passenger. "By utilizing the
surface lines for local traffic", wrote Vreeland, "and for
carrying long-distance passengers to and from the nearest subway stations, it would be possible to very greatly
reduce the number of subway stations which would otherwise be necessary, thus materially increasing the speed
and efficiency of the underground service.

"The transfer system which we propose, by which
the underground lines and the surface lines would be
operated as one system, would establish means of expedi-
tious communication between all parts of Manhattan isl-
and for a five-cent fare. Such a comprehensive result is,
of course, possible only with underground lines operated
in connection with a complete network of surface lines."

The letter also set forth that the Metropolitan company had in operation about three hundred miles of surface lines, and that the plan would relieve congestion on
many overcrowded roads. In the course of time the
West Side underground line could be extended from
Thirty-fourth street up Eighth Avenue to the Harlem
River. The proposed terminus in the Bronx was the
point at which most of the surface lines converged, and
the new line, therefore, would bring rapid transit facilities "within easy reach of a much larger proportion of
the population of the Bronx than can be served by the
rapid transit line about to be opened."

Ryan in his letter said: "Under the transfer system
which we propose, by which the underground lines and

our three hundred miles of surface lines on Manhattan Island would be operated as one system, almost every person on Manhattan Island would be able to ride from his place of residence to his place of business for a single fare of five cents and at a rate of speed which would be possible only with underground lines operated in connection with a complete system of surface lines. In other words, our plan would practically bring rapid transit to the door of every citizen.''

This proposal was taken under consideration by the Rapid Transit Commission, which proceeded to study the entire situation and to devise a comprehensive plan which would not only insure proper rapid transit development for the present but also provide logical extensions for the future. It will be remembered that the Chief Engineer had been called upon to report to the board a system of routes to serve these purposes. These reports were submitted in 1904 and 1905, and in May of the latter year the board began adopting routes and general plans and continued to do so until the map of the city had been grid-ironed with routes for rapid transit railroads. The first lines laid out were those in Third, Lexington, Seventh and Eighth Avenues in Manhattan; then followed various loop lines connecting Manhattan and Brooklyn, a line in Fourth Avenue, Brooklyn, one in Eastern Parkway, Brooklyn and another in Jamaica Avenue, Brooklyn, to Jamaica in Queens.

In the same month, May, 1905, a new law went into effect depriving the Board of Aldermen of the authority to give the municipal consent to the construction of rapid transit lines and conferring that authority on the Board of Estimate and Apportionment. The passage of this law had been forced by public sentiment which was aroused by the frequent delays of such matters in the Board of Aldermen, its long dalliance with the Pennsylvania tunnel franchise in 1904 having brought about a crystallization of this sentiment. On July 14, 1905, the Board of Estimate gave consent to the new routes.

Meanwhile the Metropolitan interests prosecuted their campaign to enlist public sentiment in behalf of their proposal. The newspapers teemed with articles pointing out the desirability of competition in the rapid transit field and the benefits to be conferred on the general public by the Metropolitan's proposal to transfer from rapid transit to surface lines and vice versa. Civic associations in all parts of Manhattan and the Bronx met and passed resolutions favoring the proposal, which were duly forwarded to the newspapers and the Rapid Transit Commission. Delegations from such societies haunted the corridors of No. 320 Broadway, where the Rapid Transit board had its offices, and clamored for hearings. Many such hearings were held and the representatives of the most congested parts of Manhattan and the most undeveloped sections of the Bronx lifted their voices to acclaim the Metropolitan scheme.

While the Metropolitan interests thus sought to array public sentiment on their side, the Rapid Transit board was engaged in studying the whole problem and considering the extension of rapid transit from the standpoint of the needs of the whole city. When the Metropolitan proposal was submitted it was referred to the plan committee of the board, which in due time reported. This report favored the laying out of a system of routes which would embody the best of the Metropolitan suggestions as well as the logical extensions of the first subway favored by the Belmont company. Such a course was followed by the board, and the engineers were set to work to draw plans.

Suddenly the community was electrified by the news that the Interborough Rapid Transit company and the Metropolitan Street Railway company had merged, and that the two immense transportation systems were hereafter to be controlled by one new company entitled the

Interborough-Metropolitan Company. For a second time the community gasped. It seemed impossible that the rival traction interests which had been at each other's throats in competition for the new rapid transit lines, should come together. Yet such was the fact, and it was not long until the cat was let out of the bag and the financial district rang with the story of how Ryan had forced Belmont into the merger by the threat of constructing a new subway to be operated in competition with the underground road into which Belmont had put his millions.

The new company was incorporated as a business, not a railroad corporation, in January 1906, with a capital of $155,000,000, 55 preferred, 100 common. It was to hold the stock of both the Interborough Rapid Transit and the Metropolitan Street Railway companies. Its first directors were: Walter G. Oakman, James Jourdan, John B. McDonald, Morton F. Plant, all of New York, and Peter A. B. Widener, of Philadelphia.

In a conversation with Mr. August Belmont in June, 1914, before quoted, he was asked about this merger.

"You remember how the street car people talked about building a system of subways and giving transfers to the surface lines", he said. "Well, we couldn't stand that kind of competition, and so we combined with them. I admit that we didn't know the exact condition of the surface car system—the interlacing of companies etc. It took us some months to get to the bottom of it. I got Shonts to do it. But when we got down to the bottom of things they were worse than we expected. But now there is hope. The old system has been reorganized, improved and put into shape where it ought to develop into a fine property. Everything will work out all right, I think."

In a Legislative investigation of the Public Service Commission, held several years later, namely in 1915-'16, it was brought out that the merger had cost the Interborough interests about $40,000,000. This loss was practically written off in 1915, when the Interborough-Consolidated Company was formed to take over the stock of the Interborough company and the old Metropolitan Securities Company, which held the stock of the surface lines taken in by the merger and later, after going through receiverships, reorganized under the name of the New York Railways Company.

Public resentment followed quickly upon public surprise. The press denounced the merger and the overcapitalization of the new company. The Rapid Transit Commission saw in the merger the collapse of competition, but nevertheless continued the laying out of routes and the preparation of plans for additional subways. In December, 1906, several of these routes had been legalized, plans for some of them made and those for others were under way. Whether to advertise for bids for construction alone, or for both construction and operation was a question on which the Commission asked the advice of the Board of Estimate and Apportionment. This course was made necessary by the Elsberg amendments to the Rapid Transit act, passed by the Legislature of 1906, which not only provided for alternative means of construction, but also limited the life of any lease of a city-owned rapid transit railroad to twenty years, with the privilege of twenty years' renewal. The Board of Estimate and Apportionment on December 7, 1906, adopted a resolution in response to the Commission's request, recommending that alternate bids be invited, first for construction alone, and second for construction, equipment and operation. The routes covered by the resolution were:

Seventh and Eighth Avenue route.

Lexington Avenue route.

Third Avenue route.

Jerome Avenue route.

Fourth Avenue and Bensonhurst route in Brooklyn.

Tri-borough route, embracing the Third Avenue

route, a route over the Manhattan Bridge to Brooklyn and part of the Fourth Avenue route in that borough.

West Farms and White Plains route.

Accordingly the Rapid Transit Commission ordered the contracts prepared so that the work might be put up for public bidding. These routes embraced nearly 100 miles of road, and the estimated cost of construction was more than $181,000,000. Of the seven routes the Commission selected the Lexington Avenue route as the one to be first advertised. This route began at the Battery and ran up Greenwich street, Trinity Place, Vesey Street, Broadway, Fifth Avenue, 35th and 36th streets and Lexington Avenue to the Harlem River, where it was to divide into three branches, one through Park Avenue and 153d street to 164th street, another through Park Avenue to 156th street and the third through Morris Avenue to 149th street. There was also to be a spur connection from Lexington Avenue through 42d street to the first subway in Park Avenue. The total length was about fourteen miles and the cost of construction was estimated at about $30,000,000. On account of the narrow width of Lexington Avenue, it was decided to make the subway in that thoroughfare a double-deck structure, with the express tracks on the lower and the local tracks on the upper level, and plans were made accordingly. The board located the stations along the line, and by the opening of the year 1907 everything was in readiness to solicit proposals.

During the years 1905 and 1906 the Rapid Transit Commission devoted a great deal of time and work to "legalizing" various rapid transit routes, in other words to obtaining the consents of the city authorities and the abutting property owners required by the statute. This involved canvassing the property owners, and as these are numerous on every route it was a considerable task to interview them all. In many cases it was a bootless task, for often the required number of consents could not be obtained and then the work of canvassing went for naught and the board had to apply to the Appellate Division of the Supreme Court for the appointment of Commissioners to investigate and report whether the proposed line should be built and for the determination of the Court to that effect in lieu of the property owners' consents. The wonder is that so many routes were legalized by the Commission. The difficulty attending the procedure is thus described in the Commission's annual report for 1906:

"The fundamental conditions of rapid transit are such as inevitably to invite the opposition of property owners to every plan which promises extensive relief. The rapid transit situation can never be dealt with in a large way except by railways which will bring passengers to the places where their daily business is carried on; that is to say, in nine cases out of ten, to the lower part of Manhattan. In this locality the streets are crooked and often comparatively narrow. The value of property is generally extremely high. The necessity for easy and cheap transportation to the outlying parts of the city does not appeal to the selfish interests of property owners. And, therefore, while it has generally been easy to secure the requisite consents in Queens, the Bronx and Brooklyn, in Manhattan it has always proved impossible, in the case of any extended rapid transit road, to obtain voluntary consents, and applications to the courts are frequently opposed. In three such cases this Board has had to encounter the most earnest and prolonged opposition to its plans."

The laying out of new routes was undertaken by the board as soon as the contracts for the Manhattan-Bronx subway and the Brooklyn extension had been let. Within six months after the subway was opened to traffic the board adopted and submitted to the city authorities plans embracing nineteen separate routes, reaching every borough of the city except Richmond. It took two years more before the constitutional consents for these lines were obtained. The proposed system was characterized by the Court as "the most stupendous scheme of municipal improvement and expenditure ever undertaken, and without a parallel in its ultimate bearing upon the destiny of the people of what we have reason for thinking will be the greatest city in the world."

With the opening of the year 1906 Herman A. Metz succeeded Edward M. Grout as Controller and therefore supplanted him in the Rapid Transit board. Metz lived in Brooklyn and he quickly undertook to forward the transit interests of that borough. He brought before the board the project for the construction of an elevated railway loop on the Manhattan side of the East River to connect the Brooklyn, Williamsburg and Manhattan bridges and facilitate travel to Brooklyn. This project had been considered by the board the year before, but no action had been taken because the board believed that the problem of communication between the bridges could be settled by the building of subways, and that the sentiment of Manhattan was firmly and irrevocably opposed to the erection of any more elevated structures in the streets.

Controller Metz, however, held that the bridges should be connected by an elevated railroad in addition to such subways as might be built, and in July, 1906, brought the matter before the board. He urged an elevated road merely as a temporary expedient, to be torn down "as soon as the subway connection is completed and the congested points at the bridges are relieved". At a later date in July the Board of Estimate and Apportionment adopted a resolution asking the Rapid Transit Commission to consider whether it was for the interest of the public that an elevated loop be built, or whether the desired result could be obtained without placing any further elevated structures in the streets. The matter was referred to the Chief Engineer of the Commission, who reported a route for an elevated connection and also a subway route. Although the elevated plan was pressed by many, the board refused to change its attitude and finally adopted plans for a loop subway, running from the Brooklyn bridge up Centre street to Delancey street extension and through Delancey street extension to the Williamsburg bridge, with a spur at Canal street connecting with the Manhattan bridge. The routes adopted also provided for a line from Brooklyn bridge down William street to Wall street, another in Grand and Desbrosses streets from Centre street to Washington street, a third in Liberty and Washington streets from William to Desbrosses street, and a fourth in Washington street, Greenwich street, Fourteenth street, University Place, Washington Square East, Wooster street and Canal street to Centre street.

On the Brooklyn side of the East River the loop subway was to run from Brooklyn bridge through Washington street to Fulton street, through Fulton, Willoughby streets and Flatbush Avenue Extension to Fulton street again, through Fulton to Lafayette Avenue, through Lafayette to Bedford Avenue, through Bedford Avenue and its extension to the Williamsburg bridge.

It being impossible to obtain consents for the Manhattan portion of the loop line, the board applied to the Appellate division and obtained a determination in lieu of such consents. It was decided to advertise for bids for construction only, leaving the question of operator for later decision. Bids for the Manhattan sections were received and the contracts awarded to the lowest bidders in the spring of 1907.

It was in June, 1907 that the last of these contracts were awarded, and the Commission went out of existence on June 30.

During the year 1906 the subway tunnel under Wash-

ington Heights was completed and in March was placed
in operation from 157th street and Broadway to the banks
of the Harlem Ship Canal. Here the terminus remained
while the old bridge at that point was replaced by a
double deck structure, as described in another chapter.
The replacement was effected in June, 1906, when the
subway trains were operated across it. The station on
the north side of the bridge, known as 225th street, remained the terminus for nearly two years, or until the
Van Cortlandt Park extension was built. This extension
carried the line nearly a mile further north. It was built
by the Rapid Transit Subway Construction Company
as extra work under its contract. The route was approved by the Appellate Division of the Supreme Court
in July, 1906, although the formal order was not entered
until the following October. The Rapid Transit Commission and the company agreed on the amount of
$675,000 as the cost of the extension, and this was ap-
proved by the Board of Estimate and Apportionment on
November 23, 1906. Work was begun immediately and
completed in the early part of 1908, when the extension
was opened to traffic.

Before the subway had been in operation one year
complaints as to inadequate service were made to the
Commission. As traffic grew these complaints increased
in number, and in March, 1906, the Commission appointed
a sub-committee of two members and the Chief Engineer
to investigate the question of service. The contract with
the city provided that the operating company should
"meet all reasonable requirements of the public in respect of the frequency and character of its railway service to the full limit of the capacity of the railroad." This
committee found the service defective in certain particulars and so reported on March 22, 1906. It is interesting to note from this report that the company was
then running eight car express trains in the rush hours
and five car express trains in the middle of the day and

late at night. The committee found that the express service was inadequate on Sundays and recommended that the company operate seven or eight car trains instead of five car trains during the whole day; also that eight car trains be operated on the express tracks on week days all day long, and that the local train service during the rush hours should be increased. These suggestions were transmitted to the company, which at once put them into effect.

Additional means of ventilating the subway along the trunk line from Brooklyn Bridge to 96th street were provided during the year 1906. In the summer of 1905 many complaints were made of the excessive heat and poor air. The Rapid Transit Commission retained Professor George A. Soper, of Columbia University, to make a further study of air conditions. He made an investigation covering the last five months of 1905 and reported that, while the air in the subway was hotter than the air in the streets in summer, it was not deleterious to health and would not have any bad effects if proper sanitary precautions were taken to keep the subway free from dust and odors.

The engineers of the Commission made a careful study of the ventilation problem. They found that before operation began the subway was cooler in summer and warmer in winter than the streets. After trains began running the opposite condition was found to prevail in summer, the air in the subway being from five to ten degrees warmer than that in the streets above. This increase in temperature was caused by the friction of train movement, the grinding of brakes etc. and to a small degree to the animal heat thrown off by the many passengers. While the air was renewed often enough to be sanitary, it was believed that more frequent renewals would improve it as well as the ventilation. Accordingly the engineers, with the consent of the Commission, caused a number of additional ventilating cham-

bers to be constructed between stations, fourteen between
Brooklyn Bridge and Fifty-ninth street. In these and in
the existing chambers constructed when the subway was
built they installed blowers and louvres, for the purpose
of facilitating the escape of air from and ingress of fresh
air into the subway. The louvres were simply large iron
shutters hung on axles so that they normally remained
closed but were forced open by the rush of air caused by
the passage of trains. At stations, too, some of the vault
lights were removed and replaced by ventilating gratings.
The effect of these improvements was felt during the next
summer, when the heat in the subway was found to be
much less than in the previous year.

An experimental cooling plant also was installed in
the Brooklyn Bridge station. Two artesian wells were
sunk and the water from them was pumped into a series
of pipes installed on each side of the station. Air is
pumped through these pipes in counter current to the
water, becoming cooled in the passage, and is then delivered to the station platforms by ducts overhead. This
device worked satisfactorily, and tests in warm weather
showed that it kept the temperature in the station about
five degrees lower than it was on the street, whereas it
had been seven degrees higher during the previous summer.

CHAPTER XV

THE year 1907 will be forever memorable in the transit annals of New York City, for it marked the passing of the Board of Rapid Transit Railroad Commissioners and the creation of the Public Service Commissions, one of which (the First District Commission) was charged with the old board's powers and duties in respect of rapid transit construction.

Why the change? The reader of history may well ask that question, for it is only answerable by those who lived at the time and witnessed one of the curious phenomena of free government. One would suppose that the Rapid Transit Commission, having triumphed over so many difficulties and successfully built the first subway, would have been crowned with laurel by their contemporaries and continued indefinitely in their official places. Yet precisely the opposite transpired. Instead of being commended, they were condemned, not because they had not done well with the first subway, but because it was such a great success that they had not multiplied it fast enough to suit those who, now that underground travel was a demonstrated success, clamored for new underground roads all over the city! Because the old board had not ended the crush at the Brooklyn Bridge, because it had not built subways into Brooklyn, and Queens and in other parts of Manhattan, it was denounced by the press, which clamored for its abolition.

Giving all due credit to the old Commission, it must be said in fairness that there was some ground for complaint. It procrastinated unduly, deliberating and negotiating when it should have been acting. But it did not deserve the odium heaped upon it. However, a public sentiment against it was created and it had to go. Com-

plaints against the board became so frequent, criticism of
its inaction so vociferous that it got a bad name. Before
the subway which it had brought into being was two
years old, demands in and out of the press were being
made for its removal.

Denunciation was at its height when Charles E.
Hughes, elected Governor in 1906, began his career as a
public officer in January, 1907. To impress upon him the
need of action in the transit field, a committee of Brooklyn men invited him to "come and see for himself" the
horrors of the crush at the Brooklyn Bridge. The Governor came, saw and was conquered. He assured the
Brooklynites that he would do something to end such
conditions, and he kept the promise. With his advisors
the Governor set to work to devise an agency which in
the name of the State should supervise and regulate the
corporations performing a public service under franchises
granted by the public. The result was the Public Service
Commissions act, which passed the Legislature of 1907
and was approved by the Governor as soon as passed.
This law created two commissions of five men each, to
be appointed by the Governor by and with the consent
of the State Senate, and gave them the power to supervise and regulate railroad and street railroad companies,
gas and electric light companies etc. both as to their
finances and the service rendered. One commission was
given jurisdiction over the First District, comprising the
City of New York, and the other over the Second District,
embracing the rest of the State. The law also repealed
the act creating the Board of Rapid Transit Railroad
Commissioners and devolved their duties on the Public
Service Commission for the First District. As this rapid
transit work was entirely for the benefit of New York
City, it was provided that the expenses of this commission, save and except the salaries of the five commissioners, the Secretary and Chief Counsel, should be paid
by the City. To attract a fit type of men the salaries of

PUBLIC SERVICE COMMISSION, FIRST DISTRICT,
1907 — 1911

1. John E. Eustis;   2. Milo R. Maltbie;
3. Chairman William R. Willcox;
4. Edward M. Bassett;   5. William McCarroll.

the commissioners were fixed at $15,000 a year each, that of the Secretary at $6,000 and that of Counsel at $10,000. These salaries amounted to $91,000 for each commission. In the Second District all other expenses are paid by the State out of appropriations made by the Legislature; in the First District all other expenses were paid out of the City Treasury. The law was amended in 1916 so as to make payable by the state all expenses of the Commission for the First District except those incurred for rapid transit purposes which were continued as a charge against the City.

The act took effect July 1, 1907, and on that day the First District Commission appointed by Governor Hughes met and organized. It was composed of William R. Willcox, of Manhattan, a lawyer, former Park Commissioner and at the time of his appointment Postmaster of New York; William McCarroll, a business man of Brooklyn; Edward M. Bassett, a lawyer and former member of Congress, of Brooklyn; Milo R. Maltbie, of Manhattan, then Secretary of the Municipal Art Commission; and John E. Eustis, of the Bronx, a lawyer and former Park Commissioner of that borough. Willcox, McCarroll and Eustis were Republicans; Bassett and Maltbie Democrats.

By the terms of the law the new commission took over the staff of the old Rapid Transit board, and the work of the engineers went along, with scarcely any interruption. Additions to the staff were made as rapidly as possible, and in the selections little if any attention was paid to political considerations. The men were chosen for fitness and competency alone. The first appointment made was that of Secretary, and for that position the Commission chose Travis H. Whitney, a lawyer, a Republican and at the time Secretary of the Citizens' Union. He remained Secretary of the First District Commission for nearly nine years and was appointed a member of the Commission by Governor Whitman in 1916

Abel E. Blackmar, now a Justice of the Supreme Court, was appointed Counsel but he served only one year, when he was appointed and later elected to the Supreme Court bench. He was succeeded by George S. Coleman, who served until 1917, when he was succeeded by William L. Ransom, the present incumbent.

For a time George S. Rice, Chief Engineer of the old board, acted in similar capacity for the commission, but in 1908 he was succeeded by Henry B. Seaman, who served until 1910, when he resigned and Alfred Craven, the Deputy Chief Engineer of the old board, became Acting and later Chief Engineer of the commission, a position he held until 1916 when he was made Consulting Engineer and Daniel L. Turner was appointed Chief Engineer. The Commission fixed the salary of the Chief Engineer at $15,000 and it remained at this figure until 1913, when it was increased to $20,000. In 1916 it was again made $15,000.

One of the first acts of the new Commission was to inaugurate the Interborough-Metropolitan investigation. Clothed with inquisitorial powers by the Legislature and having authority to examine books of account and compel the attendance of witnesses, the Commission immediately received requests for an inquiry into the famous merger. It adopted a resolution for such an investigation and retained the late William M. Ivins, a leading member of the bar, to act as special counsel for the inquiry. Hearings began in August and continued until October, 1907. Officers of the Interborough and Metropolitan companies were examined under oath, and soon the precarious financial condition of the surface lines was exposed. The testimony showed that some of the subsidiary companies of the Metropolitan street railway system had been taken over at extravagant rentals; that others were excessively capitalized; that dividends had been paid out of funds not derived from earnings and that money had been wasted in a variety of ways.

Toward the close of the investigation creditors of the New York City Railway Company, the company which operated the surface lines for the Metropolitan, filed petitions in court alleging insolvency and asking for the appointment of receivers. The petitions were granted and the company went into the hands of receivers, Adrian H. Joline and Douglas Robinson being appointed. Later Frederick W. Whitridge was named separate receiver for the Third Avenue Railroad Company and its subsidiaries. For three years and more the properties underwent rehabilitation and reorganization, emerging finally as the New York Railways Company, which took over the old Metropolitan lines, and the Third Avenue Railway Company, which took over the lines of the Third Avenue Railroad Company. Complete new equipments were purchased and the properties put in first class operating shape.

It was during this investigation that the word "acceleration" was coined into a local meaning. Lemuel E. Quigg, who handled for the Ryan-Whitney interests the publicity campaign in support of the Metropolitan offer to build subways for free transfers to and from the surface lines, was examined as to the methods he employed. He told how he had caused the organization of various civic associations to meet and pass resolutions in favor of the Ryan subway offer; also of hiring lawyers and others to appear at public meetings to advocate the cause.

"Did you do anything more?" was one of the questions asked him in this connection by Mr. Ivins.

"Yes", replied Mr. Quigg, "I even wrote some of the speeches with which they confounded the arguments of our opponents."

At another time Mr. Ivins asked whether he did all this to influence public sentiment.

"Not so much to influence it, as to accelerate it; I think accelerate is the proper word", replied the witness.

The press and public seized on the new word as a

fitting designation of the effective form of influence employed, and "acceleration" since has been resorted to by numerous parties who sought to influence or arouse public or official sentiment in their favor.

The new board at once began a study of the rapid transit situation, with the view of affording relief at the earliest possible time. It had inherited from the old board four different rapid transit projects—the Brooklyn extension of the first subway; the Van Cortlandt Park Extension of the Broadway branch of the subway; the Centre Street loop subway and the Fourth Avenue (Brooklyn) subway. It wisely determined to push these projects to completion while devising plans for further amplification of facilities.

Both the Brooklyn and Van Cortlandt Park extensions were in course of construction when the new Commission came into existence. Work on both was continued under the new regime and pushed to successful completion.

The other two projects were not so far advanced. Contracts for the construction of the Centre Street loop subway had been awarded by the old board, as told in the preceding chapter, but actual work had not been started. The new Commission made radical changes in the plans, enlarging the bore of the subway by providing for a height of fifteen feet as against thirteen feet and for a width of fifteen instead of twelve feet for each track. It also reduced some of the heavy grades provided for in the old plans. The contractors accepted the revised plans and proceeded with the construction of the subway.

In the case of the Fourth Avenue subway in Brooklyn matters were even less advanced. The old board had adopted the route and general plan for this line, which was to run from the Centre Street loop subway in Manhattan over the Manhattan Bridge, under Flatbush Avenue Extension to Fulton Street, under Fulton Street to

Fourth Avenue and under Fourth Avenue to Fort Hamilton. It was found that two tracks of the first subway occupied a part of this route in Fulton Street and if made part of the proposed Fourth Avenue line would make it difficult for any company other than the Interborough, the operator of the first subway, to operate it. The new Commission, wishing to produce a line which would be attractive to an independent company, modified the route by diverting it from Fulton Street around through Ashland Place and thence into Fourth Avenue, thus avoiding the Interborough tracks. Meanwhile it had held public hearings on the route and started its engineers to work on detail plans.

At the same time a study was made of the situation in Manhattan and the Bronx, with the view of laying out a new subway. This study was completed during the first six months, and on December 31, 1907, the Commission adopted the Broadway-Lexington Avenue route. This was a combination of routes adopted by the old board, with some modifications. As adopted by the new Commission the Broadway-Lexington Avenue route began at the Battery, ran up Greenwich street to Vesey street, through Vesey to Broadway and up Broadway as far as Ninth street, where it turned eastward through private property to Irving Place, ran up Irving Place into Lexington Avenue and up Lexington Avenue to Harlem River; under the Harlem River by tunnel to Park Avenue and 138th street, the Bronx, where it divided into two branches, one running up Mott, River, Gerard and Jerome Avenues to Woodlawn Road, and the other through 138th street, Southern Boulevard and Westchester Avenue to Pelham Bay Park.

While the engineers were preparing detail plans for this route the Commission studied the financial situation, for the City was close to its constitutional debt limit of ten per cent. of the assessed value of the realty within its boundaries and could not at the time provide funds for such an extensive piece of work. It was estimated that the construction of the Broadway-Lexington route would cost about $50,000,000. As a beginning or path-finder, the Commission decided to advertise for bids for the construction of a part of the Fourth Avenue subway in Brooklyn, estimated to cost about $16,000,000. Advertising was begun in February, 1908, and bids were opened in March for six sections, extending from Manhattan Bridge to Fourth Avenue and Forty-third street, Brooklyn. In May awards were made for the six sections to the lowest bidder in each case, and the contracts were sent to the Board of Estimate and Apportionment.

A Democratic administration controlled the city. George B. McClellan was Mayor and Herman A. Metz Controller. Both had been ex-officio members of the Rapid Transit Commission, and neither looked with particular favor on the new Commission, appointed by a Republican Governor and having a Republican majority. They naturally regarded the building of rapid transit lines in the city a purely local function and did not like to see it entrusted to a State Commission over which the City authorities not only had no control but in which they had not even a representation. The new law provided that all the expenses of the new Commission, aside from the salaries of Commissioners, Secretary and Counsel, should be paid by the City of New York, and yet the City was denied any control of or supervision over such expenses. The Commission was authorized to draw on the Board of Estimate and Apportionment for such expenses, and if the bill were not paid was empowered to apply to the Court to compel payment.

The Fourth Avenue subway contracts were the subject of the first difference. Controller Metz, who in the Rapid Transit Board had been the staunch friend of the Fourth Avenue project, now took a decided stand against it. The contracts as transmitted by the Public Service Commission, were referred to him for certification, and he reported to the Board of Estimate and Apportionment that they proposed to commit the City to an expenditure of $16,000,000, and that the City was so close to the debt limit that he could not certify the contracts. Jefferson M. Levy brought a tax-payer's action for an injunction to restrain the Board of Estimate and the Controller from approving the contracts on account of the City's financial condition. A temporary order was served and action on the contracts was postponed pending the report of Benjamin F. Tracy, whom the Court appointed referee to ascertain the exact borrowing capacity of the City as of June 30, 1908.

About a year later the referee reported that the City on the date named had a clear margin of about $54,000,-000, which of course was more than ample to finance the construction of the Fourth Avenue subway. The matter was taken to the Court of Appeals, however, and that tribunal in October, 1909, confirmed the referee's findings. The temporary injunction was immediately dissolved, and the administration, just then facing a general election for new City officers, made haste to approve the contracts and appropriate the necessary funds. Upon this action the Public Service Commission asked the contractors who had put in the lowest bids for the six sections of the work in May, 1908, whether they were prepared to carry out the contracts on the figures then submitted, and on receiving affirmative answers proceeded to execute the contracts. Ground was broken with appropriate ceremonies on November 12, 1909, in Flatbush Avenue Extension, Brooklyn, on one of the contracts of the Bradley Contracting Company, William R. Willcox, chairman of the Public Service Commission turning the first shovel-full of earth. Thereafter the work continued without serious interruption to completion.

Meanwhile the Public Service Commission was seeking in every way to clear the pathway for additional sub-

way building. Two courses were open—to increase the
City's borrowing capacity and to get the law amended
so that investment in rapid transit leases would be more
attractive to private capital than it was under the Elsberg amendment which limited such leases to twenty
years. The Commission found that bonds issued for
water works were excluded by the State constitution
from the obligations considered in figuring the debt
limit, and that this exemption was made because the
works were self-supporting properties. There was equal
reason, therefore, for exempting the bonds issued for
the construction of docks and the city subway, which
were also self-supporting. Accordingly the Commission
drafted and sent to the Legislature of 1908 an amendment to the constitution providing for the exemption of
bonds issued for the docks and the subway.

The promptness with which this was done speaks well
for the Public Service Commission. Organized on July
1, 1907, it had not been in office six months when it dis-
closed the weakness of the city in the matter of borrowing
capacity and applied the obvious remedy. Its action
later made possible the undertaking of rapid transit
expansion on an extensive scale. Constitutional amendments must pass two sessions of the Legislature and then
be approved by a vote of the people at a general election
before becoming effective, and this amendment was approved successively by the sessions of 1908 and 1909.
In the latter year it was submitted to popular vote and
duly approved, and the Legislature of 1910 passed the
legislation necessary to put it into effect. The immediate
result was the expanding of the borrowing capacity of
the City of New York by an amount estimated at $120,-
000,000, and thanks to the prompt action of the new
Commission this came at the very time when it was
imperatively needed to enable the City to embark upon
a generous policy of rapid transit expansion.

During the same period the Commission formulated

and sent to Albany many amendments to the Rapid Transit act drafted with the view of lessening the rigors of that statute. The twenty years' lease clause was repealed and instead the Public Service Commission was empowered to make leases of city-owned rapid transit lines for any period deemed advisable. The most important of these amendments were passed in the sessions of 1909 and 1912. In the popular mind it is doubtful if the Commission received any credit for these legislative achievements, yet their importance is unquestionable. Without them and the constitutional change the city would have been absolutely unable to enter upon the comprehensive scheme of subway building later undertaken.

While these matters were pending in the Legislature the new Commission continued its study of the transit situation and sought to devise a comprehensive plan for rapid transit extension in all boroughs of the city. Having adopted the Broadway-Lexington Avenue route for Manhattan and the Bronx, it tried to adapt certain routes in Brooklyn for connection with it. Thus the so-called Tri-borough plan was evolved early in 1908. The City had spent millions in building the Williamsburg and Manhattan bridges over the East River, and as yet these bridges were giving no rapid transit service. The Commission wisely decided to put them into use in the new rapid transit system, and made them links in the Tri-borough chain to connect Manhattan and Brooklyn lines. On the Brooklyn side it adopted the Fourth Avenue subway running to Fort Hamilton and Coney Island, and the Broadway-Lafayette subway running from the Williamsburg bridge out Broadway, Brooklyn, to Lafayette Avenue and back through Lafayette Avenue to a junction with the Fourth Avenue subway at Fulton street. The Williamsburg and Manhattan bridges were to be used to connect these lines with the Centre Street loop subway in Manhattan. In 1908 and 1909 the engineers of the Commission prepared detail plans for this system, which, it was estimated, would add 45 miles of new road and cost about $147,000,000.

While the plans were being prepared the Commission sought to ascertain whether any private company would join the city in the new enterprise. Immediately after the Legislature of 1909 passed the amendments to the Rapid Transit act eliminating the twenty years' lease provision the Commission invited proposals from all the prominent street railroad companies. It held large ideas as to the extent of the rapid transit improvements which should be made and felt that, even with the enlarged debt limit, the City would not be able at once to provide all the funds required. Consequently it sought to get private companies who might become bidders for a lease of such lines to contribute out of their own funds toward the cost of construction.

On June 30, 1909, the Interborough Rapid Transit Company submitted a proposal to build third tracks on the Second, Third and Ninth Avenue elevated lines, to lengthen station platforms in the first subway so that ten car express and six car local trains might be operated and to build certain extensions of the subway with its own money, provided the City would authorize their construction as "extra work" under the original McDonald contract for the first subway. The company offered the City the option of building the new subway extensions with its own funds or having them built at the company's expense and operated at a fixed rental like the first subway or under a profit sharing arrangement by dividing profits with the City after paying operating expenses and other costs. In return the company asked for a lease of the new lines to be coterminous with the existing lease of the first subway, which would expire in 1954, and for practically perpetual franchises for the elevated railroad additions.

This proposal provided for the extension of the subway from Forty-second street up Lexington and Third

Avenues to and under the Harlem River to a junction with the first subway at 149th street; the extension of the subway on the West Side of Manhattan south from Times Square through Seventh Avenue, Varick Street and West Broadway, Canal Street and the Manhattan Bridge to a junction with the first subway in Brooklyn and two tracks south of Canal Street to Battery Park; also to extend the Sixth and Ninth Avenue elevated line from 149th Street across McCombs Dam bridge and up Jerome Avenue in the Bronx to 194th Street; to extend the Second Avenue elevated road across the Queensboro bridge to Long Island City, and finally to sell to the City and to operate as part of the subway system the Steinway tunnel, owned by Interborough interests, already built under the East River from 42d Street, Manhattan, to Long Island City, in Queens Borough.

The Commission gave long and serious consideration to this offer, but finally rejected it on August 27, 1909, for various reasons, chiefly because it did not provide for an adequate scheme of extension. The Commission in its letter to the company, however, plainly indicated its willingness to consider a further proposal which would more adequately meet the needs of the City. This was the beginning of an exchange of correspondence between the Commission and the company, which lasted for two years. Conferences accompanied the passage of letters, and steady progress was made, although at times the differences between the parties seemed to be irreconcilable.

While these negotiations were being carried on a momentous change and one having an immediate bearing on the rapid transit situation occurred in the City government. In the election of 1909 William J, Gaynor was elected Mayor, and while he was the Tammany candidate, the other City officers and the members of the Board of Estimate and Apportionment were elected by the Fusion forces. The new Board of Estimate, which organized in

January 1910, consisted of William J. Gaynor, Mayor; William A. Prendergast, Controller; John Purroy Mitchel, President of the Board of Aldermen; George McAneny, Borough President of Manhattan; A. E. Steers, Borough President of Brooklyn; Cyrus C. Miller, Borough President of the Bronx; Lawrence Gresser, Borough President of Queens, and George Cromwell, Borough President of Richmond. Mr. Gresser was later succeeded as Borough President of Queens by Maurice E. Connolly.

With the advent of the new government the official atmosphere cleared. The new Board of Estimate adopted an attitude of friendliness and co-operation toward the Public Service Commission, and thereafter both boards worked in harmony. The Board of Estimate appointed a special Transit Committee consisting of McAneny, Miller and Cromwell, and this committee worked hand in hand with the Public Service Commission and actively participated in the conferences and negotiations which marked the years 1910 and 1911 as particularly notable for rapid transit progress.

Following the rejection of the Interborough proposal of 1909, the Commission resolved to bring matters to a focus by advertising for bids for the Tri-Borough system, as above outlined. While the engineers were busy preparing detail plans, counsel to the Commission under its direction proceeded to draft the necessary contracts. To test the attitude of private capital toward sharing the construction cost or assuming it altogether, the Commission drew up two different forms of contract—one providing for construction, equipment and operation by the bidder, in other words a private capital contract, and the other contract for construction alone, the City to bear the cost and to provide an operator later. The contracts were completed during the summer, the required public hearings were held, the detail plans were finished and on September 1, 1910, the Commission began adver-

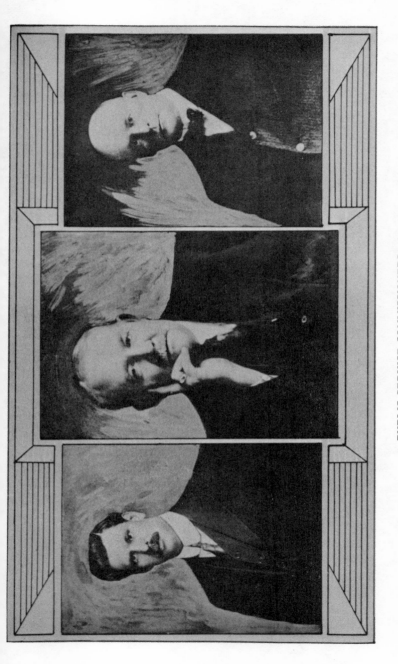

PUBLIC SERVICE COMMISSIONERS 1913.

1. George V. S. Williams. 2. Edward E. McCall, Chairman. 3. J. Sergeant Cram.
Milo R. Maltbie and John E. Eustis Were the Other Members.

tising for bids. The bids under the private capital form were set for opening on October 20 and those under the municipal construction form for October 27.

When October 20 came not one bid was received under the form of contract for construction, equipment and operation by private capital, but on October 27 several responsible contractors submitted bids for the construction of various parts of the system. While the private capital contract covered the whole Tri-Borough system, the other form embraced only the Broadway-Lexington Avenue line, the Broadway-Lafayette Avenue line and the Canal Street line, for the reason that the city's funds were limited and it was thought prudent to limit the extent of the bidding to an amount to which it would be safe to commit the City.

While the failure to receive bids for private capital construction was a disappointment, it was not an unexpected result. The Interborough company, which was the most likely bidder, preferred other routes to those embraced in the Tri-Borough system and also objected to the terms of the contract, which were deemed too onerous by the operating company. The Commission, therefore, felt that it would be wise to await another proposal from the company, which indicated that it was ready to make another offer. No action, therefore, was taken on the construction bids received October 27, but they were held under advisement.

The Hudson and Manhattan Railroad Company, which operated the so-called McAdoo tunnels under the Hudson River, was then under the management of Hon. William G. McAdoo, who later became Secretary of the Treasury under President Wilson. Mr. McAdoo took up the Tri-Borough matter, and early in November 1910, shortly after the bids were opened, his company submitted to the Public Service Commission a proposition to equip and operate the whole Tri-Borough system if constructed by the City and connected with the Hudson and Manhattan line.

This offer spurred the Interborough company to further effort, and on December 5, 1910, that company made another proposal, which came so near to meeting the views of the Commission as to the needed extensions that it changed the whole aspect of the situation. While it was under consideration the Hudson and Manhattan company, in accordance with a time limit placed in its letter, withdrew its proposal, leaving only the Interborough offer before the Commission.

This proposal offered to construct certain extensions of the subway to cost $128,000,000, providing the City would contribute $53,000,000 thereof, the extensions to be as follows:

Down Seventh Avenue from Times Square, down Varick street, West Broadway and Greenwich street to the Battery, with a branch from Greenwich street through Liberty street, under the East River to Pineapple street, Brooklyn, and through Pineapple and Fulton streets to a junction with the terminus of the first subway, and an extension from that terminus under Flatbush Avenue to Eastern Parkway and through Eastern Parkway to Buffalo Avenue; also an extension under Lafayette Avenue from Flatbush Avenue to Broadway, Brooklyn.

Also an extension of the first subway from 35th street and Park Avenue under private property at 42d street to Lexington Avenue and up Lexington Avenue to and under the Harlem River to 138th street, whence one branch would run to a connection with the West Farms branch of the subway, and through Mott Avenue, 153d street, and River Avenue to 157th street, with an elevated extension up River Avenue to 162d street where a connection would be made with the proposed Jerome Avenue extension of the Ninth Avenue elevated railroad; another branch to run through 138th street, Southern

Boulevard and Whitlock Avenue to Westchester Avenue, continuing as an elevated road over Westchester Avenue to Pelham Bay Park.

Also an elevated extension of the West Farms branch of the subway from its terminus at 180th street out White Plains Road to Gun Hill road, where it would connect with the proposed extension of the Third Avenue elevated line.

It was also proposed that the company should turn over to the City the Steinway tunnel, providing the City would complete it at a cost estimated at $1,500,000. Included in the offer also was the company's previous proposal to add a third track to the Second, Third and Ninth Avenue elevated lines and extend the Ninth Avenue line across the Harlem River and up Jerome Avenue to 194th street—all at its own expense.

The so-called Steinway tunnel was about completed when the Public Service Commission was created in 1907. It was projected by William Steinway, later Rapid Transit Commissioner, who got a charter for it from the Legislature. This charter was acquired by the New York and Long Island Railroad company, the stock of which was acquired by the Interborough Rapid Transit company, which supplied most of the funds to build the line. Its charter required that it should be in operation by January 1, 1907, but it was not completed by that date, and the City of New York brought suit and had its franchise to operate declared void. The courts, however, held that the title to the physical property remained in the trustees of the New York and Long Island Railroad company, through whom the Interborough company proposed to turn it over to the City for completion. It runs from 42d street, Manhattan, from a point between Lexington and Third Avenues, under 42d street and the East River to Jackson and Van Alst Avenues, Long Island City, in Queens. In 1908 the Interborough company placed its cost up to that time at about $8,000,000. This included nearly $900,000 paid for real estate.

CHAPTER XVI

DUAL SYSTEM OF RAPID TRANSIT ADOPTED BY COMMISSION AND BOARD OF ESTIMATE.

AFTER subjecting the Interborough offer of December, 1910, to rigid scrutiny, the Commission came to the conclusion that, with some slight amendment, it would be a satisfactory one for the City to accept, and accordingly transmitted a copy of it to the Board of Estimate and Apportionment, with a letter indicating the Commission's attitude. The law did not require its submission to the Board of Estimate in advance of the Commission's approval, but the Commission had decided to co-operate with the City government in all ways and desired the latter to be thoroughly informed of every step taken in planning for rapid transit extensions for which the City would have to pay. It went further and invited the Board of Estimate to confer with it and to participate in its conferences with the Interborough company. The invitation was accepted, that Board, as before mentioned, designating a special Committee—Messrs. McAneny, Miller and Cromwell—to represent it. Then began a series of conferences which were to culminate in the adoption of the Dual System of Rapid Transit. Results showed the wisdom of this conciliatory policy, for thereafter both boards worked with perfect, mutual understanding, and as representatives of the City presented a united front to the private companies seeking rapid transit franchises.

These conferences started with only the offer of the Interborough company under consideration, but before they had progressed very far the field was widened by the receipt by the Commission of an offer from the Brooklyn Rapid Transit Company, which operated the elevated railroads in Brooklyn and Queens, to equip and operate certain new subways if built by the City, both

CITY OFFICIALS WHO APPROVED DUAL
SYSTEM CONTRACTS

1. William J. Gaynor, Mayor in 1913.

2. William A. Prendergast,
Comptroller in 1913.

in Manhattan and Brooklyn, provided the City would give it the rights to build certain extensions of and additions to its elevated roads, and to operate all of them as one system.

This proposal was dated March 2, 1911. In it the Brooklyn company suggested that the City build, in addition to the Tri-Borough lines, a new subway running from the Battery up Church street to Broadway, up Broadway to 42d street and thence up Seventh Avenue to Fifty-ninth street, with an extension easterly to a connection with the Queensborough bridge; also that the City construct another tunnel under the East River from the vicinity of the Battery to connect with the proposed Broadway subway in Manhattan and with the Fourth Avenue subway in Brooklyn; that the Fourth Avenue subway be connected with four rapid transit lines extending southward and eastward, of which one was to be an extension of the company's Third Avenue elevated line to Fort Hamilton, another a four track elevated railroad on New Utrecht Avenue from 39th street to 52d street with a two track extension from there over the old West End route to Coney Island; a third to be a three track elevated railroad over the Sea Beach railroad right of way from 62d street to Coney Island and the fourth a two track elevated road over the old Culver line down Gravesend Avenue from Tenth Avenue to Coney Island —the work to include the elimination of all grade crossings on all these former steam railroads.

It was also proposed that the City build a tunnel under New York Bay to connect the Fourth Avenue subway in Brooklyn with Staten Island; also that the Fourth Avenue subway be extended through Flatbush Avenue to Prospect Park Circle, there dividing into two branches, one continuing out Flatbush Avenue to a connection with the Brighton Beach railroad of the company's, and the other out Eastern Parkway to Pitkin Avenue, with an elevated extension from that point to a connection with the former Kings County Elevated line at Snediker Avenue.

The company also asked for the rights for a third track on its Fulton street, Broadway and Myrtle Avenue elevated railroads and to build the following extensions of elevated lines:

An extension of the Kings County line from the old City Line through Queens to Jamaica; a connection between the Myrtle Avenue and Broadway lines; the reconstruction of the Lutheran Cemetery surface line as an elevated road; and a new elevated line from the Williamsburg to the Queensborough bridge.

The company also asked for the use of the Centre Street loop subway in Manhattan and a connection between both Williamsburg and Manhattan bridges with the new Broadway subway in Manhattan.

The proposal suggested that the City should build the subways and that the company should equip and operate them, upon terms to be agreed upon, in connection with its elevated railroads, and that the reconstruction and extension of the latter should be paid for by the company. It offered to accept terms "not less favorable than those presented in any other offer now under consideration by your Commission and the Board of Estimate and Apportionment."

Probably nothing like the Dual System conferences ever had been held in New York City before, and certainly they will not be duplicated in the near future. A group of ten or a dozen men met around the big oak table in the committee room of the Public Service Commission on the fourteenth floor of the Tribune building at No. 154 Nassau Street—or rather on the thirteenth floor, for the Tribune skyscraper is one of the few big office buildings in the city which was planned with deference to the "13" superstition. It has no floor numbered 13, but the thirteenth floor is numbered 14. On this floor the offices of the Commissioners and Secretary were located, and the

room used for the conferences was a room fronting on
Spruce street and devoted to the meetings of the Committee of the Whole. If its old oak table could speak, it
would tell of many an interesting passage in the famous
negotiations when expenditures of hundreds of millions
of dollars were discussed as an ordinary business conference would discuss those of a few thousands.

Men of brains and financial might met around that
conference table. At the head sat William R. Willcox,
chairman of the Commission, usually flanked by George
McAneny, chairman of the Board of Estimate's Committee. Scattered around the sides were the other Commissioners, namely William McCarroll, Edward M. Bassett, Milo R. Maltbie and John E. Eustis; the other members of the Board of Estimate committee, Cyrus C. Miller
and George Cromwell; the representative of the Interborough company, usually Theodore P. Shonts, its president, infrequently August Belmont, the chairman of its
Executive Committee and often Richard Reid Rogers,
of its legal staff. After the Brooklyn Rapid Transit
company submitted its offer its president, Col. Timothy
S. Williams and its counsel, A. M. Williams and George
D. Yeomans took their seats at the conference table. A
few joint conferences were held, but usually Interborough matters and Brooklyn Rapid Transit matters were
discussed at different times. And many a battle royal
was fought. The companies were bent on getting the
best terms they could out of the City, and the City's rep-
representatives were demanding more than they
could get from the companies. So keen was this
competition that at the close, while each side felt that it
had made a good bargain it also felt keen regret that it
had been compelled to yield so much to the other. This
was well illustrated by Mr. Shonts after one of the final
conferences. He was asked if his company had conceded
certain points to the City's representatives and replied:
"I was fairly well dressed when I went into that

room, but they've taken away everything but my shirt, and they would have had that if we hadn't adjourned.''

The entrance of the Brooklyn company into the field was welcomed by the City. For some time the Commission had been trying to get it interested in rapid transit extension, but the old management of the company was averse to it. When Timothy S. Williams became president, however, its policy changed and he welcomed the opportunity which the plans of the Public Service Commission afforded to expand his system. His participation not only introduced competition into the situation, but it gave the City the desired opportunity to make the new system really comprehensive by fully developing the rapid transit field in Brooklyn and Queens as well as in Manhattan and the Bronx. One of the reasons for the rejection of the first Interborough proposition was that it did not do enough for Brooklyn, and the appearance of the Brooklyn company provided for a vast expansion of the Brooklyn lines.

Within six months after the conferences began all parties had agreed to the fundamentals of a scheme for rapid transit construction and operation. Considering the vastness of the project and the conflicting interests which were reconciled and joined in it, it was little short of wonderful that any agreement at all was reached and truly remarkable that it had been reached in such a short time. The result was mainly attributable to William R. Willcox and George McAneny, who were the leaders of the City's forces.

On June 5, 1911, the City's conferees sent to the Board of Estimate and Apportionment a report—now known as the Joint Report. This report recommended that, under contracts which should contain terms satisfactory to the City, certain new rapid transit lines should be built and owned by the City, with contributions toward

TRANSIT COMMITTEE OF BOARD OF
ESTIMATE AND APPORTIONMENT

1. George McAneny, President, Board of Aldermen;

2. George Cromwell, Borough President of Richmond;

3. Cyrus C. Miller, Borough President of the Bronx.

construction cost by the Interborough and Brooklyn companies, and that some of them should be leased for operation to the former and some to the latter. The fact that two companies were to be concerned caused the project to become known as the Dual Plan, and in a short time it was appropriately named the Dual System of Rapid Transit.

In substance this Joint Report provided that the Brooklyn company should operate the Fourth Avenue subway in Brooklyn, then under construction by the City, the Centre street loop subway in Manhattan already built by the City, and a new subway running from lower Manhattan up Broadway to about Fifty-ninth street, with proper connections with the Brooklyn lines, and should make certain extensions of its elevated roads in Brooklyn and Queens, the whole system to be linked together and operated under contract with the City for a five cent fare.

It also provided that the Interborough company should operate the various extensions of the first subway, to be built jointly by the City and the company—each contributing half the cost, but the ownership to remain in the City. These extensions included practically all of the Tri-Borough system north of Forty-second street, Manhattan, a line down Seventh Avenue from Times Square, a new tunnel under the East River and the extension of the first subway through Eastern Parkway, Brooklyn, to Buffalo Avenue, thence by elevated extension through East 98th street and Livonia Avenue to New Lots Road, with a branch down Nostrand Avenue; all of these extensions to be operated under contract with the City as a part of the first subway and for a five cent fare. In addition it was provided that the Interborough with its own money should add a third track to the Second, Third and Ninth Avenue elevated lines and build certain extensions of those lines; also that the company should turn over to the City the Steinway tunnel and operate it as part of the subway.

The report laid down certain terms to which each of the companies must agree if the City were to undertake the building of the lines proposed. Among them were: that the rate of fare on each company's system, including transfers, must be five cents; that the term of lease for the City-owned subway lines should be forty-nine years; that the City have the right of recaption at any time after ten years; that the City should share equally with the companies in the surplus profits of all lines owned by the City; that the City should retain the right of supervision over all contracts and over the accounting systems. It was also proposed that the existing leases of the Interborough company for the first subway should be "leveled" so as to expire at the same time as the new leases. The City was also to share equally with the Interborough company in the net profits of the elevated lines in excess of the average net profits on existing lines for the two years from July 1, 1909, to June 30, 1911.

It was also provided that a "preferential" payment out of the earnings should be made to the Brooklyn company to represent "its net profits from operation of the existing lines included in the agreement" as of the year ending June 30, 1911.

Under the proposed agreements the Joint Report estimated the division of cost as follows:

For construction—By the City $123,200,000; by the Interborough $54,800,000; by the Brooklyn company $26,400,000—a total of $204,400,000.

For equipment—By the Interborough $21,000,000; by the Brooklyn company $24,000,000—a total of $45,000,000. This made the cost of the entire system $249,400,000.

The Joint Report which was approved by the Board of Estimate and Apportionment, provided that, if either company refused to accept the terms offered by the City, the lines allotted to it should be offered to the other company upon the same terms. This provision unexpectedly came into use, for the Interborough company refused to accept the terms laid down in the Joint Report and on July 21, 1911, the Board of Estimate and Apportionment formally notified the Public Service Commission that it would approve contracts for the construction of the new subways provided for in the Joint Report, all for operation by the Brooklyn company, which had signified its willingness to take the lines offered to the Interborough company in addition to its own allotment.

This led to the immediate beginning of construction. It will be remembered that the Commission had received bids on October 27, 1910, for the construction of certain sections of the Lexington Avenue subway in Manhattan. Now the Commission communicated with some of the lowest bidders on such sections and found them still willing to accept the contracts on the figures then submitted. Accordingly the Commission proceeded to execute four contracts with the Bradley Contracting Company, the lowest bidder for as many sections of the Lexington Avenue line. The awards were made on July 5, 1911, just one month after the Joint Report had been submitted to the Board of Estimate and Apportionment. They were for the construction of a four track subway on Sections 6, 8, 10 and 11 of Route No. 5, the Broadway—Lexington Avenue line, covering the following parts:

Section 6, from 26th street to 40th street; Section 8, from 53d street to 67th street; Section 10, from 79th street to 93d street; Section 11, from 93d street to 106th street. The total contract prices for these four sections were $13,388,965.55.

The four contracts were approved by the Board of Estimate and Apportionment on July 21, 1911, and on July 31 ground was broken at Sixty-second street and Lexington Avenue with appropriate ceremonies and in the presence of thousands of citizens. The first shovelfull of earth was turned by William R. Willcox, chairman of the Commission, and addresses were made by him, George McAneny and others.

As fast as the Public Service engineers turned out the plans the Commission awarded construction contracts for other sections of the work, on the understanding that the Brooklyn company was to be the operator. On August 1 the contract for Section 12 of the Lexington Avenue subway was awarded to the Oscar Daniels Company for $2,825,740.74; on October 10 the contract for Section 15 of the same line to the Hagerty-Drummond Company for $3,820,129.75; on October 31 the contract for Section 13 to the Bradley Contracting Company for $4,071,416.50; on December 8 the contract for Section 9 to the Patrick McGovern Company for $1,961,997. This placed under contract all of the Lexington Avenue line from 53d street to 157th street, except the tunnels under the Harlem River (Section 14) which were let in May 1912 to Arthur McMullen and Olaf Hoff for $3,889,775.05.

Three of the Broadway sections of the same line were placed under contract early in 1912. In January the Commission awarded the contract for Section 3, in Broadway between Howard and Bleecker streets to the Underpinning and Foundation Company for $2,295,-086.50; the contract for Section 2, between Murray street and Canal street to the Degnon Contracting Company for $2,355,828.50, and in March the contract for Section 2A, between Canal and Howard streets, to the O'Rourke Engineering Construction Company for $912,351.60. Thus in nine months after the Interborough had withdrawn from the field the Commission had let contracts aggregating more than $35,000,000.

The withdrawal of the Interborough company, however, was not permanent. During the winter of 1911 and 1912 overtures were made to the Commission by Samuel Rea, then Vice-President of the Pennsylvania Railroad Company, for a resumption of negotiations with the Interborough company, for the reason that the Seventh Avenue subway if built would tap the Pennsylvania station at 33d street and for the benefit of his patrons Mr.

RAILROAD PRESIDENTS WHO SIGNED DUAL
SYSTEM CONTRACTS
1. Timothy S. Williams, New York Municipal
Railway Corporation. 2. Theodore P. Shonts,
Interborough Rapid Transit Company.

Rea wanted that line to connect with the first subway, instead of with the Brooklyn lines. Accordingly conferences with the Interborough company were resumed, and on February 27, 1912 it submitted a new offer, which was approved by the Public Service Commission and the special committee of the Board of Estimate and Apportionment. As the Brooklyn company was willing to forego its assumption of the Interborough lines of the Dual System, the committee on May 22, 1912 submitted to the Board of Estimate a report approving the last Interborough offer. This report gave to the Interborough for operation the lines alloted to it in the Joint Report of 1911 upon similar but somewhat modified terms. The supplemental report was adopted by the Board of Estimate, which notified the Commission that it would approve contracts with the two companies drawn in accordance with the terms of the report.

Meanwhile the Legislature was asked to amend the Rapid Transit Act so as to permit the City to enter into the proposed contracts, or rather to clear up certain provisions which left doubt as to the powers of the City. These amendments were incorporated in the Wagner Bill, which was passed by the 1912 session and approved by the Governor.

There was also an appeal to the courts. The Interborough and Brooklyn Rapid Transit companies had sought the aid of bankers to raise the large amounts of money which would be needed to finance the new undertakings should agreements be reached with the City, and the bankers, at least J. P. Morgan and Company to whom the Interborough had applied, insisted that there should be a judicial approval of the proposed contracts before they would agree to finance them. Accordingly in February, 1912, an action for injunction was brought by the Admiral Realty Company to restrain the Public Service Commission, the Board of Estimate and Apportionment and the two transportation companies from entering into

the proposed contracts. Similar actions were brought by
John R. Ryon and John J. Hopper, taxpayers. The three
actions were heard together and progressed as one case
through the courts.

The defendants demurred to the complaints and the
first argument, made before Supreme Court Justice Abel
E. Blackmar was upon the demurrer. The chief arguments
were made by Daniel P. Hays, of Hays, Hershfield and
Wolff for the Admiral Realty Company; by Clarence J.
Shearn for John J. Hopper; by Willard N. Baylis for
John R. Ryon; by George S. Coleman for the Public Service Commission; by Louis H. Hahlo, Assistant Corporation Counsel, for the City; by Richard Reid Rogers for
the Interborough company and by Charles A. Collin for
the Brooklyn Rapid Transit Company.

All the complaints alleged that the proposed contracts
would violate the constitution of the State of New York
for two main reasons:

First—That the proposed provisions for preferential
payments to the companies out of the earnings of a rapid
transit railroad owned by the City would constitute a
loan of the City's credit in violation of that part of Section 10 of Article VIII of the constitution reading:

"No county, city, town or village shall hereafter
give any money or property, or loan its money or
credit to or in aid of any individual, association or
corporation, or become directly or indirectly the
owner of stock in, or bonds of, any association or
corporation; nor shall any county, city, town or village be allowed to incur any indebtedness except for
county, city, town or village purposes. * * *"

Second—That the Rapid Transit Act, by virtue of
which the proposed contracts would be made, is a local
act and therefore in conflict with that part of Section 18
of Article III of the constitution which says:

"The Legislature shall not pass a private or local bill * * * granting to any corporation or individual the right to lay down railroad tracks * * *"

In the arguments and briefs counsel for the defendants relied largely on the decision of Judge Haight in the famous case of the Sun Publishing Company against the Mayor of New York, before alluded to, brought to restrain the building of the first subway. In that case the court held that the constitutional provision invoked "should be construed with reference to the evils it was intended to correct", and that the provision "was not intended to nor does it prohibit municipalities from constructing their own roads and paying therefor when necessary and authorized by the Legislature." Other cases also were cited. The Supreme Court sustained this view in the Admiral Realty and allied cases, for on April 3, 1912, Judge Blackmar upheld the demurrer and held the proposed contracts constitutional. The cases were appealed, but the decision was affirmed both by the Appellate Division and by the Court of Appeals, the decision of the latter being handed down on June 29, 1912.

Within the next seven months the Public Service Commission did a monumental piece of work in preparing and getting the assent of the two companies to the Dual System contracts. This work was done mainly by the law department of the Commission, and the formulating and actual drafting of the important agreements was the work of Assistant Counsel LeRoy T. Harkness.

While the drafting of the contracts was under way a political change in the State government occurred, which later had a bearing on the Dual System contracts. In the election of that year (1912) William Sulzer, Democrat, was elected Governor, succeeding John A. Dix. Dix, who was elected in 1910, was also a Democrat, and during his term of office the terms of two of the Public Service Commissioners expired—Edward M. Bassett and William

McCarroll, the former a Democrat, the latter a Republican. Dix appointed Democrats to succeed both, J. Sergeant Cram in Bassett's place and George V. S. Williams to succeed McCarroll. Shortly after Sulzer was inaugurated the term of William R. Willcox, Republican and chairman of the Commission from the beginning, expired, and the Governor named Edward E. McCall, a Democrat, and a Supreme Court judge, to succeed him.

Willcox, who had done so much to bring about the Dual System agreement, desired to complete the contracts and execute them before retiring from office. In this wholly natural ambition he had the cordial support of the Commission staff, which worked night and day to whip the contracts into final shape and get them approved by the two traction companies. Conferences were held morning, noon and night, sometimes at the Commission offices, sometimes at the Chairman's house and finally at rooms hired for the purpose in the Manhattan Hotel at 42d street and Madison Avenue. At this hotel the final touches were given, the proofs from the printer read and passed by the Commission and representatives of the companies.

Meanwhile a storm of attack and public criticism raged about the heads of the Commissioners. Certain newspapers denounced the contracts as vicious, declared the terms unduly favorable to the companies and correspondingly bad for the City and urged on the Governor the appointment in Willcox's place of a man who would upset the proposed agreements. And they received a measure of support, although there is little question that popular opinion was largely in favor of the contracts. In official life Milo R. Maltbie, a member of the Commission, and John Purroy Mitchel, President of the Board of Aldermen and a member of the Board of Estimate and Apportionment, opposed certain of the terms and finally the whole contracts.

It was in such an atmosphere that Willcox worked during the month of January, 1913, to get the contracts approved. In spite of the strong opposition he felt certain of a favorable vote both in the Commission and in the Board of Estimate and Apportionment if he could once get the contracts printed in a form that would be acceptable to all parties to them. And after all it was a mechanical obstacle which turned the scale. The final proofs were approved at the Manhattan Hotel at two o'clock one morning in January, 1913, and orders were given the printer to go ahead. It was then found that the press capacity of the printer who had set all the type was so limited that it would take a week or more for him to turn out the completed copies. A printer with the largest press rooms in the City was communicated with by telephone, in the small hours of the morning, and it was arranged that he should get the type of most of the contracts from the first printer and do the press work. The type was transferred the next day, and the presses began humming, but it was too late. The opposition, fearing Willcox's success, got out an injunction to prevent the approval of the contracts by the Commission. John J. Hopper brought a tax-payer's action to restrain the Commission from approving the contracts, on the ground, among others, that they involved a waste of public funds. This proceeding effectually tied the hands of the Commission and prevented approval of the contracts before Willcox's term expired on February 1, 1913.

On February 3 following Governor Sulzer appointed Edward E. McCall, then serving as a Justice of the Supreme Court in the First District, to succeed Willcox. Judge McCall did not wish to leave the bench, but yielded to urging and accepted the new appointment, which was immediately confirmed by the Senate. While the Hopper case was pending he entered upon a study of the subway contracts, and in a few weeks after his appointment the Court dismissed the application for an injunction, leaving the Commission free to act. Upon the request of

Clarence J. Shearn, attorney for Hopper, the Commission, which under Willcox had held the public hearings required by the statute in January, called additional public hearings, which were held at the City Hall during the month of February, and at which all opponents of the Dual System contracts had another chance to be heard. At these hearings John Purroy Mitchel, afterwards Mayor, opposed the contracts and George McAneny defended them.

A hitch occurred in February over one of the contracts —the certificate to the Manhattan Railway Company granting the rights to build and operate additional tracks on the elevated railroads in Manhattan and the Bronx owned by that company but under lease for 999 years to the Interborough company. The Manhattan company was controlled by George J. Gould, the son of Jay Gould, and he and his board of directors objected to the terms of the certificate. In this emergency the Commission drafted a new certificate made out to the Interborough company, the lessee, conveying the identical rights in the same terms to which the Manhattan company objected. A public hearing on this certificate was called for March 15, but before that date the Manhattan Company and the Interborough Company came to an agreement, by which the former agreed to accept the certificate and the latter to increase the amount allowed the Manhattan Company under the 999 year lease for office expenses etc. When the hearing was held this inter-company settlement was announced, and the Commission took no further action on the certificate drafted for the Interborough Company. While this certificate rests today among the forgotten documents of the Commission, it probably was a potent factor in changing the Manhattan Company's attitude.

Meanwhile the Commission went ahead with the other contracts. On March 4, 1913, the day President Wilson was inaugurated, it formally adopted the two operating contracts and the several certificates and transmitted them to the Board of Estimate and Apportionment for approval. These contracts were:

Operating contract with Interborough company, providing for construction by the City, with a contribution from the company, and operation by the company of the Lexington Avenue, Seventh Avenue, Eastern Parkway and other subway lines.

Operating contract with the New York Municipal Railway Corporation a new company formed by the Brooklyn Rapid Transit interests to enter into the Dual System agreements, for the construction by the City, with a contribution by the Company, and for operation by the company of the Broadway, the Fourth Avenue, the Canal Street, the Fourteenth Street and the Centre Street Loop subway lines.

Certificate to the Interborough company granting rights to build and operate extensions of the Second, Third and Ninth Avenue elevated lines.

Certificate to the New York Municipal Railway Corporation granting rights to build and operate elevated extensions of the Jamaica Avenue, Liberty Avenue and Luthern Cemetery lines.

Certificate to the New York Municipal Railway Corporation granting rights to build and operate additional tracks on the Fulton Street, Broadway and Myrtle Avenue elevated lines.

Trackage agreement between Interborough and New York Municipal companies for operation of trains of latter over the new rapid transit lines in Queens to be leased to the Interborough company by the City.

Trackage agreement between the City and the two companies for joint use of such lines by the two companies.

The Commission was divided in the adoption of these instruments. The vote on the two operating contracts and on the trackage agreements was three to two, those in the affirmative being Chairman Edward E. McCall,

Commissioners John E. Eustis and George V. S. Williams; the negative, Commissioners Milo R. Maltbie and J. Sergeant Cram. On the certificates for extensions and third tracking the vote was four to one, Commissioner Milo R. Maltbie alone voting in the negative.

After the hearing on March 15 the Commission formally adopted the certificate to the Manhattan Railway Company for the third tracking privileges by a vote of three to one, Commissioner Milo R. Maltbie casting the negative vote and Commissioner J. Sergeant Cram being absent. On the same day it was transmitted for approval to the Board of Estimate and Apportionment. On March 18 the Commission sent to the Board of Estimate requisitions for the appropriations needed to carry out the contracts, namely: For the Interborough contract $28,200,000 in addition to $35,135,637.84 previously registered on account of contracts already let; and for the New York Municipal contract $60,000,000 in addition to $40,501,991 previously registered on account of contracts already awarded. On the same day the Board of Estimate approved the contracts and granted the requisitions.

On the next day, March 19, 1913, the Commission met in public session in its large hearing room on the third floor of the Tribune building, and in the presence of many citizens, including members of the Board of Estimate and other City officials, executed the contracts. Theodore P. Shonts, president, Frank Hedley, vice-president and H. M. Fisher, Secretary of the Interborough company signed for that company; D. W. McWilliams, Secretary, and E. T. Jeffery, director, for the Manhattan Railway Company; Timothy S. Williams, president and H. A. Bullock, Secretary, for the New York Municipal Railway Corporation.

For the City the contracts were signed by Edward E. McCall, Chairman and Travis H. Whitney, Secretary of the Public Service Commission for the First District. Chairman McCall performed a graceful act by requesting

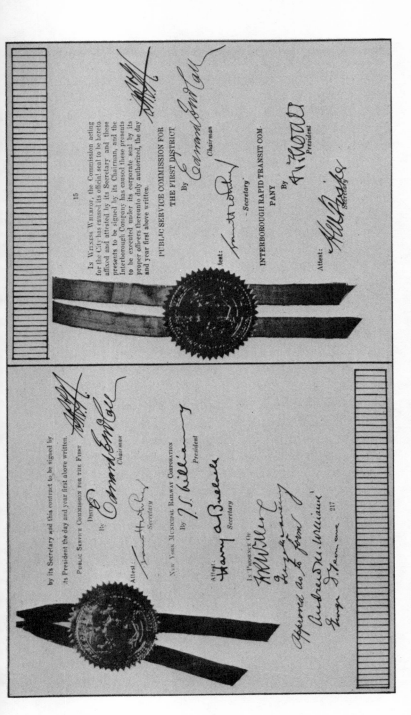

DUAL SYSTEM CONTRACTS

LAST PAGE OF OPERATING CONTRACT AND CERTIFICATE SHOWING SIGNATURES.

William R. Willcox, his predecessor in the chairmanship, to attest his signature, which he did, so that, though Mr. Willcox could not sign as chairman, his name nevertheless appeared on the contracts he did so much to bring about. The same compliment was paid George McAneny, who also attested the Chairman's signature on the same documents. Each company then submitted to the Commission for approval a mortgage upon all its property and an application to issue bonds under it. The Interborough mortgage was for $300,000,000 and its proposed bond issue $160,957,000; that of the New York Municipal company $100,000,000 and its proposed bond issue $40,000,000. The Commission approved both mortgages and both bond issues.

CHAPTER XVII

EXTENT, IMPORTANCE AND COST OF THE DUAL SYSTEM OF RAPID TRANSIT.

TO appreciate the extent and importance of the Dual System one must know the limitations of the existing rapid transit lines at the time the agreements were made. Outside of the Hudson tunnels, or McAdoo tubes, the rapid transit facilities of the city were divided between the Interborough Rapid Transit Company and the Brooklyn Rapid Transit Company. The former operated the first subway in Manhattan and the Bronx with a short branch to Brooklyn and the elevated railroads in Manhattan and the Bronx; the latter the elevated railroads in Brooklyn and Queens boroughs. It was these two companies that joined the City in the Dual System agreements, and those agreements provided for the amplification and extension of the lines of both.

The Interborough company controlled and operated 73 miles of single track in the City subway, and 118 miles of single track on its elevated roads. The Dual System provided additional City-owned lines to the extent of 149 miles of single track subway and elevated railroad; elevated railroad extensions of ten miles of single track and additional tracks on such roads amounting to ten miles more. In other words the single track mileage of the Interborough system was to be increased from 191 to 360 miles.

At the same time the Brooklyn company controlled and operated 105 miles of single track on its elevated railroads. The Dual System added to this 110 miles of single track in new City-owned lines and 35 miles of single track extensions of the elevated roads, together with nearly ten miles of additional tracks. This increased the company's single track mileage from 105 to 260. Taking both companies together the total single track mileage of the Dual System is 620, against a prior existing mileage of 296.

The new contracts, therefore, provided for more than doubling the existing rapid transit mileage—an increase never before attained or even contemplated. In the past the rapid transit system had been a slow, natural growth. First came the elevated railroads, which served the needs of the city for twenty years; then the first subway, which with the elevated roads met all demands after a fashion for the next ten years. Then came the Dual System, which promised to more than double all that had gone before for thirty years in the short space of time needed to build it, estimated at five years! Even now, with the Dual System approaching completion, there are comparatively few who realize the extent of the traffic revolution it will bring about. It is probable that it will cause a great shifting in the tides of travel, and that may mean a shifting of centers of importance, with resultant effect on real estate values.

Single track mileage is taken as the unit of comparison here because it is the true test of a railroad's capacity. While the total of such new trackage will be about 324 miles, the actual length of new road will be only about 90 miles. This is because some of the new lines will have six, some four, some three and some two tracks. Of course there will be no single track roads. The double track line is the smallest unit permissible in a large city, and where express service is desired three or four tracks are required.

In the selection of routes for the new lines the aim was to provide needed extensions for existing lines and to build new lines into sections either wholly without or lacking in rapid transit faciities. In the Interborough territory the City's first concern was to provide extensions for its own subway. This subway ran the length of Manhattan Island in zig-zag fashion—from the Battery up the East Side to 42d street, then across town to

Broadway and up the West Side to 242d street with a branch out Lenox Avenue and other streets to Bronx Park at 180th street. It was decided to extend the East Side line to the north and the West Side part to the south so as to make two subways instead of one—a complete line up and down the East Side and a complete line up and down the West Side. This was done by extending the first subway from 42d street at the Grand Central terminal over to Lexington Avenue and up Lexington Avenue to the Harlem River; and by extending it from 42d street at Broadway down Seventh Avenue and other streets to the Battery. These additions alone mean two complete, four track subways up and down the length of Manhattan Island—a virtual doubling of the existing road.

As adopted the Lexington Avenue line begins in Park Avenue at about 40th street, where it leaves the first subway. It runs thence under private property (the site of the old Grand Union hotel) and diagonally across 42d street to the New York Central property at the northwest corner of Lexington Avenue and Forty-second street, and under that property to Lexington Avenue at about 43d street. The line then runs up Lexington Avenue to the Harlem River, and under this river by tunnels to a point near 135th street. For this entire stretch, a distance of nearly one hundred blocks, it is a four-track road.

At 135th street the road forks into two branches, each having three tracks. The one to the West runs up Mott and River Avenues to Jerome Avenue and up Jerome Avenue to Woodlawn Road. At 157th street and River Avenue the underground part ends and the line continues as an elevated road up Jerome Avenue.

The branch to the East runs through 138th street to Southern Boulevard, through Southern Boulevard to Whitlock Avenue and out Westchester Avenue to Pelham Bay Park. It is a subway to Whitlock Avenue, where it crosses the Bronx River by bridge and continues out Westchester Avenue as an elevated railroad.

While these two branches provided for the territory tributary to Jerome Avenue on the West and for that in the extreme East of Bronx borough, they did nothing for the intermediate ground. It was therefore decided to extend the Lenox Avenue branch of the first subway from its terminus at 180th street, Bronx Park, through private property to White Plains Road and up White Plains Road to 241st street, near the northerly city boundary. This is an elevated railroad with three tracks.

These improvements were wisely correlated with the improvements of the company's elevated railroads in the Bronx, for which the contracts provided. Plans were made to connect the new lines so that they could be operated by elevated as well as subway trains. The Sixth and Ninth Avenue elevated line terminated at 155th street and the Harlem River. An extension was provided over the Putnam Division bridge across the Harlem River, leased from the New York Central Railroad Company by the Interborough for the purpose, through East 162d street by a tunnel through the Sedgwick Avenue hill and thence as an elevated road to a junction with the Jerome Avenue line at 162d street. This will permit elevated trains from the Sixth and Ninth Avenue lines to continue over the new line in Jerome Avenue to its terminus at Woodlawn Road.

The Third Avenue elevated terminated at Fordham. It was decided to extend it northward through Webster Avenue to Gun Hill Road and through Gun Hill Road to a junction with the new line in White Plains Road, so that elevated trains from the Third Avenue line may run over the White Plains Road line to its terminus at 241st street. A connection was also provided between the Lenox Avenue branch of the first subway and the new Jerome Avenue branch, which will permit an interchange of trains between the Lexington Avenue and the old sub-

ways. Another connection is made between the Third
Avenue elevated line and the Lenox Avenue branch of
the first subway where they intersect at about 149th
street.

From Times Square, at Broadway and 42d street, the
first subway as it comes down Broadway was extended
into Seventh Avenue, down Seventh Avenue and Seventh
Avenue Extension to Varick street, through Varick street
to West Broadway and thence through Greenwich street
to a connection with the first subway at the Battery.
From Times Square down to Park Place it is a four
track line entirely under ground. At Park Place two
tracks continue over the route named to the Battery,
while two others diverge and run under Park Place, the
U. S. Postoffice and Beekman street to William street,
down William street to Old Slip and thence under the
East River by tunnels to Clark street, Brooklyn, and
through Clark and Fulton streets to a junction with the
first subway near Brooklyn Borough Hall.

As the first subway has two tracks entering Brooklyn
by tunnels this will give the Interborough company four
tracks to that borough—exactly doubling its present
facilities. It was also decided to extend the first subway
in Brooklyn from its terminus at Flatbush and Atlantic
Avenues out Flatbush Avenue to Prospect Park Plaza
and thence into Eastern Parkway and out that street to
Buffalo Avenue as a four track, underground road; and
from Buffalo Avenue as a three track elevated road
through East 98th street and Livonia Avenue to New
Lots Avenue. From Eastern Parkway a two track subway was provided under Nostrand Avenue to Flatbush
Avenue.

With the exception of the elevated extensions referred
to, all these new lines were built and will be owned by
the City, although equipped and operated by the Interborough company. They will for some time at least pro-

vide handsomely for the rapid transit needs of Manhattan, the Bronx and part of Brooklyn.

It was deemed necessary also to provide for Queens Borough, and to this end the City took over the Steinway tunnel from the Interborough interests and planned for its extension on both sides of the East River. As previously stated this tunnel is a two track underground and under river railroad running from Forty-second street, Manhattan, to Long Island City. Under the Dual system it is extended on the West to a junction with the first subway at Times Square, and on the East to Queensborough bridge plaza in Long Island City. It is now known as the Queensboro Subway.

From Queensborough bridge Plaza the City builds and leases to the Interborough with trackage rights to the Brooklyn company, two new elevated railroads, one running northward through Second Avenue to Ditmars Avenue, Astoria; the other eastwardly through Queens Boulevard and Roosevelt Avenue to Alburtis Avenue, Corona. Each of these roads will have three tracks. The Steinway tunnel extension will be connected with them at the Plaza, so that trains from it may operate both to Astoria and to Corona. The company is also given the right to connect with them its Second Avenue elevated line in Manhattan, by an extension built over the Queensborough bridge, so that elevated trains also may run to Astoria and Corona.

The company also got the right to complete the third tracks for express service on its Second, Third and Ninth Avenue elevated lines.

By the inclusion of the New York Municipal Railway Corporation, generally referred to as the Brooklyn Company, in the Dual System agreements there was made possible a much greater expansion of rapid transit facilities in Brooklyn and Queens than if the new contracts had been confined to the Interborough company. Before the agreements were made the Brooklyn elevated lines terminated on the Manhattan side of the Brooklyn and Williamsburg bridges. Here the throngs of incoming passengers from all parts of Brooklyn and Queens were discharged every morning, to find their way as best they could to their places of business in Manhattan. The "bridge crush" had become notorious, and it was resolved to end it once for all in the Dual System arrangement. To do this not only were new facilities provided for the Brooklyn company on the Brooklyn side, but a distributing system in Manhattan was planned to serve all of this company's lines entering the borough by bridges or tunnels. This is the Broadway subway, a four track line destined to serve the business part of Manhattan or that part of it south of 59th street.

The Broadway subway begins in the southern part of Manhattan in Whitehall street, where the tunnel from Montague street, Brooklyn, enters the borough. It runs thence as a two track line under Whitehall street across town to Morris street, turning thence into Trinity Place and continuing up Trinity Place and Church street (these two being really one thoroughfare) to Vesey street, where it turns into Broadway. The line passes under a corner of Old St. Paul's churchyard in the rear of the church, thence into Vesey street and from Vesey street curves under the old Astor House property and into Broadway just south of the U. S. Postoffice building. Here the line changes to a four track line, and continues under Broadway northward to 42d street. Here it descends to pass under the first subway and continues northward under Seventh Avenue to 59th street, where the four track line ends; two tracks curve into 59th street and continue to Fifth Avenue, where they swing into 60th street and extend under that street to the East River and into a new tunnel to be built to Long Island City. Here the two tracks will come out of the ground and join the new elevated lines on the Queensborough Bridge Plaza.

STATION AT PELHAM PARKWAY, WHITE PLAINS ROAD EXTENSION
Type of Ornamental Concrete Construction.

Four other City-owned subways were leased for operation to the Brooklyn Company—the Centre Street loop subway and the Canal Street subway in Manhattan and the Fourth Avenue subway in Brooklyn and the Eastern District subway in Manhattan and Brooklyn. When the Dual System agreements were made the Centre Street and Fourth Avenue subways were nearly completed and they were adjusted to the Brooklyn part of the system.

The Centre street loop, as before stated, was built to connect the Williamsburg, Manhattan and Brooklyn bridges. It consists of a four track underground railroad extending from the Manhattan terminus of the Brooklyn Bridge northward under Centre street to Delancey street and eastwardly under Delancey street to the Williamsburg Bridge, with a two track spur at Canal street connecting with the Manhattan Bridge. In August 1913 the two westerly tracks in this subway were placed in operation in connection with the Broadway elevated railroad in Brooklyn, the trains from which now run through the loop subway to the Chambers street station in the basement of the new Municipal Building, instead of stopping as formerly at the end of the Williamsburg bridge. The two easterly tracks south of Canal street were placed in operation in June, 1915, as part of the Fourth Avenue subway, and the two easterly tracks north of Canal street were devoted to the Williamsburg Bridge operation.

The Fourth Avenue subway is a four track underground road running from the Brooklyn end of the Manhattan Bridge through Flatbush Avenue Extension to Fulton street, Ashland Place and Fourth Avenue to 86th street, near Fort Hamilton. The Dual System contracts provided for its extension through 38th street with two, three-track elevated lines to Coney Island, one running from 38th street down New Utrecht Avenue, 86th street and Stillwell Avenue and the other from 38th street down Gravesend Avenue and Shell Road, both terminating at a common terminal at Coney Island. It was further provided that the company should at its own expense reconstruct its Sea Beach line as a four track railroad and connect it at 65th street with the Fourth Avenue subway, thus providing another line to Coney Island. From Flatbush Avenue Extension, or from Fulton street near the Extension, another connection was planned. This is a two track railroad running under Fulton and St. Felix streets to Flatbush Avenue and thence under Flatbush Avenue to a junction with the Brighton Beach railroad at Malbone street. A further connection with Manhattan was provided by a two track underground line running from the Fourth Avenue subway in Flatbush Avenue Extension just west of De Kalb Avenue through Willoughby street to Montague street and down Montague street to and under the East River to Whitehall street, Manhattan and a connection with the Broadway subway.

In June, 1915, the Fourth Avenue subway was opened for traffic from Manhattan to Coney Island by the Sea Beach connection. Two tracks, a combination of local and express tracks, were used for the first operation to Sixty-fifth street and the Sea Beach tracks from there to Coney Island. For this service the two easterly tracks in the Centre street loop south of Canal street are used. Two tracks in the Fourth Avenue subway after crossing the Manhattan Bridge descend and pass under the Centre street loop and run under Canal street to a junction with the new Broadway subway in Manhattan.

Aside from the Fourth Avenue system just described the City also agreed to build for operation by the Brooklyn Company a new subway from Manhattan to East New York. This is known as the 14th Street—Eastern line. It begins in Fourteenth street, Manhattan, at Sixth Avenue, runs eastwardly as a two track, underground road through 14th street to and under the East River to North Seventh Street, Brooklyn, through North Seventh street to Metropolitan Avenue, to Bushwick Avenue, to

Johnson Avenue, where it becomes an elevated railroad and continues over the Long Island Railroad right of way, parallel to Wyckoff Avenue, and thence southeasterly to a junction with the Broadway elevated railroad in East New York.

All the above lines are built and paid for by the City and leased to the Brooklyn Company for operation, except of course the Sea Beach line, which is a reconstruction of the company's own property. In addition, the Dual System contracts granted to the company the rights to make extensions of and additions to its existing elevated railroad lines as follows:

An elevated connection between the Broadway and Myrtle Avenue lines and an extension of the latter to Lutheran Cemetery.

An elevated extension of the Broadway line from its terminus out Jamaica Avenue to Grand Avenue, Jamaica, in Queens Borough.

An elevated extension of the Fulton street line from the old City Line, at the boundary between Brooklyn and Queens, out Liberty Avenue to Lefferts Avenue, Richmond Hill, Queens Borough.

Also to build and operate a third track on each of the Broadway, Myrtle Avenue and Fulton street elevated lines.

All of such improvements are to be made at the company's expense.

The completion of this system means nothing less than a revolution in Brooklyn-Manhattan travel. Heretofore, owing to track limitations, no real express service was possible on the Brooklyn elevated roads. The third tracks on the Fulton street, Myrtle Avenue and Broadway lines permit of the addition of express trains. This in itself will greatly lessen existing congestion. The Fourth Avenue subway and its connections provide ample means of access to the Coney Island beaches—a long felt want. The Broadway subway in Manhattan gives all lines a proper and convenient outlet.

Both leases with the companies run for forty-nine years. In general the terms are the same in each contract; that is each company agrees to contribute a certain amount toward the cost of construction of the City-owned lines, to build the company-owned lines with its own funds and to provide the necessary equipment for all lines at its own expense, although title to the equipment on City-owned lines is to vest in the City.

Each company is to charge only five cents for fare on any parts of its system and is to give free transfers at all intersections, but no transfers will be given between the lines of one company and those of another, nor will the Interborough company be required to transfer from its elevated lines to the City's subway lines or vice versa. Each company is to share equally with the City the surplus profits from operation.

In the Interborough contract provision was made for the synchronizing of its leases, that is to bring the old and new leases to a common expiring date. Under the old leases covering the first subway the company had until 1954 to operate the Manhattan-Bronx part of the line and till 1940 the Brooklyn extension, with the privilege of twenty-five years' renewal in each case. These leases the company naturally regarded as very valuable, for it was making about $6,000,000 a year out of the operation of the subway. It would not listen to any curtailment of the life of the leases unless the City would agree to compensate it for the profits to be expected in the period curtailed. It was finally agreed that a preferential payment equivalent to these profits should be provided for in the new lease, that the company should terminate the old agreement and consent to a new lease for old and new lines for 49 years. The amount of the preferential agreed upon was $6,335,000 a year, as representing the average annual profits under the old leases for the two years ending June 30, 1911.

As Mr. Belmont pointed out in his remarks previously quoted, the first suggestion of a preferential payment came from the Brooklyn Rapid Transit Company. It was proposed in that company's offer of April 25, 1911, as a part of the terms of operation. These terms provided for the pooling of all receipts from both city-owned and company-owned lines and, after paying out of them operating expenses, etc., the payment to the company of "an amount equivalent to the net earnings of the existing lines operated by the Brooklyn Rapid Transit system in connection with the proposed new lines, as of the year preceding the beginning of operation under the proposed contract with the City." As these earnings were increasing every year, the conferrees for the City felt that the present earnings, which were known, would be a better guide than future earnings, and it was finally agreed that the preferential should be equivalent to the average annual net profits for the two years ended June 30, 1911. And thus it went into both contracts. In the Brooklyn company contract the amount of the preferential payment is $3,500,000 a year.

The first deductions from the pooled receipts, to be made even in advance of the preferentials, included: To the City such rentals as were due from the Interborough Company for the first subway; taxes and governmental charges of all kinds against each company; twelve per cent. of the revenue for maintenance exclusive of depreciation; for depreciation, five per cent. from the Interborough and three per cent. from the Brooklyn Company. Then come the preferential payments, and after them: six per cent. on the company's investment for construction and equipment, out of which an amortization fund must be set aside; to the City by the Interborough Company an amount equal to 8.76 per cent. on the City's expenditures for construction; one per cent. of the revenue to be paid into a contingent reserve fund. The surplus remaining is to be divided equally by the City and company.

It was agreed that the City through the Commission should prepare and award in the manner provided by the Rapid Transit Act all construction contracts on City-owned lines, but that in case of contracts which would be paid for in part by the companies a draft thereof should be submitted to the company affected for its criticisms and suggestions before it was finally adopted by the Commission. Such contracts also were to include the company as one of the parties, and the funds applied for such purposes by the company should be disbursed by it direct to the construction contractor.

The Interborough company agreed to contribute $58,000,000 and the Brooklyn company $13,500,000 toward the cost of construction of City-owned lines, and in addition the latter agreed to bear the cost of building the connection between the Canal street subway and the Broadway subway to connect the latter with the Fourth Avenue subway in Brooklyn, which was estimated at about $500,000. The total contribution, therefore, of the Brooklyn company is generally placed at $14,000,000. Of the Interborough's contribution it was agreed that $3,000,000 was to be allowed the company for the transfer to the City of the Steinway tunnel.

It was also provided that the Brooklyn company at its own expense should reconstruct its existing lines where necessary, to link them up with the City-owned lines, so that both could be operated together as parts of one system. This involved the reconstruction of the company's Brighton Beach line between Malbone street and Church Avenue, the reconstruction of the Sea Beach line as a four track road, the elevation of existing tracks and the construction of additional two tracks on the Brighton Beach line between Neptune Avenue and Coney Island, the construction of a new union terminal at Coney Island for the Brighton Beach, the Sea Beach, the New Utrecht and Gravesend Avenues lines and the extension of station platforms and other needed alterations—all under plans to be approved by the Commission.

Heavy security was demanded of both companies. Each was required to deposit with the Controller of the City $1,000,000 in approved securities and also to file a bond in the sum of $1,000,000. It was arranged that the special deposit should be returned to the company in instalments as its contribution to the cost of construction was paid; as each quarter of the contribution was expended a quarter of the deposit was to be returned.

To provide for a settlement of disputes between the parties to each contract an arbitration court was created. Each side names one arbitrator and the third is named by the Chief Judge of the Court of Appeals, or in his failure to act by any of the Associate Judges of the same Court in the order of their seniority, or in their failure by the President of the New York Chamber of Commerce. Personal claims by either company against members of the Public Service Commission or of the Board of Estimate and Apportionment on matters connected with the contracts are barred.

The City is given complete control over expenditures by the companies under the contracts. The companies agree to supervision by the Public Service Commission and to provide for such inspections as the Commission may wish to make. They must keep proper accounts, permit their examination and submit to the Commission for approval any contract or mortgage in connection with their contributions toward the cost of construction. All contracts affecting the maintenance and operation of the railroads extending for more than one year or involving more than $50,000 must be approved by the Commission, which may also prescribe systems of accounting and forms of vouchers and payrolls. The Commission may object to any item of expenditure as improper and the company must hold the same in a suspense account until the matter is adjusted, or, in case of failure to agree, arbitrated.

All equipment is to be purchased by each company at its own expense, but title to that on City-owned lines when accepted by the Commission becomes immediately vested in the City. All equipment must be of the best character "known to the art of urban railway operation." At the proper time the Commission may order the company to begin providing equipment, which shall be ready to put into operation any part of the road as soon as completed.

January 1, 1917, was fixed as the date for the beginning of "initial" operation of the completed system, but provision is made for the temporary operation of such parts of the lines as may be ready before the whole system is finished. Such temporary operation is to be conducted on the same terms as are provided for the operation of future extensions of the Dual System, which are slightly different from the terms for permanent operation. If there is a deficit from such operation, it is provided that the company may deduct the amount of such deficit from the revenue before making any payments to the City.

There are special provisions in the contract with one company which do not appear in that with the other. For instance, the Brooklyn company is permitted for ten years to purchase its power instead of generating it; and in the Interborough contract there is a provision for the "exchange of legs" of the first subway if at any time the City should exercise its right of recapture, so that it may take over a complete operating line instead of a fragment of one of the new lines.

So much for the contracts for City-owned lines. The rights for the extensions and third tracking of existing elevated railroads owned by private companies were conferred in separate "certificates", granted under other

TWO VIEWS OF DUAL SYSTEM
CONSTRUCTION
1. Deep Cut on 162nd Street Connection;
2. Reinforced Concrete Construction in
the Bronx.

provisions of the Rapid Transit Act. The companies were given franchises for such improvements to run for 85 years, subject to the right of the City to take them over at any time after ten years from the date of the contract upon proper payments.

A third tracking certificate, as stated above, was granted to the Manhattan Railway Company, the owner of the elevated railroads in Manhattan and the Bronx operated by the Interborough company under lease. Prior to this time the company had in use a third track on the Ninth Avenue line extending from Fourteenth to 116th Street, and a third track on the Third Avenue line extending from Forty-second to 129th street; also portions of the Second Avenue line had some third tracks. There was some question as to the rights for either one or both of these extra tracks, and the affirmation or confirmation of such rights was one of the considerations in the Dual System contracts. The latter beyond this confirmation granted rights for a third track on the Second Avenue line in addition to those on the Ninth and Third Avenue lines, which were expanded to extend the third tracks from the Battery to 155th street on the Ninth Avenue, and from Pearl street to 145th street on the Third Avenue line. In places four and even five tracks were authorized.

During the negotiations there was a great deal of discussion as to the amount of compensation the City should receive for the grants for additional tracks, and more as to the method by which it should be determined. It was finally decided and so nominated in the certificate that, after operation began, the company should pay to the City annually from the receipts of each station served by the additional tracks an amount equal to two per cent. of the excess of such receipts over the receipts of the same station for the year ending June 30, 1911, or for a corresponding portion of such year. These payments are to continue for twenty-five years, when the rental is to be readjusted for the next twenty years and again readjusted each twenty years thereafter. In case the City and the company cannot agree on the readjustment, the matter may be settled by arbitration or by appeal to the courts. In no case, however, is the readjusted rental to be less than that provided for the first twenty-five years.

Ten years after operation begins the City is authorized to purchase and take over the additional tracks so installed, but not for purposes of railroad operation. This condition was deemed advisable because the City has no power to take over the original tracks and therefore could not operate the third tracks in the event that it came into possession of them. The recapture provision, therefore, is valuable only in that it will save the City from condemning and paying full value for the third tracks if at any time it decides to purchase the line or to condemn the original tracks and remove the whole structure from the streets. When the right of recapture accrues, namely ten years after operation begins, the City must pay cost plus 15 per cent. for the property, but this percentage decreases each year thereafter until at the end of 85 years the City gets the property without any payment whatever.

The certificate for additional tracks granted to the Brooklyn company, while substantially the same, differs in some particulars from that granted to the Manhattan company. The most important point of divergence is in the terms of compensation to the City. Instead of a percentage of receipts, or excess of receipts due to the new tracks, the earnings of the elevated roads upon which additional tracks are built shall be pooled with the receipts of the subway lines operated by the Brooklyn company and payments made to the City in accordance with the operating contracts for the City-owned lines. The reason for this is that the Brooklyn elevated roads are to be operated as parts of the City-owned system, while the

Manhattan elevated lines are to be operated separately and not as parts of the subway system.

Three Brooklyn lines are covered by the certificate for additional tracks, namely, the Broadway, the Fulton Street and the Myrtle Avenue lines. The right on the Broadway line extends from the Williamsburg bridge to East New York; on the Fulton Street line from the Brooklyn bridge to the Queens boundary; and on the Myrtle Avenue line from Broadway to Wyckoff Avenue. As in the Manhattan certificate more than one additional track is authorized in places. The grants run for 85 years and the property may be purchased and taken over by the City at any time after ten years on the same terms as are laid down in the Manhattan certificate.

Certificates for the extensions of elevated lines are somewhat different in their terms. Instead of a percentage of excess profits, the City is to receive as rental for the extensions of the Manhattan elevated railroads, operated by the Interborough company, one half of the excess profits over the average net profits of the existing elevated lines for the years 1910 and 1911, fixed in the certificate at $1,589,348, from which there is previously deducted the rental paid under the additional track certificate. The other terms are substantially the same as those in the third-tracking certificate. The franchise runs for eighty-five years, but the City has the right to take over the roads at any time after ten years upon paying cost plus 15 per cent., the percentage declining every year until at the end of the grant the property passes to the City without any payment.

The extensions for which authorizations are granted by the certificate to the Interborough company are: The Webster Avenue Line, the Eighth Avenue and 162d Street Connection, the Queensboro Bridge Line and the West Farms Subway Connection. The Webster Avenue Line is an extension of the Third Avenue elevated road from its terminus at Fordham northward through Webster Avenue to Gun Hill Road and eastward through Gun Hill Road to a junction with the elevated extension of the Lenox Avenue branch of the first subway in White Plains Road. The Eighth Avenue and 162d Street Connection is an extension of the Sixth and Ninth Avenue elevated lines from their terminus at 155th Street and Eighth Avenue over the Putnam Division Bridge across the Harlem River and through East 162d street to a junction with the Jerome Avenue elevated extension in River Avenue of the Lexington Avenue subway. The Queensboro Bridge line is an extension of the Second Avenue elevated road over the Queensboro bridge to a junction with the new rapid transit lines to Astoria and Corona. The West Farms Subway Connection is an elevated line joining the Third Avenue elevated road with Lenox Avenue branch of the first subway and running from about 143d street through Willis and Bergen Avenues to the subway line, which is an elevated road at that point.

The certificates to the New York Municipal Railway Corporation for elevated extensions in Brooklyn and Queens are substantially similar to the certificates for additional tracks granted to that company. These extensions are to be made a part of the whole system, and the City will get compensation for them out of the earnings thereof in the manner provided in the main operating contract. That is the receipts of all lines and extensions will be pooled, and the City will share with the company in the surplus profits remaining after paying operating expenses and other charges fixed by the contract. The grants are to run eighty-five years, with the same provision for recapture after ten years as are embodied in the Interborough certificates.

The extensions covered by these certificates to the Brooklyn company are: The Jamaica Line and the Liberty Avenue Line. The Jamaica Line is an extension of the Broadway elevated road from its terminus near Crescent street out Jamaica Avenue to Grand street, Jamaica.

The Liberty Avenue Line is an extension of the Fulton street elevated road from its terminus at the Brooklyn-Queens boundary out Liberty Avenue to Lefferts Avenue, Queens.

At the time the Dual System contracts were signed the total cost of the work, including construction and equipment, was estimated at $330,000,000. Had it not been for the World War this estimate might have been approximated in the result, but the increase in prices of materials, cost of labor, etc., has largely augmented the figures. The original estimates provided for an investment of $164,000,000 by the City of New York, $105,000,000 by the Interborough Rapid Transit Company and $61,000,000 by the Brooklyn company. It is now known that the City's expenditure will equal or exceed $200,000,000 and that the investment of each of the companies will be much heavier than the estimates, so that the entire, ultimate cost of the system will be about $400,000,000. This exceeds the cost of the Panama Canal.

Since the adoption of the Dual System contracts opinion has been divided as to their merits—that is, whether they were a good or a bad bargain for the City. They were both. They were good in the enormous increases of rapid transit facilities which they assured at a time when the city was sorely in need of relief. They were bad in that they assured the operating companies a continuation of large profits and placed the burden of carrying deficits from operation upon the City, besides giving the companies first call on the revenues. Time alone will show whether the good or the bad predominates. The primary object in building rapid transit railroads is to provide quick transportation service for the people; whether the operation of such roads will bring a monetary return to the City is secondary. There is no question that the Dual System will fulfill the first; whether the second will be realized only the future can tell. Had the Dual System negotiations failed, however, the plight of the

city would have been serious, for the building of new
lines would have been delayed and the burden of constructing them would have been placed wholly on the
municipality, the resources of which would not have permitted such a large addition to the rapid transit system
as was made possible by the co-operation of the companies under the Dual System agreements.

CHAPTER XVIII

DECKED ROADWAY METHOD OF CONSTRUCTION—PROBLEMS
MET IN THE WORK.

IN the contract for the construction of the Brooklyn
extension of the subway there was a new provision,
born of the experience in underground work gained in
the building of the first sections, for the carrying on of
operations without unduly disturbing the street surface
or interfering with its traffic. In prosecuting the first
contracts in streets where the subway was to run close
to the surface, the contractor tore up the street pavement
and began excavation just as he would for a gas main
or a sewer, leaving the opening in the street a gaping
wound in the surface until the steel structure was completed, when the backfill would be placed and the pavement restored.

As large areas were badly obstructed for months
at a time, this method of working seriously interfered
with traffic and also greatly injured the business of the
tradesmen having stores in the area affected by making
access to their places so difficult as to discourage visitors.
The extreme of this evil was felt in Forty-second street
between Park Avenue and Broadway. Trade in the shops
along the street fell off so that some merchants closed
their places and others continued with reduced profits.
Complaints poured in upon the Rapid Transit Commission, which wisely decided to prevent a repetition of such
interference with normal conditions if its engineers could
find a way.

The engineers were equal to the emergency and devised what has since become known as the "decked roadway" method of subway construction. It was first tried
in building the extension of the subway down Broadway
from City Hall to South Ferry, and it was so successful
that it was embodied in all future specifications. This

method consists in replacing the ordinary street pavement
with a temporary plank roadway strong enough to support the usual street traffic and excavating for the subway underneath it. As depth is attained in the excavation huge timbers properly braced are erected beneath
the decking, which is kept in place till the steel frame
of the subway is erected, when the temporary decking is
removed, the backfill placed and the street pavement restored. The plan had two merits, first the business of
merchants along the route and the ordinary street traffic
were not interfered with, or if so only to a bearable degree, and, second, it kept the work of construction out of
sight and thereby minimized interference from the outside. Since it was introduced in 1902 more than twenty
miles of subway have been built according to the cut and
cover method.

This method of work involved another departure
in the treatment of gas pipes encountered in the route
of a subway. Covering the excavation produced a confined space between the bottom of the cut and the street
decking, so it was feared that, should a gas pipe be injured so as to leak, the escaping gas would mix with the
air in the cut and produce that highly explosive com-
pound which when ignited works tremendous damage.
To safeguard the work, therefore, the ''by-passing''
method was devised. That is, the service pipes were removed from the mains and carried around the cut in by-
pass pipes either laid close to the curb on the street surface or supported on trestles above the sidewalks. In
either case the gas was removed from the cut and possible
explosions were prevented.

Only the engineers and contractors actually engaged
in the work could tell of the thousand other problems
encountered and solved during the construction of the
subways. Almost every section had its own peculiar
obstacles. For instance, in tunneling under the East
River the contractor had to combat the water under the

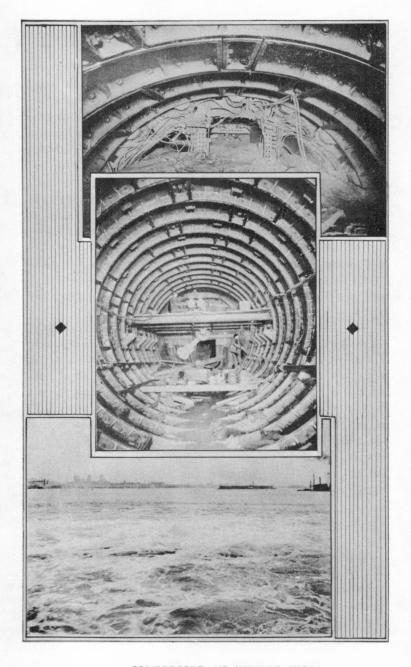

COMPRESSED AIR TUNNEL WORK

1. Tunnel Heading Filled With Mud Following a "Blowout"
2. Erecting Iron Rings of Tunnel; 3. Surface of East River
at Point of "Blowout."

river bed while he was pushing the tubes across. The hydraulic shield and compressed air were invoked. The shield was pressed forward a few feet a day, the workmen, or "sand-hogs", excavating the material in front of it and installing the cast iron rings of the tubes under its protection, the water in the material above being driven out by compressed air introduced into the workings through pipes connected with compressors on the surface.

Two of the most remarkable accidents ever recorded in compressed air work happened during the construction of the subway tunnels under the East River, and the second, although eleven years later, was almost a duplicate of the first. In each case a man was blown out of the tunnel by the force of the air, through the river bed and through the water to the surface and yet came out alive.

The first accident occurred in 1905 during the construction of the Battery-Joralemon street tunnel of the first subway. As frequently happens, a "blow-out" took place. That is, the compressed air found a weak spot in the roof of the tunnel and began escaping. In such cases the usual treatment is for the men in the tunnel to heave bags of sand or clay into the vortex and thus stop the leak. On this occasion Dick Creedon, a workman employed by the contractor, attempted to plug the air hole with a bag of sand. The pressure of the air was so strong, however, that the "blow-out" sucked both bag and man into the vortex and forced them through thirty feet of sand and silt up into the waters of the river. On reaching the surface Creedon began swimming and was soon picked up by a boat, apparently none the worse for his marvellous experience. The "blow-out" was repaired by dumping tons of sand from scows immediately over the break.

The second of these accidents occurred in 1916 in the Whitehall-Montague street tunnel of the Dual System subways, also under the East River. A "blow-out" occurred in the north tube a short distance out from the Brooklyn shore. The shield had just been shoved ahead for the placing behind it of another ring of the tunnel tube. Four workmen were about to place the top "breasting" board in its new position just ahead of the shield, when there was a rush of air and three of the four disappeared. They were sucked into the vortex and through twelve feet of sand to the river bottom. One of them, Marshall Mabey, shot up through the water and into the air on the top of a geyser which eye witnesses thought reached a height of forty feet above the surface. When he dropped back into the water he began swimming and was soon picked up by a boat sent out from the contractor's dock. He was practically unhurt. His companions were less fortunate. One was found unconscious in the river forty minutes after Mabey was rescued, but efforts to resuscitate him were unavailing. The body of the other was not recovered until the next day. It is supposed they were struck by some hard substance in their passage through the river bottom and either killed or made unconscious and then drowned. The break was repaired by placing a blanket of clay in the river bottom.

All of Manhattan Island is underlain with rock, but it is closer to the surface in the northern part of the island than elsewhere, so that a subway running close to the surface of the streets passes through soft sand in the southern part and through solid rock in the northern part of the island. At low places, too, it must be built below water line. These varying conditions produced varying problems and taxed the ingenuity of the engineers to meet them. In the sand district the sides of the cut had to be buttressed with stout timber sheeting to prevent their falling in, while in the rocky section great stretches of tunnel were built with the walls of the cut unsupported except by the solidity of the rock itself. At many places, however, the rock is treacherous, and here great care had to be exercised. Whenever such rock was encountered the prudent contractor made assurance doubly sure by buttressing the rock walls with heavy timber braces. Natural mistakes were made on occasion in "diagnosing" the character of the rock, and in such cases gravity caused slides of varying dimensions. A notable instance was the slide in Park Avenue near Thirty-seventh street referred to in a previous chapter.

Along Lafayette street near Canal street the subway passed through marshy ground, in places below the tide water level. Here pumps had to be used to keep the excavation clear of water while the work proceeded. It was also difficult to get a foundation of sufficient stability for the subway structure. Such conditions here and in other parts of the line made waterproofing necessary, and the first subway was liberally swathed in a coat of asphalt blankets to keep it dry. The waterproofing, it was found after the subway was opened, was impervious to air as well as water, with the result that it tended to keep the heated air, generated in the tubes by the friction of wheels and machinery, from escaping. In the later built subways this result was avoided by reducing the waterproofing.

Perhaps the most difficult piece of work in the sand district during the construction of the first subway was the excavation in front of Trinity church in lower Broadway on the Brooklyn extension. This extension runs down Broadway from the City Hall to Bowling Green, where it turns eastward and runs under the East River to Brooklyn, two tracks, however, continuing down Broadway to the Battery. It was found that the foundation of the church spire was built on sand and extended only nine feet below the sidewalk level. As the subway was to be twenty-four feet down, it was feared the excavation in the street, which was to be only nine feet away from the spire foundation, would undermine it. To prevent this the work was done in three pockets. The cen-

tral pocket was first excavated and in it was placed a
mass of concrete for the floor and sidewall of the subway,
the sand at the side being held up meanwhile by steel
sheeting which was left in place after the work was finished. The pockets on either side of the central one were
then treated in the same way in succession. After the
work was done and the subway wall and floor were built
in front of the church it was found that there had been
no settlement of the spire.

Another interesting piece of work on the first subway
was the placing of the bridge over the Harlem ship canal
near the old Kings Bridge, on the Broadway branch.
The City already had a single deck bridge at the point,
which was used for ordinary highway traffic. To accommodate the subway trains it was necessary to replace this
bridge with a double-deck structure to carry ordinary
traffic on the lower and the subway trains on the upper
deck. The new steel bridge was assembled in sections on
false work resting on barges anchored nearby. When it
was ready to install, similar barges bearing cribbing were
floated under the old bridge at low tide, and as the tide
rose the old structure was lifted clear of its anchorages
and floated away, when the new bridge was floated into
the vacant place and lowered into position as the tide
receded. The old bridge was floated down to 207th street,
where it is now doing duty as a highway bridge. On several other occasions the rise and fall of the tide were
utilized in this way to facilitate engineering operations.

Considering the magnitude of the work, the Dual
System subway and elevated roads have been built
with surprisingly little disturbance of normal conditions.
Thanks to the cut and cover method of construction,
traffic in the streets under which the new tunnels were
built has gone on day by day with slight inconvenience to merchants along the routes. Of course, no such
work could be done without inconveniencing somebody,
but the inconvenience has been trifling compared to the

trouble caused by the building of the first subway. The work was also remarkably free from accidents.

A perfect record in this respect was spoiled by two of the worst accidents attending the Dual System construction, and singularly enough both occurred in the same month and within a few days of each other. Both were due to the collapse of the temporary street decking, but the causes were different. The first took place in the Seventh Avenue subway on September 22, 1915, and the second followed in the Broadway subway on September 25.

The first was by far the worse. Just before eight o'clock in the morning, when rush hour traffic on the street surface was at its height, a blast was fired in the north heading of the excavation in Seventh Avenue, just south of Twenty-fifth street. From that point south to about Twenty-third street the avenue was decked over by planking supported by an elaborate system of timbering. As usual the two tracks of the surface car line, with their ties and concrete bed, were also supported in the same way so that trolley car operation might go on as usual.

It is supposed that rocks dislodged by the blast were hurled against the nearest timbers supporting the decking and with such force as to knock them down. In falling they carried with them the supporting timbers to the south for a short distance, thus leaving a stretch of the street decking and heavy car track bed hanging in the air. The weight of the decking and car tracks on the over-hang proved too much for the remaining supports, which fell in quick succession and the whole street surface between a point south of Twenty-fifth street and a point south of Twenty-fourth street, or something over a block, fell to the bottom of the cut, a distance of thirty feet.

A loaded trolley car was going north in Seventh Avenue at the time. As the tracks sank in front of it gravity forced it into the declivity and it slid to the bottom, where it landed a complete wreck. Some of the passengers were killed and others injured. Most of them got out or were helped out safe, but few escaped some slight injury. Police and firemen, with the contractor's men did heroic rescue work, but in spite of their efforts eight persons were killed. The injured were treated in an improvised hospital near by and later removed to homes or the hospitals. They numbered thirty or more. Within two weeks the contractors had the debris removed and the steel work of the new subway in place. It was found that the collapse of the decking had been stopped where the steel work ended, namely just north of Twenty-third street. When the pavement was replaced it rested on solid steel.

Panic over this accident had scarcely subsided when the second collapse took place. This was on a section of the new subway in Broadway. On Saturday evening, September 25, at about seven o'clock about seventy-five feet of the temporary street decking on the west side of Broadway just north of Thirty-eighth street sank into the excavation, falling about thirty feet. Fortunately there were few persons on the street at the time, and only one was killed. There was a taxicab standing at the curb when the pavement caved in, and it fell to the bottom of the cut, a distance of about twenty-five feet. The chauffeur had left it a moment before and was safe on the sidewalk when his machine went down.

The timbering on the east side of the street held, so that only the decking on the western half fell in. The two trolley tracks hung in air and though they sagged badly they did not break and fall. It was only by the quick action of the motorman of a southbound car that a repetition of the trolley accident in Seventh Avenue was averted. He saw the street sink ahead of him, quickly applied the brakes and then reversed his power, sending the car backwards from the very brink of the yawning pit. The New York Railways Company rewarded him for his presence of mind, which no doubt saved the passengers from injury and possible death.

This accident was caused by a slide of rock from the west side of the cut. The rock in this section is known by the engineers as treacherous, and wherever it looked suspicious extra precautions were taken to brace it. Here, however, there was a hidden seam which did not reveal itself until hundreds of tons of rock moved laterally into the cut, knocking down the nearest timbers supporting the street decking and causing the collapse. The timbering was exactly the same kind as that used in Seventh Avenue—in fact the same contractors who had the Seventh Avenue work also had the Broadway contract. They used a combination of steel beams and timbers which was supposed to be particularly strong. Engineers of the Public Service Commission, however, held that any timbering would have given way if subjected to such a strain and did not find fault with the method used.

The authorities took prompt action. The Public Service Commission opened an office at the scene and its engineers at once began the work of repairing the damage. The Mayor appointed a committee of engineers from the various City departments to investigate and this committee examined all contracts on which timbering was used to support the street decking and made recommendations for certain minor changes to strengthen the same. These were put into effect by the engineers of the Public Service Commission, which also appointed a board of three consulting engineers from other cities to study and report on the work. This board consisted of Edmund S. Davis, of Boston, Henry H. Quimby, of Philadelphia and D. C. Jackling, of San Francisco. Mr. Jackling could not serve and the work was done by Messrs. Davis and Quimby, who made a report in October, 1915, which in general approved the style of timbering used, made certain recommendations for improvement and suggested the employment of an engineer skilled in mining timber work to supervise all timbering. The Commission acted on the recommendations and added a mining engineer to its staff in the person of H. G. Moulton, who served throughout the remaining period of construction.

More than two years before the decking accidents, namely in June 1913, a fatal slide of rock occurred in the Lexington Avenue subway work near 56th street. At this point the lower or express tunnel passes through rock, and as it was known to be treacherous the contractor installed timbering to support the roof and sides of the tunnel. One night a large portion of the roof gave reveal itself until hundreds of tons of rock moved laterally way and the enormous weight of many tons of rock thrown suddenly on the timbering caused it to fail. Eleven workmen were caught in the tunnel and buried by the cave-in. All were dead when taken out.

There were several other accidents due to slides of rock, but none of great proportions. These caused some loss of life. The number of fatal accidents was small considering the magnitude of the work.

In closing this chapter a word about the engineers of the Public Service Commission seems appropriate. At the height of construction the force numbered more than 2,000 employes. Its functions were many, but may be summarized under the following classifications:

Studying traffic and population trend and laying out and surveying routes for rapid transit lines.

Making general and detail plans for the construction of rapid transit roads and designs for elevated structures, subway and elevated stations.

Reconstructing sewers interfered with by rapid transit lines and making plans therefor.

Inspecting materials entering into rapid transit construction.

Supervising actual construction of subways, elevated railroads and sewers, including passing on plans submitted by contractors or operating companies.

ENGINEERS OF PUBLIC SERVICE COMMISSION.

1. **Daniel L. Turner,** Chief Engineer, 1917. 2. **Alfred Craven,** Chief Engineer, 1912 to 1917.

3. **Robert Ridgway,** Engineer of Subway Construction.

The inspection of materials was thorough and extensive. Every bit of sand and cement used for the concrete work, every ton of steel placed in the structures, all bricks, lumber and mortar used in the work, all marble or other stone going into it, all tiling for stations, plumbing and station fittings of every description—all had to pass the scrutiny of these engineers. The proper inspection of lumber, steel and cement involved the dispatching of competent men to the mills and other producing plants in distant states, but this was done and many such men maintained for years in out of town places. This saved the rejection of unfit materials after they had been delivered on the ground, resulting in economy for both the city and the contractor.

During the greater part of the Dual System work the engineering staff of the Commission was headed by the following men:

Chief Engineer—Alfred Craven, followed by D. L. Turner.

Engineer of Subway Construction—Robert Ridgway.

Deputy Engineer of Subway Construction—Daniel L. Turner.

Engineer in Charge of Designs—Sverre Dahm.

Electrical Engineer in Charge of Equipment—Clifton W. Wilder.

Engineer of First Division—J. O. Shipman.

Engineer of Second Division—J. H. Myers.

Engineer of Third Division—C. V. V. Powers.

Engineer of Sixth Division—F. C. Noble, followed by George S. Rice.

Engineer of Seventh Division—F. W. Carpenter.

Engineer of Sewer Division—L. D. Fouquet.

Engineer of Tunnel Division—C. M. Holland.

Engineer of Track Division—R. H. Jacobs.

General Inspector of Material—George L. Lucas.

Engineer of Station Finish Division—Jasper T. Kane.

Engineer of Subsurface Structures—Charles N. Green.

Consulting Mining Engineer—H. G. Moulton.

Consulting Engineers—Gibbs and Hill and Alfred Noble.

CHAPTER XIX

RAPID TRANSIT IN BROOKLYN.

RAPID TRANSIT development in Brooklyn naturally followed the successful operation of the elevated railroads in New York, although several years elapsed before the growth of Brooklyn reached a point which demanded better and quicker transportation than was afforded by the horse car lines. These had multiplied with great rapidity in the period between 1850 and 1870, when New York's first elevated railroad began practical operation. But by that time Brooklyn had grown to be a city of 400,000 people, and the demand for rapid transit was already insistent. It had been partially supplied by the Long Island Railroad and other steam roads leading to Coney Island, but aside from these the city itself had no means of rapid transit.

The first project of note was that of the Brooklyn Steam Transit Company, chartered in May, 1870, for the purpose of building an elevated railroad from the East River to Flatbush. The charter covered both underground and elevated construction, allowed two or more tracks and gave wide choice of a route, which was to run from Fulton Ferry to the southern limits of Prospect Park in such streets as might be found most convenient. It permitted the use of steam or any other power except horses. The company was to provide both first and second class cars, but in the city limits was not to charge more than ten cents for a first class fare. The capital was to be $3,000,000 with power to increase it to $7,000,-000, and the right to extend the line to and through any towns of Kings County was granted. At least one mile of road must be built within three years.

The list of incorporators included the names of many men then and afterwards famous in the civic life of Brooklyn. Among them were Samuel McLean, Seymour

L. Husted, Henry E. Pierrepont, Alfred S. Barnes, A. A. Low, Archibald M. Bliss, Jacob I. Bergen, Cyrus P. Smith, John Lefferts, William C. Kingsley, Simeon B. Chittenden, Benjamin F. Tracy and Alexander B. Powell.

The project, however, came to naught. The length of the proposed road was more than five miles, and its estimated cost more than $5,000,000. Subscriptions to the capital stock came in slowly, and the panic of 1873 made the financing all the more difficult. In that year it was reported in the press that only $500,000 had been subscribed, and after many ups and downs the company went out of existence, the Court of Appeals in 1879 deciding that it had forfeited its charter by its failure to build in the specified time. The company had broken ground to begin work on June 1, 1878.

Meanwhile the company destined to operate the first elevated railroad in Brooklyn was organized. This was the Brooklyn Elevated Railroad Company, which was chartered in 1874 with $5,000,000 capital to build a "silent, safety" road from the end of the proposed Brooklyn Bridge, then just started, to Woodhaven in Queens, through several Brooklyn streets and Fulton Avenue, East New York. It was also to have a branch to Fulton Ferry. It was provided in the charter that steam locomotives might be used for motive power, but that they should not emit smoke or cinders and that the noise of operation should be lessened by suitable devices. The latter provisions seem to have been honored mainly in the breach.

The incorporators included Jacob Cole, Cornelius B. Payne, John H. Burtis, Abraham Lott, B. F. Clayton, John L. Nostrand, Job Johnson, Florian Grosjean, John Q. Kellogg, Joseph F. Bridges and other well known citizens of the time. Burtis was elected president and Kellogg secretary.

Like similar projects in Manhattan this scheme had its ups and downs and its tragedies. Among the latter the pitiful story of Q. Kirkup, an English engineer takes first rank. In England Kirkup had been connected with John Stephenson, the father of railroading, and with an only daughter had come to this country with some money. In March, 1875, he became connected with the Brooklyn Elevated Railroad Company, drew its plans, solicited funds and devoted his whole time and means to the scheme for two years. After vainly trying to put the company on its feet he died in extreme poverty. His work, his honest life and his sacrifices have earned for him a place in the history of rapid transit.

The directors quarreled and Burtis resigned as president. Various schemes were tried to raise money. A promoter named Whibeck was employed, and one of his methods was to open with prayer the meetings he got up to stimulate interest in the enterprise. In May, 1876, Burtis was re-elected president and the company obtained from the Common Council a resolution changing its route so as to pass through Willoughby street, Gold street, DeKalb avenue, Grand avenue, Lexington avenue and Broadway. This caused a popular outburst of opposition, and an agitation ensued, led by such men as the Rev. T. DeWitt Talmage, which resulted in the veto of the grant by Mayor Schroeder.

It was then decided to build according to the original route, and on May 24, 1876, ground was broken at the corner of Reid and Lexington avenues. Mayor Schroeder himself turned the first shovel-full of earth, but in his address justified his previous action in vetoing the new route. The company's workmen then dug pits and installed a few foundation stones for pillars, and these stones came into use later when the road was built. After they were placed, however, no more work was done for some time.

An internal fight over plans ensued. Kirkup had drawn plans for a two-track elevated road, substantially like those finally adopted, but Nostrand did not like them

PUBLIC SERVICE COMMISSION, 1917.

Left to Right — Travis H. Whitney, William Hayward, Oscar S. Straus, Chairman;
Henry W. Hodge, Charles S. Hervey.

and submitted a set of his own. Another director became enamored of a single rail device and urged its adoption. This was an invention of General Roy Stone and had been placed in trial operation over a gorge in Fairmount Park, Philadelphia, at the Centennial Exposition then in progress. It was described as "a triangular trestle work like the letter A, with one rail on top, over which engine and cars hung like a saddle on a horse's back." Nothing came of this plan.

It is a singular thing, however, that just thirty years later, namely in 1906, an English engineer, F. B. Behr, who had patented the same idea, was demonstrating the scheme in New York and trying to get the Board of Rapid Transit Railroad Commissioners to give him a franchise to build and operate a mono-rail line on substantially this plan from the heart of Brooklyn to Coney Island. Behr proposed to operate it by electric motors and claimed to be able to attain a speed of one hundred miles an hour with perfect safety to the passengers. He failed in his efforts to get a franchise.

In 1877 and 1878 the Brooklyn Elevated project languished. Other rapid transit schemes attracted public attention. Deacon Richardson negotiated the lease of Atlantic Avenue to the Long Island Railroad Company. In June 1878 the Brooklyn Steam Transit Company, previously referred to, then dominated by S. B. Chittenden, broke ground for its road on Atlantic Avenue, but Deacon Richardson caused railroad iron to be piled over the excavations and hired men to drive off the other company's workers if they dared to remove it.

The style and form of the first elevated road in Brooklyn were settled in 1878 by a Rapid Transit Commission appointed on the petition of property owners by Mayor Howell, under the Act of 1875. This commission consisted of J. W. Adams, N. H. Clement, C. J. Lowrey, J. Y. Culyer and Felix Campbell. Several plans were submitted to the commission, which finally decided on the type of road later built and thus sounded the death knell of the "silent safety" and "saddle-back" devices. It was this commission which organized the Kings County Elevated Railroad Company, which was later to put into operation Brooklyn's second elevated railroad system. Boston capitalists got a large share of the original stock, and for some time there was continued agitation against "foreign" capital gobbling up the Brooklyn franchise.

In 1879 the Brooklyn Elevated Railroad Company was reorganized. R. B. Floyd-Jones, a well known Long Islander, acquired control and brought in the most picturesque figure in Brooklyn's rapid transit history, W. Fontaine Bruff. Bruff was an English engineer, who parted his hair as well as his name in the middle. He was one of the early types of the breezy, energetic promoter, and while he spent money lavishly he seems to have had a talent for gathering it in, and is credited with infusing life into the languishing project and bringing about the road's construction. When he finally got the work started he would drive to it each morning in a stylish carriage, with a liveried coachman. He brought bankers into line and for a time funds rolled in upon him at the rate of $90,000 a week. He was elected president of the company in January, 1879.

In the meantime the Kings County Elevated Railroad Company became active, under the presidency of Judge H. G. Bond. Unable to get the consents of property owners in the required number, it applied to the courts for a commission to determine the necessity of the road. In March 1879 the court appointed J. G. Hewlett, S. B. Bartow and Thomas E. Silliman. In April it became known that the Brooklyn Elevated had let a contract in February for the construction of its line to Floyd-Jones. Then ensued a fight between Bruff for the Brooklyn company and Bond for the Kings County company, which wanted a franchise for a part of the route of the former. In spite of opposition Bruff started work with sixteen men on May 12 at the corner of Reid and Lexington avenues. The police, who had announced that this would not be permitted, promptly stopped the work and arrested all hands. Later they were released on bail, and next day Bruff resumed operations with another gang. They, too, were arrested, and work then was suspended pending the action of the courts. Finally the defendants were discharged and Bruff was permitted to resume work.

While these events were in progress the Brooklyn aldermen approved the franchise of the Kings County company. The act aroused a storm of indignation and Mayor Howell vetoed the grant and rebuked the aldermen, who promptly passed it over his veto. The fight for the franchise was then taken into court. Meantime Bruff had put in the foundations for his elevated columns at every point on the Brooklyn company's line touched by the Kings County company's franchise or had erected scaffoldings or iron work. He had 700 to 800 men engaged. On October 9, 1879, the Court of Appeals decided against the Kings County company, leaving the field clear for the Brooklyn Elevated.

During the year 1880 materials came in slowly, construction work lagged and a fight on Bruff began. In October the directors quarreled and many resigned. Finally on the application of one director, Edward S. Keeler, the Supreme Court ended Bruff's reign by appointing Richard G. Phelps as receiver for the company. His appointment was attacked and after much litigation he was ousted and John B. Lydecker and Samuel M. Schaeffer were confirmed as receivers. They issued $2,500,000 in receivers' certificates and built two miles and a half of elevated structure, from Hudson avenue and Prospect street to Bedford and Lexington avenues. Then the money ran out and work stopped.

From that time to 1884 little was accomplished. In 1881 the Common Council adopted a resolution permitting the Brooklyn Elevated company to change its route

so as to include Myrtle avenue and part of Fulton street
in its franchise. Mayor Howell vetoed it and the aldermen were enjoined from passing it over his veto. On the
last day of the year, however, they did so in the face of
the injunction and all were arrested. After a hearing in
January, 1882, they were sentenced to jail for from ten
to thirty days each. They actually were incarcerated for
a short time, but were released on legal proceedings pending trial. In the following November most of them had
to go to jail for a brief period.

In 1884 the Brooklyn Elevated was reorganized, taken
out of the receivers' hands and successfully financed to
completion. This was brought about principally by
Frederick Uhlman, who acted as chairman of the Bondholders' Committee. The first mortgage, which was held
by the Farmers' Loan and Trust Company, was fore-
closed, and on May 12, 1884, the property was bought in
by Uhlman on behalf of the trustees for the bondholders
for $100,000 in excess of the receivers' certificates. On
May 29 articles of incorporation were filed for the Brooklyn Elevated Railroad Company, with the following
named directors: Frederick Uhlman, Alfred J. Pouch,
Stephen Pettus, Elbert Snedeker, Hugo Rothschilds, Edward Lauterbach, Charles J. G. Hall, Abram J. Harden-
berg, Leonard Lewisohn, Adolph Landenberg and Henry
W. Putnam. On June 1 Putnam was elected president,
Hall vice-president, Snedeker treasurer and Pettus secretary.

Thereafter everything went smoothly. An extension
of time was obtained from the Legislature and work all
along the line was pushed. The first rail was laid in January, 1885, and on May 13 following the first five miles
of road was placed in operation. Mayor Low, then Brooklyn's chief magistrate, participated in the opening ceremonies, and the people hailed the first rapid transit line
with great enthusiasm.

The route as it began operation was from York and

Washington streets along York to Hudson avenue, along Hudson to Park avenue, along Park to Grand avenue, along Grand to Lexington avenue, along Lexington to Broadway and along Broadway to East New York. George B. Cornell was the chief engineer who finished the road. The main part of it is now (1917) operated as the Broadway line of the New York Consolidated Railroad Company, of the Brooklyn Rapid Transit Company's system.

Similar vicissitudes marked the career of the Kings County Elevated Railroad Company, already referred to. It was organized in December, 1878, about a year after the charter was granted. Judge Bond, of Brooklyn, above mentioned, formed the company which accepted the franchise and took up the work of getting property owners' consents. Failing to obtain the required number, the company appealed to the court. A commission to determine was appointed and reported favorably, but the General Term refused to confirm the report on the ground that the construction of the road would destroy private property. Judge Bond became discouraged and dropped the project.

A combination was then formed by General James Jourdan and H. J. Davison, of Brooklyn, and William Foster Jr., of New York, which attempted to resuscitate the scheme. They made another effort to get consents but failed, although they met with more encouragement than their predecessors. They obtained the appointment of another commission by the court, and again the commission made a favorable report. Judge Gilbert, of General Term, confirmed the report but left his decision sealed and sailed for Europe before its consideration was taken up formally by the court. Judges Barnard and Dykman gave judgment that the decision was incompetent and that Judge Gilbert would not have rendered it had he known all the facts. After this defeat William Foster

Jr. became discouraged and withdrew from the enterprise.

Davison and Jourdan, having faith in the project, formed a new combination, which after many ups and downs resulted in the company which built the road. It was involved in continuous litigation, which it fought successfully to the Court of Appeals. The directors of this company were Edward A. Abbott, James O. Sheldon, Henry J. Davison, Wendell Goodwin, Henry J. Robinson, Harvey Farrington, James Jourdan and William A. Read. Jourdan was president.

The contract for construction was given to the Phoenix Bridge company, which built the road from Nostrand avenue through Fulton street to the Bridge and Fulton Ferry. This part of the line was placed in operation April 24, 1888. Ground had been broken at the corner of Fulton street and Red Hook Lane in the fall of 1885. The line is now a part of the Fulton street elevated road operated by the New York Consolidated Railroad Company.

Another pioneer project in rapid transit in Brooklyn was the Union Elevated Railroad Company. This was organized in 1886 to build certain lines, which as soon as constructed were leased to the Brooklyn Elevated Company to operate. The first line opened was the Hudson avenue branch, running from the Long Island Railroad station through Flatbush and Hudson avenues and connecting with the line of the Brooklyn Elevated from Park Avenue to the Fulton Ferry. By 1890 the Union had constructed eleven miles of elevated road, all operated by the Brooklyn Elevated. In the same year the two companies were consolidated under the name of the Brooklyn Union Elevated Railroad Company. The combined capital was $13,000,000 and the total length of the combined roads was eighteen miles.

Within a few years all the various elevated companies were acquired by the Brooklyn Rapid Transit Company, which also absorbed most of the surface car companies of

Brooklyn. The same interests control them today. As told in a previous chapter, the Brooklyn Rapid Transit Company joined the City of New York in the Dual System agreements of 1913 and organized the New York Municipal Railway Corporation to enter into the contract with the City. In preparation for this step the elevated railroad companies were merged under the name of the New York Consolidated Railroad Company, which operates the old lines together with the new lines leased to the New York Municipal Railway Corporation.

Aside from the projects mentioned Brooklyn like New York was filled with rapid transit schemes during the period of organization and construction. Many never got beyond the paper stage, while others flourished for a time only to fail in the end. Among the unusual ones was the Gravity Railroad. This was projected in 1888 by an engineer named Henning. His plan was to connect Brooklyn with New York by two tunnels under the East River, starting from each side at the surface of the ground and descending to and under the river at a grade sufficient to carry the cars from one side to the other by the force of gravity alone. In 1890 the East River Tunnel Company was incorporated to build the tunnels and to operate them partly by Henning's gravity system and partly by cable power. The scheme was never carried out. Henning calculated that he could shoot his trains under the river in one minute and a half.

CHAPTER XX

THE HUDSON AND MANHATTAN TUNNELS UNDER THE HUDSON RIVER.

PLANS for bridging over or tunnelling under the Hudson River were formed about the middle of the Nineteenth Century, but it was not until 1873 that they took definite shape. In that year the Hudson River Tunnel Company was incorporated to build a tunnel under the Hudson to connect New York City with the railroads terminating at Jersey City, New Jersey. Its president was De Witt C. Haskin, a man of bold and determined character whose project for boring a highway under the mighty river was far ahead of his times. He failed, but his idea lived and was carried out a third of a century later by men who then could command the skill and experience lacking in Haskin's day.

It was in November, 1874, that Haskin's company began work. His plan contemplated a tunnel 26 feet wide by 24 feet high to accommodate two tracks. The tunnel was to have an iron shell, with a lining of brick masonry three feet thick. The first work was to sink a shaft on the New Jersey side about 100 feet from the river at the foot of Fifteenth street, Jersey City. This shaft had been sunk to a depth of twenty feet, when the Delaware, Lackawanna and Western Railroad Company started injunction proceedings. This and other litigation stopped the work for five years. It was resumed in 1879, when the shaft was completed to a depth of 60 feet and from the bottom a heading for the tunnel was started. Compressed air was used to support the roof and keep out the water, but without the shield now so universally used.

The engineers in charge of the work were Spielman and Brush, and they changed the plans to provide for two tunnels instead of one, each to be of elliptical shape and to carry one track, and to be 18 feet high and 16 feet wide. In July, 1880, the North tunnel had been driven 280 feet and the South tunnel 15 feet, when a bad "blow-out" of air occurred, letting the river water into the works and drowning about twenty men. It took six months to sink a pneumatic caisson alongside and regain entry into the tunnel. Before the accident the tunnel had been allowed to get both out of grade and out of alignment, and some of the brick lining had cracked.

In May, 1881, General William Sooy Smith took charge as chief engineer, but remained only one year. During that time work was resumed and a caisson was sunk on the New York side at the foot of Morton street. The work continued with varying fortune until November, 1882, when it was stopped for lack of funds. At that time the North tunnel from New Jersey had been driven 1,542 feet, the South tunnel 570 feet and the North tunnel from New York 74 feet. In December of that year Trenor W. Park, who had suceeded Haskin as president of the company, died at sea and was succeeded by C. G. Francklyn.

Additional funds were obtained and the work was resumed in April, 1883, at the New York end, but in August the money gave out and operations again were suspended. The suspension lasted until April, 1887, when work was resumed on the New Jersey side, but was again suspended in September, when the Jersey North tunnel was out 1,840 feet from the shaft.

In 1889 bonds were floated in England and work was once more resumed, this time with S. Pearson and Sons, of London, as contractors, and William R. Hutton as engineer. By the end of the year the North tunnel from Jersey City had been driven 2,000 feet from the shaft, although a bad "blow-out" marked the progress of the work. At this point the contractors introduced the use of the tunnel shield, which was installed in 1890, and thereafter the work was pursued by this method. A year later the North tunnel reached a point 3,700 feet out, which was about 700 feet across the New York State line. In August, 1891, however, another financial crisis arose, following the great Baring failure, and the company found it impossible to procure funds. Accordingly work was again suspended, with the North tunnel bored to a point 3,900 feet out. In 1892 the contractors, S. Pearson and Sons, filed a lien for $20,000 on the tunnel. The British company failed to advance the needed money and the work was practically abandoned for ten years.

In the meantime, namely in 1899, the tunnel was sold under foreclosure and purchased by Stetson, Jennings and Russell, a New York law firm, acting for the bondholders. In 1902 the project was revived by the New York and Jersey Railroad company, organized by William G. McAdoo, a New York Lawyer, who subsequently became Secretary of the Treasury in President Wilson's cabinet. This company acquired the old company's rights and resumed work in 1902, with Charles M. Jacobs as chief engineer. It applied at once to the Board of Rapid Transit Railroad Commissioners for a perpetual franchise under the New York rapid transit act for tunnel rights from Morton street, Manhattan, to the New Jersey State boundary under the Hudson River, there to connect with the partially built tunnel from Jersey City. The franchise was granted by the Board on July 10, 1902, but was not approved by the Board of Aldermen and the Mayor until the following December.

As the tunnel was to run southward on the New Jersey side to the Pennsylvania Railroad terminal in Jersey City, it was decided to get a franchise for an additional tunnel under the river from that point to lower Manhattan. For this purpose a new company, known as the Hudson and Manhattan Railroad company, was organized in 1903. The new company applied to the Board for another perpetual franchise for two more tubes, to run from a point between Liberty and Fulton

**MODERN STEEL CAR TRAINS OPERATED IN
NEW YORK SUBWAYS**

1. Train of Interborough Rapid Transit
Company; 2. Train of New York Consolidated Railroad Company.

streets, Manhattan, under the Hudson River to the State line, there to connect with similar tubes to be built out from Jersey City. This was granted by the Board on November 24 and approved by the Aldermen and the Mayor late in December, 1903.

Meanwhile the work was proceeding rapidly under the management of Mr. Jacobs. In March, 1904, the North tunnel was "holed through" and in September, 1905, the South tunnel headings were joined. In the same month work was begun on the downtown tunnel.

On March 2, 1904, the New York and Jersey Railroad Company made further application to the Board for an extension of its tunnel route from the Manhattan terminus at Greenwich street and West Tenth street to Sixth Avenue and thence northward under Sixth Avenue to Thirty-third street, and for a perpetual franchise therefor. This was denied by the Board, which was unwilling to grant perpetual rights in such a case, involving one of the principal north and south avenues of New York City. On May 5, 1904, the company made application for a "limited term" franchise for the Sixth Avenue line, but on May 24 withdrew it and substituted one for an extension from Christopher and Greenwich streets easterly under Christopher and Ninth streets to Third avenue. Property owners in Sixth avenue objected to the abandonment of the proposed extension under that thoroughfare to Thirty-third street, and the Board finally agreed to offer the company a franchise for it subject to recaption by the City in twenty-five years, and a franchise in perpetuity for the Ninth street extension as far as Fourth avenue. The company was willing and accordingly the Board granted the franchise for both extensions on these conditions on December 22, 1904.

The franchise provided for the extension of the two-track subway from the previous terminal at Greenwich, West Tenth and Christopher streets easterly under Christopher street to Sixth Avenue, whence two tracks should proceed northward under Sixth avenue to Thirty-third street and two tracks eastwardly under Ninth street to Fourth avenue. Stations were located in Christopher street between Greenwich and Hudson streets; Christopher street and Sixth avenue; in Sixth avenue at Fourteenth, Eighteenth, Twenty-third, Twenty-eighth and Thirty-third streets.

As rental it was provided that the company should pay to the City annually fifty cents per foot for each linear foot of single track railroad for ten years after beginning operation and one dollar per foot thereafter until the rental under the original franchise of 1902 should become subject to readjustment. A further payment of $9,000 per annum was provided for, such amount being equivalent to three per cent. of $300,000, the estimated annual gross earnings of the extensions. This payment was to be made for ten years, after which the amount of it was to be five per cent. of the gross earnings of the extensions. All payments were to be readjusted at the end of each twenty-five years.

This certificate was approved by the Board of Aldermen in February, 1905, with a slight modification allowing the granting of permits for street openings by the City officials. Having failed to get the consents of property owners, the company applied to the Appellate Division of the Supreme Court, which confirmed the favorable report of its commissioners on June 14, 1905. On the following day the company began construction of the Sixth Avenue extension.

The Hudson and Manhattan Railroad company, which held the franchise for the down-town tunnels of the line, also failed in obtaining property owners' consents and applied to the court. Commissioners were appointed and reported favorably, and the Appellate Division confirmed their report on June 14, 1905. Construction work on this line began September 5, 1905.

On December 1, 1906, the various companies of this system, including the New Jersey and New York corporations, were consolidated with the Hudson and Manhattan Railroad Company, which thenceforward conducted the management and operation of the new lines. Work was pushed forward without undue delay and operation of the "Hudson Tubes", as the line came to be called, was begun on February 25, 1908, more than thirty-three years after the work had been started by Haskin. The motive power is electricity generated in a plant in Jersey City and supplied by the third rail method.

At the Manhattan terminal of the downtown tubes the Hudson Terminal building was erected, with the station in the basement. This building, a 22 story "skyscraper", was erected by the Hudson Companies, a separate corporation formed in 1905 to handle the construction and real estate operations for the Hudson and Manhattan Railroad company. The financing was done by the banking firm of Harvey Fisk and Sons, Messrs. Pliny Fisk and William M. Barnum of that house having been closely connected with the enterprise. The total cost of the system and its equipment was about $70,000,000. Mr. McAdoo remained president of the Hudson and Manhattan Railroad company until he went into the cabinet in 1913, when he was succeeded by Wilbur C. Fisk. Mr. Jacobs remained chief engineer to the end and was assisted by J. Vipond Davies as deputy chief engineer.

In 1909 the Hudson and Manhattan Railroad company applied to and received from the Public Service Commission for the First District a franchise for an extension of the tunnel from its present terminus at Sixth Avenue and Thirty-third street northward under Sixth Avenue and curving under Bryant Park to Forty-second street and the Grand Central station of the New York Central system. Owing to unfavorable financial conditions this extension has not yet been built.

The system as it operates today is a great addition

to the transportation facilities of New York City. It carries about 70,000,000 passengers a year and the traffic is steadily growing. Many of these are commuters who live in New Jersey and do business in New York, formerly dependent on the ferry boats. In 1912 the company connected its lines with the Pennsylvania Railroad and now operates through trains from New York City to Manhattan Transfer and Newark. Incoming passengers on the Pennsylvania may change to Hudson and Manhattan trains at the Transfer and continue their journey through the tubes to downtown Manhattan without extra charge. On the Jersey side the tubes connect directly with the Erie and Lackawanna railroad terminals.

All steel equipment is used in the tunnels, the cars having center side doors and steel uprights as well as straps for standing passengers. The closing of the last door gives the electric signal to the motorman to start the train.

On February 25, 1915, the road had been in operation seven years. In that time it had carried 329,357,277 passengers without the loss of one life. Operated to its full capacity, it is estimated that it can carry 220,000,000 passengers a year, so that the present traffic is about one-third of the maximum.

The tunnels lie at an average depth below the bed of the Hudson River of 25 feet, although the deepest point in them is 101 feet below the surface of the water. The total weight of the iron rings used in their construction is 111,000 tons, and 925,000 barrels of cement were used in the concrete work.

The company is now operating about eight miles of road, of which a little more than three miles lie in New York and a little less than five in New Jersey. The total length of single track is more than eighteen miles. It has 226 steel passenger cars each forty-eight feet long and capable of seating forty-four persons. The capital stock is about $45,000,000 and the outstanding bond issues aggregate about $76,000,000.

The Hudson Terminal buildings are among the mammoth office buildings of the world. They have twenty-two floors above and four floors below the street level. They contain 4,500 rooms and 877,900 square feet of rentable area. The gross revenues from the buildings in 1914, including rentals, were $1,723,671.73.

There is more than has been told in the story of New York's rapid transit undertakings, but to present it all the limits of a single volume would be exceeded. For instance, the evolution of the rapid transit car, from the flimsy wooden boxes used on the first elevated railroads to the ponderous and expensive all-steel, electric cars operated in the subways of today, is in itself an interesting story of the scientific and mechanical progress of the last half century. The adaptation of electricity to traction purposes, too, and the recounting of the many and rapid advances in this branch of electrical engineering would in itself provide material for a volume. But these and other phases of rapid transit development were purposely omitted in order to present in sufficient fullness the narrative of invention, legislation, construction, negotiation, private ownership and public ownership during Fifty Years of Rapid Transit, set forth in the preceding pages.